DRAGONS
AT YOUR
DOOR

DRAGONS AT YOUR DOOR

How Chinese Cost Innovation Is
Disrupting Global Competition

MING ZENG AND
PETER J. WILLIAMSON

HARVARD BUSINESS SCHOOL PRESS
BOSTON, MASSSACHUSETTS

11 10 09 08 07   5 4 3 2 1

ISBN: 978-142210-208-4

Library of Congress Cataloging-in-Publication Data is forthcoming.

The paper used in this publication meets the requirements of the American
National Standard for Permanence of Paper for Publications and Documents in
Libraries and Archives Z39.48-1992.

Contents

Preface and Acknowledgments   vii

Introduction   I
Dragons at Your Door

1   Disrupting Global Competition   27
How Did They Get Here So Fast?

2   Cost Innovation   57
The Chinese Dragons' Secret Weapon

3   Loose Bricks   89
Rethinking Your Vulnerabilities

4   The Weak Link   123
Limitations of the Chinese Dragons

5   Your Response   149
Winning in the New Global Game

Conclusion   193
Charting the Future

Notes   205
Index   211
About the Authors   237

Preface and Acknowledgments

We chose the title of this book in order to emphasize a key point: that as leading Chinese firms go global, they are adopting strategies that challenge some of the basic assumptions on which a lot of companies from the United States, Europe, and other developed markets depend to remain profitable. Just like any other form of disruptive competition, this powerful and unorthodox challenge threatens to knock complacent incumbents off their perches. We will certainly argue that the new wave of competition from China hitting the global market demands a resolute response from established companies—if they are to continue to succeed. But lest careless (or unscrupulous) readers be tempted to see this book as portraying a "them-and-us" battle between China and the United States (or other developed countries), let us debunk any such misconception at the outset.

No doubt there is some tough competition ahead, with corporate winners and losers on both sides. Far from being a zero-sum game, however, the emergence of Chinese companies as significant players in the global market promises new benefits to the world's consumers and new opportunities to those established companies that choose the right responses and execute them well. While there will be casualties, an outcome that also sees more global alliances between Chinese and foreign firms is much more likely than universal descent into a destructive economic conflict.

Our cooperation itself is a microcosm of some of the potential benefits of treating the rise of Chinese companies as an opportunity. A Chinese native, Ming grew up with China's economic reform and since his return to China in 2002 he has spent his days (and nights) working closely with Chinese firms, sharing their joy, struggle, and pain as they moved forward. Peter first went to China back in 1983; since then, as well as keeping a close eye on the development of Chinese firms, he has also spent a lot of time with leading multinational firms to figure out their Asian and China strategies. Together, we see China's rise from the perspectives of both sides. Such cooperation as we already see happening between companies such as Lenovo and IBM, Alibaba and Yahoo! is likely to become a major trend in the near future.

Rather than being the product of recent trade spats or fears that American or European jobs are being exported, therefore, the genesis of this book lies in a cooperation that began in 1998 when the two of us first met at INSEAD in Fontainebleau, right after the 1997 Asian financial crisis. It struck us that, despite being surrounded by Asian doom and gloom, China's economy was doing remarkably well, and Chinese companies such as Huawei, Lenovo, and Haier were emerging from the fray as winning competitors in their home market. We started to wonder how these companies had managed to come from seemingly nowhere to capture a disproportionate share of the Chinese market, not only against competition from their domestic rivals, but from well-resourced and experienced multinational companies as well. So we began to explore a hunch: that what set these companies apart was not only competent management and good execution, but their strategies as well. Perhaps they were doing something different? This question began our research on how the dragons might be bringing a disruptive strategy, that we later dubbed *cost innovation*, to your door.

What we didn't anticipate was just how far and how fast Chinese firms and the Chinese economy would move. With hindsight, it turned out that starting from about 1998, two decades after China began opening up to the outside world, China's economy and its leading companies really took off toward becoming a global force. We were fortunate to be tracing the evolution of Chinese firms over what proved to be such a historic period in their development.

We didn't have any idea, either, what a daunting task we had set ourselves. Fortunately, the hard grind of following twists and turns at the company level, rather than focusing mainly on macro trends, proved to be an extremely rewarding experience. Much has been written about the remarkable transformation of China, its economic development, and both the opportunities and difficulties foreigners confront in making money in China. But few authors have zeroed in on one of the driving forces of China's recent achievements—its companies—nor the implications of their rise. With the help of this perspective, we have concluded that the emergence of Chinese multinationals will fundamentally change the global competitive game. Unfortunately, very few outside China yet understand this and how important it is to get prepared.

The impact will be felt well beyond the confines of corporate boardrooms. China's rapid integration into the global economy, adding 1.3 billion consumers and a labor force of 800 million to the world's total, can't help but change the global economic equilibrium broadly. It will initiate transition to a new economic structure with changes in the division of labor between regions, reorganization of multinational firms, and new alliances among companies (and countries) over the next decade. All companies, workers, and governments have to find their new role if they are to survive and prosper as the global map is redrawn. The key purpose of this book is to explain one of the most powerful drivers of these shifts—cost innovation by leading Chinese companies—and how managers should prepare for the different future that it will shape.

Given the complexity of the topic, we have had to make some difficult decisions about what to include, especially when it comes to discussing some of the broader economic and political context around the core argument or delving into the specifics of management processes inside particular companies. We have chosen to put the focus on the dragons' innovative strategies; for example: how they are using their low costs in creative ways to build sustainable competitive advantage; where they are choosing to target their limited resources to maximize the chances of successfully breaking into the global market; and how they are reinventing the classic experience curve. We believe that only if managers gain a full understanding of these strategies will they be equipped to develop viable responses. It is also here that we believe Western managers have most to learn from the way the dragons are challenging conventional wisdom and the greatest opportunities to leverage these ideas by using their own unique capabilities and experience. Moreover, because Chinese companies have yet to pioneer really new management processes (as the Japanese did with Total Quality Control or Just-in-Time), we have placed less emphasis on describing aspects of strategy implementation. It's not because we think good execution is unimportant (clearly it is a prerequisite for success), but because it's an area where the dragons arguably haven't brought much that's new.

Of course, this may change in the future: more innovation in management processes may happen as Western and Chinese management heritages increasingly intermix. Much else will also change: writing a book concerning companies in China inevitably means trying to hit a moving target. But we have tried to identify sustained shifts from within the mix of fact, fiction, and random noise that makes up the mass of news about China and its companies that now hits the wires daily. We are therefore confident that the main conclusions of this book will prove resilient. Only time will tell if we were right.

Acknowledgments

In the course of our research, we have visited many companies and interviewed hundreds of executives—both from Chinese and multinational firms. It is impossible to list them all. Special thanks to Liu Chuan Zhi, Zhang Rui Min, and Ma Yun for providing valuable guidance that helped us to understand the inner workings of budding Chinese firms over the years.

Thousands of students and participants in executive programs in China and around the world, too numerous to mention by name, have contributed directly or indirectly to this book with their challenging questions, feedback, and advice—all of which has shaped our thinking along the way. To each and every one, our sincere thanks. Many people have also provided capable assistance throughout the long research journey. Liu Yong, Zirui Tian, and He Xiaoming have been particularly helpful in data collection and analysis over the last two years, along with Kevin Foley, Zhang Yu, and many others at different stages of the project.

Our thinking has benefited greatly from discussions with our colleagues at INSEAD's Euro-Asia Centre, particularly Professors Ben Bensaou, Henri-Claude de Bettignies, Arnoud De Meyer, Philippe Lasserre, Gordon Redding, and Helmut Schutte, as well as Ming's colleagues at Cheung Kong Graduate School of Business in Beijing, particularly Professors Bing Xiang, Larry Lang, Daqing Qi, Aimin Yan, and Yunkui Xue.

We would like to thank the anonymous reviewers who made important comments on an earlier draft. We also gratefully acknowledge the financial support of INSEAD and Cheung Kong Graduate School of Business for this ambitious research project over the last nine years.

Finally, our thanks go to Astrid Sandoval, the editor who navigated through the difficult task of improving the exposition and clarity of our argument and who, through gentle prodding, saw this project through to completion.

Despite the excellent help we enjoyed from these many quarters, misinterpretations and deficiencies, of course, remain fully our own.

—Ming Zeng and Peter J. Williamson
Beijing and London, December 8, 2006

Introduction

Dragons at Your Door

FORGET THE IDEA that the rise of Chinese competitors simply means cheap, low-quality imitations flooding world markets. Chinese companies are starting to disrupt global competition by breaking the established rules of the game. Their tool of choice is *cost innovation*: the strategy of using Chinese cost advantage in radically new ways to offer customers around the world dramatically more for less. Cost innovation has three faces:

- First, Chinese companies are starting to offer customers high technology at low cost. Computer maker Dawning, for example, has put supercomputer technology into the low-cost servers that are the everyday workhorses of the world's IT networks. This novel strategy is demolishing the conventional wisdom that high technology is restricted to high-end products and segments. And it is interrupting the game whereby established global competitors maximize their profits along the product life cycle by only slowly migrating new technology from high-priced segments toward the mass market.

- Second, the emerging Chinese competitors are presenting customers with an unmatched choice of products in what used be considered standardized, mass-market segments. Goodbaby, for example, offers a product line of over sixteen hundred types of strollers, car seats, bassinets, and playpens—four times the range of its nearest competitor—all at mass-market prices, thus challenging the idea that if customers want variety and customization, they have to pay a price premium.

- Third, Chinese companies are using their low costs to offer specialty products at dramatically lower prices, turning them into volume businesses. For example, consumer appliance maker Haier has transformed the market for wine-storage refrigerators from the preserve of a few wine connoisseurs into a mainstream category sold through America's Sam's Club at less than half the then-prevailing price. The end result: Haier has a 60 percent market share, while yesterday's niche players have been left floundering. This new Chinese competition is challenging the notion that specialty products must forever remain low-volume and high-priced.

The cost innovation challenge presented by Chinese companies is disruptive because it strikes at the heart of what makes many businesses in high-cost countries profitable today. It threatens their ability to earn high margins on high technology. It undermines their ability to extract a price premium by offering customers more product variety and greater customization. And it means that even if they use their specialist knowledge to move upmarket into niche segments—above the fray of low-cost competition in the mass market—they risk being blown away as the Chinese explode these niches into volume business.

Imagine a world where high technology, variety, and customization, along with specialist products, are available to customers at dramatically lower prices; a world where the value-for-money equation offered to global consumers has been transformed by

Chinese multinationals. Could you survive this kind of dramatic change in the competitive climate?

This new era of global competition is not far-fetched. It is precisely the disruption to existing business models that the emerging Chinese dragons are now unleashing. It means we must all learn to cope with a world that will soon see a cost revolution, whether we are prepared or not.

Cost Innovation in Action

The dynamics of how cost innovation can be used to displace established competitors from the core of a market, and the consequences that follow, are nowhere better illustrated than in the case of China International Marine Containers Group (CIMC). Already global number one in terms of volume in 1996, today CIMC is six times larger than its nearest competitor, dominating the world of shipping containers with more than 55 percent global market share. But far from being just a low-end, volume producer, it has penetrated every segment of the container market. Driven by its corporate slogan "learn, improve, disrupt," CIMC has captured one segment after another, including products with sophisticated refrigeration, state-of-the-art electronic tracking, internal tanks, folding mechanisms, and customized features—all niches that specialist European container makers believed they could defend, despite their high costs. In 2005 it bought up 77 patents from a bankrupt competitor Graaff—ironically the German firm from which CIMC licensed its first refrigeration technology back in 1995. One year earlier it acquired a 60 percent shareholding in Clive-Smith Cowley, the British company that invented the proprietary "Domino" technology that allows empty containers to be "folded" for ease of back-hauling.

As a result, CIMC is now a major force in setting the new global standards for container transportation. The company's goal is to repeat its successful strategy as it diversifies into a range of modern transportation equipment, including the trailers used by trucking companies around the world.

Strength in the China Market Establishes the Launchpad

Most of the emerging dragons begin by establishing a strong position in China. Because the China market is typically fragmented between too many competing firms due to China's system of protectionist provincial governments, pulling ahead of these numerous rivals is no easy task. Those who rise to the top, therefore, have already experienced a baptism of fire. This means they already have well-honed skills in paring down costs and squeezing the maximum benefit from limited resources.

CIMC is no exception. Far from being an overnight success, it began life in 1980 as one of the first Sino-foreign joint ventures in China. It was initially established as a partnership between China Merchants Holdings (one of the vehicles established by China's State Council to invest in projects promoting international trade) and East Asiatic Company, the Danish trading company (founded in 1884 when Captain H. N. Andersen shipped his first consignment of Thai teak logs to Europe) that had built trading and shipping operations throughout Asia.

CIMC's first container rolled off the line in 1982, but a combination of inexperienced management and a downturn in the market led the company near disaster; in 1986 production was shut down and most of its employees laid off. CIMC was subsequently restructured, but even by 1990 it was a minor producer, making less than ten thousand containers a year. It found itself competing with more than twenty other container producers that had sprung up across China, attracted by the high margins on a business with low barriers to entry and a breakeven of only a few thousand units.

When Mai Boliang, the current president of CIMC, was appointed in 1991, he set about an aggressive expansion plan that would enable CIMC to pull away from its Chinese competitors. Taking advantage of new regulations that opened the way for initial public offerings (IPOs) in China, he floated the company on the Shenzhen Stock Exchange in 1993 and used the money to buy up Chinese competitors that were struggling as the demand cycle suffered a downswing. These acquisitions enabled CIMC to expand to five massive plants; by 1996, it was number one in China. Given the huge size of the China market, this already made it one of the largest players in the world—large enough to gain the economies of scale necessary to become cost competitive in manufacturing compared with its established global competitors.

The fact that most of the emerging dragons, like CIMC, venture into the global market only after building a strong position in the China market has two important implications for Western managers. First, it means that where a market is underdeveloped or nonexistent in China the dragons lack one of the foundations of their strategy. Conversely, if China becomes a lead market in particular business (as has happened in DVD players and is beginning to happen in mobile phones) then the strategy of becoming strong in China first, leaves the dragons well-placed to attack the global market.

The second implication is that Western companies that decide not to fight the emerging dragons aggressively on their own turf in China leave themselves exposed in the long term. By leaving a leading Chinese competitor to build strength and scale unchallenged, global competitors are likely to be storing up trouble. Moreover, when the dragon makes a foray into the global market, Western incumbents that have avoided serious commitment to China are left facing a completely unfamiliar competitor.

Finding the Loose Brick

Like most of its Chinese cousins, when CIMC set out to expand its market share abroad it looked for a loose brick in established competitors' defenses. These loose bricks are not always obvious to an incumbent, and as we will explore in detail in chapter 3, identifying these weaknesses and developing strategies to eliminate them turns out to be an important element in countering the threat of disruption from new Chinese competitors. CIMC found a classic loose brick in the combination of standard, low-priced containers and the way its rivals accounted for profits.

As global competition in the container market intensified, prices plummeted; a standard container that had sold for $2,850 in 1995, for example, netted only $1,300 by 1999. In consequence margins on sales were squeezed to only 3 percent. CIMC recognized a silver lining in this otherwise dismal picture—its international competitors, mainly in Korea and Japan, must be suffering even more severely.

It was here that CIMC identified a loose brick. It knew that its Asian competitors were almost all part of diversified conglomerates that regularly reassessed the relative returns on investment across their businesses. CMIC could be almost certain that its rivals' head-office accountants would be telling their bosses that standard containers were unprofitable "dogs" in their portfolio, and it wouldn't take much more pain before these companies decided to exit the market.

CIMC therefore set about stepping up the competitive pressure on the business line it guessed its rivals regarded as the least attractive to defend—a loose brick it had a chance to dislodge. CIMC focused its innovation efforts on an all-out push to remove cost from every activity in its business. By streamlining its processes for procurement of raw materials, benchmarking and rationalizing the activities in each plant, accessing international finance to cut its cost of capital, and looking for more efficient ways to transport containers, it was able to squeeze 33 percent out of material costs and 46 percent out of its manufacturing and overhead costs. More efficient transportation alone saved $5 million per annum.

These initiatives across the entire range of activities meant that CIMC extended its cost advantage far beyond the differential in wage rates, so that even when competitors began to move their manufacturing to China to take advantage of lower labor costs, they couldn't produce a finished container as cheaply as CIMC. As CIMC won orders, its total volume expanded, kick-starting a virtuous cycle in which growing economies of scale continued to reinforce its cost advantage. By 1996 it was churning out 199,000 units—about one in five of every new container manufactured in the world—and became global number one by volume.

Moving Upmarket

Having secured its scale and cost advantages in the production of standard containers, CIMC's strategy was to use cost innovation to move upmarket and carve out a large share of more sophisticated products.

Its chance to break out of the low end came when the Asian financial crisis hit in 1997. CIMC's diversified rivals, especially the Korean companies, were hard hit and needed to offload non-core businesses. Their unprofitable container operations were high on the list for disposal. The specialized competitors in Germany, meanwhile, were seeing their business dry up because the crisis eliminated their customers' ability to pay premium prices. CIMC took full advantage of this situation.

High Technology at Low Cost. CIMC began by investing $50 million in a new subsidiary, the Shanghai CIMC Reefer Containers Co., Ltd., to manufacture refrigerated containers (or "reefers" as they are known in the trade). It then entered into a licensing agreement with Graaff Transportsysteme GmbH, a specialist producer that had innovative, proprietary, and widely accepted technologies for the manufacture of the insulated panels used in reefers.

CIMC paid Graaff license fees on twelve patents used in the new operation. In addition, Graaff received 2 percent equity in the venture and $750,000 for selling one of their existing production lines, to be dismantled and shipped to China, along with the services of Stephan Teepe, a recognized German expert in the sector who was appointed chief engineer of the new Shanghai plant.

But CIMC's objective went far beyond imitating an established player. Instead its strategy was to use its lower cost design and engineering resources to improve on the technologies it had acquired as well as to apply them to create a broader product range than its global competitors. In short, cost innovation to deliver technology at low cost and variety at low cost.

CIMC quickly absorbed the German technology and then set about scaling it up and making improvements. According to Teepe: "When the production line was imported from Germany it had a capacity of 10,000 TEUs [twenty-foot equivalent units] per annum. Over the next five years CIMC technicians fundamentally reengineered the manufacturing process four times, applying advanced technology borrowed from the auto industry."[1] This allowed CIMC to gain a technological edge on its established competitors while still reducing its costs further.

Having brought advanced technology at low cost to the reefer business, CIMC began to drive hard to increase its market share in order to kick-start a new cycle of cost reduction through scale economies and learning. Again taking advantage of the aftershocks of the 1997 Asian financial crisis, it was able to acquire Hyundai's plant in Qingdao at a bargain price—under $20 million. Through this deal CIMC gained production facilities with an estimated replacement value of $180 million, an additional line for producing reefers, and effectively removed a major competitor from the market. CIMC then expanded the capacity of its newly acquired facilities by 150 percent to 25,000 TEUs. But even in the seemingly routine task of expanding an existing plant, CIMC found ways to innovate on cost. While former owner Hyundai had budgeted $30 million to increase capacity, CIMC leveraged the experience it had gained through the Shanghai plant and used innovative approaches and low-cost engineers to get the expanded line up and running in less than six months, at just 50 percent of the cost—$15 million less than what the Korean company had planned!

CIMC then set about its next round of cost innovation: finding a way to replace the expensive aluminum used in refrigerated containers with much cheaper treated steel. It licensed steel-treatment technology from Germany and used its army of engineers to improve performance to the point where treated steel could match the performance of aluminum. CIMC then targeted the customers of the Japanese reefer suppliers who were using aluminum as their raw material—and won the business.

The impact of CIMC offering this new low-cost technology and finding a loose brick at which it could be targeted was devastating for CIMC's competitors. One by one the established Japanese players exited the market so that within eight years the last Japanese producer had closed down.

CIMC's cost innovation proved a powerful strategy: Between 1997 and 2003 it expanded production of refrigerated containers sevenfold to 63,500 TEUs to become the global leader, accounting for 44 percent of the world market.

Variety at Low Cost. Having gained dominance in the reefer segment, CIMC set its sights on extending its product line to include a wide variety of even higher-end products: containers with tanks, folding containers, and other special-purpose models.

Over the 1990s the tanker container industry had come to be dominated by South African companies. Led by Consani Engineering, Trencor, and Welfit Oddy, the South Africans controlled close to 50 percent of the world market in 1999.[2] Established since 1928 and winner of several awards for technology excellence and export achievement, Consani alone accounted for 22 percent of world production in 1999.[3]

In attacking these incumbents, CIMC again deployed the strategy of cost innovation, but this time focused on offering potential customers a wider variety of specialist models at lower cost. It began by signing a technology-transfer agreement with a British container specialist, UBH International Limited (UBHI), owner of an innovative technology (the Universal Beam Tank) that enabled the weight of tank containers to be reduced. At that time, UBHI supplied 1,800 TEUs per annum—almost 15 percent of the global market.

CIMC's second step was to reduce costs below those of the established competitors by driving for scale advantage. Within fifteen months it had built a new plant capable of producing 6,000 TEUs of tank containers per annum—almost three times the size of the incumbent global leader. Having won a large volume of business on the basis of low costs, the next step was to use its competitive Chinese design staff to expand the product line and offer more models and customization services. Key to offering this extra value added while keeping costs down was its innovative redesign of the production line to increase flexibility. CIMC was able to reduce the setup time to change models from twenty minutes to five minutes, allowing it to produce a wider variety of tank containers more cheaply than its competitors.

By 2003, CIMC had captured 30 percent of the world market in the tank container segment. In 2005, it expanded production again to become the world leader in this segment as well. The South African companies that had dominated what they viewed as a safe, high-end niche had been toppled.

Retreat to High End Leads to Defeat

In our experience, shifting focus to high-end segments is the most common strategy managers in high-cost countries are planning to adopt in response to the new competition from China. But the story of the formerly dominant South African players who found themselves competing with CIMC suggests the need for extreme caution in using this approach. The fact is, their attempt to escape the Chinese challenge by moving to successively higher-end market segments ended in dramatic failure. Trencor ceased production of dry freight containers in 1999 to focus on tanks, but by 2004 it ended manufacture of tank containers as well. Consani was placed into liquidation in January 2005.[4] Meanwhile, UBHI was effectively forced to enter an alliance with CIMC in order to maintain the viability of its "focus on the high-end" strategy.

According to its Web site UBHI believes it has "secured the future of its world-beating tank design" through its alliance with CIMC, which allows what it calls a "horses for courses" strategy whereby customized tank containers come from UBHI (just 750 TEUs per year) and the standard ones are supplied by CIMC. In another statement UBHI adds: "Whilst some observers saw this as UBHI 'selling the family silver' the co-operation [with CIMC] has proved a resounding success. Far from being viewed now as an error on the part of UBHI, the alliance of the company's trusted technology and know-how with the industrial muscle of CIMC is increasingly recognised as a model for the future."[5]

But as we will see, focusing on what one manager we interviewed called "the sunlit uplands" of the market more often than not proves ineffective. One reason is that falling volume means this strategy is difficult to sustain over the medium term. Volumes at the top end of the market tend to be small, which means it becomes more and more difficult to continue investing in the high fixed costs of R&D and product development. Established competitors are left with insufficient units over which to spread the cost once they lose the volume business and focus solely on the upper end. It is also likely that their manufacturing costs are driven up as volume falls and production becomes subscale.

Their Chinese competitors, meanwhile, have the opportunity to share the costs of maintaining expensive R&D and development departments with volume segments. Manufacturing infrastructure can also be shared. And with the fixed costs covered by mass-market volume, the Chinese can price down to margin cost if they decide to cherry-pick upmarket niches or try to explode them into much bigger markets. These dynamics mean that the relative cost disadvantage of retreating incumbents becomes ever greater as they move to successively smaller, higher-end segments of the market.

The next stage of CIMC's advance shows this cycle at work. In 1997, having secured a large share of the volume business, it could afford to establish its own R&D center. CIMC has since consistently invested over 2 percent of its revenues in research, so as its sales volumes and revenues have continued to expand, so has its total R&D budget. In an industry generally populated by medium-sized specialists with limited resources, and aided by the relatively low cost of Chinese engineers, CIMC's R&D capacity now swamps that of any of its competitors. A powerful new competitive weapon—the ability to back large-scale investigations into new technology—has therefore been added to CIMC's arsenal.

Paradoxically, therefore, the company that started out as a rock-bottom competitor, relying on cheap labor to win over the basic volume business in standard containers, now has a greater R&D capability than its volume-starved rivals who tried to move upmarket to escape CIMC's growing penetration of the low end. CIMC was able to use this new advantage in R&D capability when a shortage of the tropical hardwood used in floors of containers drove the cost of wood up to 15 percent of the total cost of making a container. In the face of declining supply from the world's rain forests, it could be anticipated that this problem would continue. So as it struggled to procure the half-million cubic feet of hardwood it used every year, CIMC began to focus its R&D capability on finding replacement materials. Many in the industry believed the problem was intractable. But after many rounds of experimentation to get the right combination of functionality, quality consistency, production efficiency, customer acceptance, and cost, CIMC came up with a suitable manmade substitute. Today it has replaced tropical hardwood in 25 percent of its container output and sees the manmade substitute virtually taking over in the future.

CIMC's R&D capabilities have also allowed it to extend the pattern of successive expansion into higher-value segments to the market for foldable containers. The panels that comprise these containers can be folded down in a "chain" onto their bases so that when containers have to be returned empty, they can be collapsed down to 20 percent of their original volume for easy transport. CIMC used its large-scale, low-cost R&D capacity to develop an alternative to the industry standard technology used for the fold-chain mechanism.

Despite being the leading company with 70 percent of the world market in "foldables," Britain's Clive-Smith Cowley got the message: as a medium-sized, specialist company it simply didn't have the resources to win a long-term race against CIMC, even with its initial technological lead. Before CIMC even finalized a prototype, Clive-Smith Cowley offered to do a deal with its Chinese rival. Such was CIMC's track record in sweeping through other high-end segments that Clive-Smith Cowley agreed to sell a 60 percent share in its business. This gave CIMC access to the "Domino" chain technology, along with an existing production line that was relocated to Guangdong.[6]

CIMC's rise from struggling entrant into the bottom end of the shipping-container business to unrivalled global leader in virtually every segment of the market—in volume, value, and technical sophistication, and R&D capability—is a wake-up call to those who still believe that moving upmarket ahead of the Chinese is the way to counter disruptive cost innovation from China. Because the Chinese are using their cost advantage across a broad swathe of activities, including R&D, design, and customization, not just in volume manufacturing, moving to successively higher-end segments is just as likely to result in bankruptcy as it is in salvation.

It might be comforting to think that CIMC and its "learn, improve, disrupt" slogan as it relentlessly moved upmarket is a special case. It is not. Look no further than China's world share of high-technology exports. In 1995 China exported $6 billion worth of goods and services classified as "high technology." By 2005 that figure was $217.6 billion, representing 28.6 percent of China's total exports.[7] In Shenzhen, which started as a Special Economic Zone across the border from Hong Kong producing cheap clothes, toys, and athletic shoes, high-technology exports have been growing at more than 45 percent per annum in recent years. By 2005 Shenzhen exported $47 billion in high-tech goods.[8] Even more significantly, some 57 percent of high-technology production was based on intellectual property owned by Chinese firms. In 2004 alone, Shenzhen companies applied for 14,918 patents. Today 90 percent of China's growing investment in R&D is made by the corporate sector.

Of course, we are not arguing that established companies should forget competing on the basis of better technology because they face disruptive competition from China. As we will see, lack of capabilities in certain types of technology and complex products is still a key weakness for China's emerging dragons, and companies that have skills in these areas can leverage them to remain successful. Instead, the message is this: don't be seduced by the idea that moving upmarket is a silver bullet for dealing with the coming wave of competition from Chinese companies. Because the challenge differs in important ways from anything we have seen before, it demands new and creative strategies in response.

Chinese Competition Is Different

Despite mounting evidence that Chinese companies are no longer confined to the bottom end of the market, skepticism about whether they represent a new kind of competition still abounds. One common argument is that the kind of strategy used by CIMC is no different from that deployed by Japanese and Korean companies in industries such as consumer electronics and automobiles.

There are, indeed, many parallels between what the Chinese dragons are doing and what their Japanese and Korean corporate cousins did before them. But that is hardly a valid reason for believing it won't be disruptive to global competition. Ask yourself: how many major U.S. or European producers are left in the consumer electronics market today? And witness the trouble the U.S. automakers are in as they continue to lose share to Asian competitors. It might more correctly be argued that the time-honored strategy of ratcheting up the value curve has proven not just disruptive but catastrophic for the companies that formerly dominated these industries.

Parallels with the rise of Japanese and Korean competitors can also be taken too far. As we will see in subsequent chapters, the emerging Chinese dragons are arguably using their cost advantage even more creatively than those who came before. Even in the early stages of their global expansion, Chinese companies aren't just competing by offering lower prices. One of the distinguishing features of these emerging dragons is the extent to which they are deploying some of the tools of product differentiation, including application of high technology to everyday products and offering of wide product lines, customization, and specialty products—all at a time while Chinese costs are still rock bottom and China is still at a very early stage in its development cycle. By contrast, it was decades before Korean companies such as Samsung and LG, for example, moved away from a strategy of simply matching the dominant competitors' offerings at lower prices and started seriously trying to differentiate themselves in the market.

Chinese companies too, so the argument goes, have little chance of becoming serious global players for decades. It's simply not possible for companies to emerge as global winners when they are headquartered in what is still on many measures a developing country, lacking international experience and with a stock of resources and capabilities that looks puny compared with the competences and infrastructure accumulated by established multinational giants from the United States, Europe, and Japan.[9]

Why, then, do we believe it be possible for the emerging Chinese dragons to have such a powerful and widespread impact on global competition so fast? After all, it took the Japanese and then Korean companies like Toyota or Samsung many decades to become major global players. Part of the answer lies in the fact that Chinese companies have been undergoing a massive, and often painful, restructuring since China began to open up in 1978. The extent to which this restructuring has transformed their competitiveness is not always fully appreciated outside China. Even more important, however, is the fact that the world environment into which Chinese companies are emerging today differs in three important ways from the conditions that prevailed in the past. These differences make the rise of Chinese companies as global competitors unique.

The first difference from earlier waves of new competition is that globalization of the world economy has created new gateways through which Chinese companies can break into the global market. The fact that barriers to global trade and investment have been continuously dropping, that international supply chains are becoming increasingly modular, that many activities are now outsourced, and that the global markets for capital, knowledge, and acquisitions are all now more open, reduces the entry barriers faced by Chinese firms. We will elaborate on exactly how these factors work to magnify the disruptive impact of Chinese competition in chapter 1.

The second unique factor is that China is probably the only country in history to have an economy opened to the world at such an early stage of its development—through massive foreign direct investment, enormous flows of trade and subsequent membership of the World Trade Organization (WTO), and links to the knowledge and experience of the large overseas-Chinese diaspora.

The scale of inward foreign investment and trade has meant that Chinese companies have been forced to learn how to compete with multinationals from day one in order to survive in their home market. Compared with their Japanese and Korean cousins, Chinese companies have had to face the cold winds of international competition almost from infancy as more than $621 billion was invested by 509,000 foreign companies (over $60 billion in 2005 alone), much of it aimed at capturing China's markets, since the doors were opened in 1978. This experience of competing with multinationals inside China gives Chinese companies a head start as they expand abroad.

The capabilities base of Chinese firms has also been lifted more rapidly and effectively through openness to the outside world. Chinese companies have gained a great deal of knowledge from multinationals in China through acting as their suppliers and customers, and as staff trained by foreign investors have hopped across to jobs with Chinese organizations. In the same way, knowledge has been infused into Chinese companies through cooperation with the overseas-Chinese diaspora. The overseas Chinese communities in Taiwan, Hong Kong, and Southeast Asia alone number over 45 million people, with a further 2 million ethnic Chinese in the United States. Among these groups are many with knowledge of leading-edge technology and extensive international business experience. These people have been active as investors and entrepreneurs in China, providing an important source of world-class capabilities to the emerging dragons. Some have returned permanently. In just one year, 2003, there were an estimated 20,000 highly qualified returnees. Of 629 members of the Chinese Academy of Science, 81 percent have studied overseas, as have 54 percent of the members of China's Engineering Academy.

This wave of reverse migration has boosted the capability of the Chinese competition to deliver high technology at low cost. Of the Chinese high-tech companies listed on the Nasdaq, for example, about half were started by returnees, who also account for many of the star Chinese ventures that have recently come to prominence such as UTStarcom, Sina, Sohu, AsiaInfo, Vimicro. Less widely recognized are the many returning Chinese who have brought back not only advanced technologies but, more importantly, modern management ideas, business experience, and links with overseas business communities.

The signs are that the contribution of returnees to capability building within China's emerging companies will only increase in the future. It is estimated that 75 percent of all the Chinese who have studied abroad since 1978 are still abroad. An increasing number of these are ready to be wooed back. And the Chinese government is now actively courting them: by 2004, China had set up more than seventy new venture parks to provide a fertile environment for returning entrepreneurs, who have established more than five thousand new businesses.

At the same time, the fact that China is still a developing country, especially in terms of its "soft infrastructure"—such as the incomplete system of property rights, inefficient markets for assets, and the still-pervasive influence of political fiat in business—means that the managers of Chinese companies enjoy competitive advantages not normally available to their rivals in the developed world. These often include access to assets and resources at below-market prices, various types of government support, and, perhaps paradoxically, very high levels of managerial autonomy. These institutional factors combine to sharpen the dragons' ability to compete with multinationals abroad as well as at home.

The impact of this unique combination of Chinese advantages is magnified by the sheer scale of China's resources and the huge size of its domestic market. Japanese and Korean companies benefited from protected home markets, but these were relatively small in the context of the global arena. China's domestic market is so large, so diverse, so rapidly growing, and so hypercompetitive that the magnitude of advantages that Chinese companies have developed at home, especially in cost and scale, means they have a much greater impact on global competition than their predecessors. China's sheer scale relative to the global market is aptly demonstrated by its global shares of production across a range of industries from low to high end, as detailed in table I-1.

TABLE I-1

Chinese global market shares of selected industries, 2005

Product	Global market share of Chinese production (%)
Television sets	40
Air conditioners	50
Refrigerators	30
Microwave ovens	51
Digital cameras	>50
Mobile phones	37
Marine containers	70
Ties	40
Toys	60
Lighters	70
Cranes	50
Sewing machines	70
Personal computers	35

Dragons at Your Door

It is clear from these statistics that CIMC's impact on the global container business is not a one-off. Chinese companies across a wide spectrum of industries and heritages have begun their assault on the global market. Lenovo, for example, hit the headlines when it successfully concluded a $1.75 billion deal to purchase 82 percent of IBM's Thinkpad PC business in December 2004—including the rights to use the IBM brand on its PCs for five years and ownership of the "Think" brand in perpetuity. The world also took notice when Chinese white goods and consumer electronics maker Haier made a bid for the venerable U.S. firm Maytag. But the real disruption to global competition won't come just from a few high-profile companies like these. Rather, China's power to change the face of global competition derives from the surge of dozens of companies few outside China have even heard of today: Galanz, which now supplies more than one in two microwave ovens sold in the global market; Wanxiang, the world's largest producer of universal joints, which has established an industry fund to buy U.S. firms in auto components (it is already talking to struggling Delphi); BYD, the world's second-largest maker of rechargeable batteries; CIMC; Shanghai Zhenhua Port Machinery Company (ZPMC), which has a 54 percent share of the world market for harbor cranes; and Pearl River Piano, which has won 15 percent of the U.S. market (40 percent in upright pianos) in just five years, and is the global volume leader, producing around a hundred thousand pianos every year.

Recently, more high-tech firms are showing strong global competitiveness. Vimicro Corporation, for example, is now among the international standard-setters in the multimedia-chip industry; it has captured 60 percent of the market for multimedia processors that drive cameras in PCs and is now making steady progress in the market for similar processors used in multimedia phones. Another example is CapitalBio, which was already indentified by *Fortune* as the "coolest international biotech firm back in 2002."[10] CapitalBio develops and commercializes a broad range of products, including biochip technology products for drug discovery research, genomics, proteomics, biosafety testing, and clinical applications. Started in 1999, the company has already filed dozens of patent applications and launched more than twenty products, including cutting-edge systems to probe gene functions. One of its main products is a small uHTS (ultra-high throughput screening) chip, which sells for a bit over $100. This chip can analyze 380 cells per hour, which is a breakthrough in R&D efficiency compared with the speed of human experts, who could only analyze at most five to six cells per day.

The growing global competitiveness of Chinese high-tech firms is also evident in the increasing numbers of successful IPOs on Nasdaq, among them China Medical, a global technology leader in the design and development of HIFU (high intensity focused ultrasound) devices for the treatment of solid cancers and benign tumors; TechFaith Wireless, one of the world's largest independent mobile phone design houses with 2005 revenue close to $100 million; and Actions Semiconductor Co., Ltd., one of China's leading fabless semiconductor companies, which provides comprehensive mixed-signal system-on-a-chip solutions for portable consumer electronics. The rise of these new Chinese competitors across a wide spectrum of industries has not always been on the radar screens of Western managers. But the fact that many of China's emerging dragons have left the starting gates in the race to become global, and that many others will follow, can no longer be in dispute.

Of course some, probably many, of the Chinese companies venturing into the global market will fail. The *dragons* we describe in this book are not necessarily representative of the general mass of Chinese firms. Instead, they are the select group of companies that are finding innovative ways to turn China's comparative advantages, especially low costs, into global competitive advantages. They have found the right strategies at the right time and have been flexible enough to ride the wave of China's fast-changing environment. And they are not just clever strategists. They are the few companies among many that have been able to back innovative strategies with quality management and excellent execution—just like other winning companies around the world.

We make no apologies for focusing on these "outliers" among Chinese businesses for three reasons. First, where these companies pioneer, many others will follow. More and more Chinese companies are learning from these dragons' approaches and are steadily building the capabilities necessary to deploy them. In this process they will not only imitate but also improve upon the basic formula. And because the "go global" strategy is an integral part of China's broader development as a nation and its goal of gaining respect commensurate with its size as a major player on the global stage, this strategy is almost certain to be sustained for decades, even if the going proves tough.

Second, incumbents would be foolish to take comfort in the fact that only a small fraction of Chinese companies who set out on the journey will become major global players with staying power. If for no other reason than the size of the Chinese market and resources behind them, the successful dragons will be big, even by world standards. We should remember that it didn't take hundreds of Japanese automakers, but just a handful of winners like Toyota, Honda, and Nissan, to send the U.S. automobile companies into a tailspin.

Third, it is not only the ultimate winners that have the potential to disrupt the accepted rules of global competition. In fact, it's some of the "kamikaze pilots" that might inflict the most damage to today's business models. As we see when any established market is disrupted by a wave of newcomers, even those fundamentally solid companies that fail to respond to the changed conditions can founder—as the recent history of the airline industry has aptly demonstrated.

As the Chinese dragons' relentless pressure to obsolete the conventional wisdom of global business gathers strength, few businesses will be immune. Sooner or later, the emerging dragons will come knocking on the door of your industry, whether you are in low tech or high tech, a mass-market or a specialized niche. The questions every manager needs to be asking, therefore, are:

- How will the dragons disrupt global competition?

- When are they likely to come knocking at my door?

- What should I be doing about it?

This book is devoted to addressing these three fundamental questions, focusing on understanding what cost innovation is, how the Chinese achieve it, how and when it will disrupt the global market, and what established multinationals and local champions alike should be doing to respond before it's too late. Our aim is to help managers whose businesses, whether they yet realize it or not, will come under threat from the disruption to global competition that the continued rise of Chinese companies as global players will bring.

In chapter 1 we will explore the unique combination of Chinese advantages that is shaping this new kind of disruptive competition, and how the emerging Chinese dragons are harnessing the new gateways being opened by globalization to move decisively and rapidly into the world market despite limited resources and experience.

Chapter 2 explains the secrets of how Chinese companies are achieving cost innovation. We show how the Chinese dragons are leveraging low-cost R&D resources to deliver high technology at mass-market prices, using a focus on process innovation to breathe new life into technologies Western companies have written off as obsolete or uneconomical, developing innovative products at a fraction of the cost of their global competitors by recombining existing technologies in new ways, riding the wave of open architecture to bypass traditional barriers to innovation, and successfully rendering established Western competitors' assets and experience obsolete by betting on low-cost, alternative technologies. Our message is straight out of Sun Tzu's ancient *Art of War*: the first step in preparing for battle is to know your enemy.[11] Only by understanding how the Chinese manage cost innovation can Western companies decide how to respond: either by learning from the Chinese or by devising a strategy for effective counterattack.

Chapter 3 looks at where Western companies are most vulnerable to the new disruptive competition from China. It sweeps away the myth that Chinese competition will impact only low-end market segments or low-technology products. We will see how cost innovation allows Chinese companies to dislodge a number of different types of "loose bricks" in the established competitors' defensive walls and hence to gain an entry point into global markets. Far beyond the obvious low-margin segments, these loose bricks include: *markets on the geographic periphery* that established players either ignore or underinvest in; *troublesome customers* who ask for nonstandard product features or services, yet balk at paying a price premium; and cozy *niche markets* that are ripe for the Chinese to shake up using cost innovation.

We then explain how the dragons, having gained an initial foothold, set up a virtuous cycle of cost, technological advance, and rapid learning until that ultimately allows them to scale the top peaks of the market, offering a product range second to none, transforming formerly protected niche markets into volume businesses.

Chapter 4 is devoted to answering the question: where are the weaknesses of these emerging dragons? This chapter will help established companies see where they might target their own responses so as to neutralize some of the Chinese competitors' advantages and exploit their limitations. We present a set of indicators to help you work out just how far cost innovation will take the Chinese dragons in disrupting your industry and how fast this new threat is likely to gather steam. This should help incumbents better anticipate the challenge they face so they can proactively build their defenses. We also show some surprising ways in which the dragons might threaten seemingly "safe" industries by coming from left field.

Finally, chapter 5 focuses specifically on how established companies can develop a strategy to respond to the new competition from China. We consider three sets of options for a successful fight-back: using your own unique technologies and capabilities for cost innovation to beat the dragons at their own game; leveraging your China operations in a new role within your global strategy; or allying with a Chinese competitor to gain advantage in the global market. Regardless of which of the various options you choose, you will see why doing nothing is not one of them.

In the conclusion we look toward the future. Reviewing what we have learned from studying the gathering wave of disruptive competition from China, we sketch out what a world of future competition between Chinese dragons, established global players, and national champions might look like and what it might take to succeed once the global competitive map has been redrawn.

I

Disrupting Global Competition

How Did They Get Here So Fast?

How were Chinese companies so quickly able to reach the point of disrupting the business models of established players from a standing start? The key to their ability to "come from nowhere" to become powerful global competitors lies in the combination of two factors: a unique combination of Chinese advantages and what Thomas Friedman aptly termed "the flattening of the world" through globalization, which has helped reduce the dragons' handicap in those areas where they are behind.[1]

Most observers intuitively understand that the fount of Chinese advantage is low-cost labor. But it is less widely recognized that the emerging Chinese dragons benefit from a confluence of related factors that allow them to deepen this basic cost advantage and to use it in novel ways to achieve cost innovation. At the same time, globalization is opening up new gateways through which companies from a developing economy can compete in world markets long before they accumulate the full range of capabilities enjoyed by established multinationals. Ten or twenty years ago it would have been a slow and difficult process for companies, even with the advantages Chinese companies enjoy, to break into the global market. Today, the structure of the global economy and, paradoxically, some of the strategies of established global players such as outsourcing, provide a fertile field for Chinese dragons to grow in world markets.

To understand how the impact of these forces might play out, we need to begin by rethinking our ideas both about the advantages Chinese companies enjoy and what globalization means for the competitive playing field.

The Dragons' Unique Confluence of Advantages

Chinese companies bring to the global market a unique set of advantages over traditional competitors, including access to low-cost talent across the spectrum, from assembly-line workers to highly skilled engineers and research scientists; the ability to use state assets and intellectual property at below their market value; even greater management autonomy versus shareholders than many of their Western counterparts; and strong personal incentives to create value, even if it means taking bold risks.

Access to Low-Cost Talent at All Skill Levels

The talent pool available to Chinese companies at low cost is unprecedented in history. While China's growth has prompted more than 150 million people to move from working the land into the nonagricultural sector, the rural labor force still numbers over 450 million, roughly two-thirds of the total workforce. And it is increasing at a rate of 10 million each year as rural children reach working age. Even if the workforce engaged solely in agriculture falls to 20 percent of the total workforce (the average for newly industrializing countries, compared with under 5 percent in developed countries), there will be an estimated pool of 340 million surplus rural workers on which expanding companies can draw. With this continual flow of underemployed workers, basic wage rates are unlikely to climb quickly, so Chinese companies will be able to draw in new, unskilled labor at low cost for decades to come. But what is even more important for the disruptive potential of Chinese competition in the global market is the huge and rapidly growing supply of highly skilled staff that companies can draw on to underpin new sorts of competitive advantage.

In 2005, for example, 3.4 million new graduates came onto the market, three times the number graduating just five years ago. Last year, China surpassed the United States in total enrollment in universities, so it now has more people studying for degrees than any other country in the world. The most popular majors were among the most relevant to the needs of commerce and industry: business administration is the top choice, followed by computer science, law, finance, communications, medicine, and English.

For these reasons, despite more than two decades of rapid growth, China's wage rates are still between 5 percent and 20 percent of those in the United States, depending on skill level and sector, and low-skilled Chinese workers earn around $1 per hour, compared with between $15 and $30 per hour in the United States or Europe.[2] Even making the most pessimistic assumptions on Chinese productivity, Chinese labor costs remain less than half of those in the United States. Certainly some wage inflation will occur, but productivity will simultaneously increase, especially as tomorrow's better-educated Chinese strive to get ahead in a fast-moving society. In all, therefore, we can expect a hefty cost advantage available to Chinese companies, right across the skill spectrum, to persist for another twenty to thirty years.

Now, as many who doubt the future strength of Chinese companies as global competitors are quick to point out, the dragons don't have a monopoly on this labor cost advantage. Foreign multinationals are also able to use low Chinese labor costs to underpin their global competitiveness as they increasingly source out of China and expand the size and depth of their Chinese operations. But here's the rub: Chinese dragons have so far proven able to exploit the potential of this advantage much more fully than their foreign rivals. Rather than only using the lower Chinese labor rates to cut their manufacturing costs, the dragons have managed to use cost innovation to exploit this advantage across the full range of activities, including design, engineering, R&D, and administration.

The implication is clear: Western companies must learn the tricks of Chinese cost innovation. Failure to do so means they won't be able to match the dragons' ability to disrupt the global market by leveraging China's low-cost talent pool in ways that go far beyond traditional sourcing strategies.

Access to State Assets and Intellectual Property at a Discount

Another factor that is fueling the cost competitiveness of China's emerging dragons is the fact that many enjoy access to state assets and intellectual property (IP) without having to pay the full market value that these assets might command if they were traded in an open global market. Let's be clear, we are not talking here about theft or corruption (although the problem is widely acknowledged in China). In most cases, the fact that Chinese dragons have been able to access assets and IP at a discount is a reflection of China's long-term transformation from central planning to a market economy, and its drive to improve the utilization of her national asset base, combined with asset and financial markets that are still underdeveloped by world standards.

Take the case of Lenovo. What is today Lenovo began life in 1984 as the New Technology Development Company of the Research Institute of Computing Technology (ICT) of the Chinese Academy of Sciences with a structure that is termed *suoban gongshi* ("institute-run enterprise"). This was an organizational form based on the principle of *guoyou minying* ("state-owned, non-government-run"), which balanced state ownership on the one hand and managerial autonomy in finance, personnel, planning, and management on the other. Lenovo's eleven founders were all scientists working for the ICT. Despite being 100 percent state funded, the ICT loaned $25,000 as a start-up capital to Legend (Lenovo's original name). In fact, the ICT was not supposed to have extra money for business investment. However, setting up companies was considered to be one of the several organizational experiments being made in China's effort to reform the existing science and technology system. So Legend was permitted to use the ICT's name and reputation to help it win business. Initially, the ICT also provided office space, utilities, and so forth to the company in kind. Moreover, people who moved across to Legend were able to maintain their state-employee benefits and their rank in the government service hierarchy; and the ICT continued to pay base salary—providing an important financial, psychological, and status safety net to those who transferred to the venture and greatly aiding its recruitment efforts. Finally, the ICT provided Legend with full access to the Institute's rich science and technological resources, both physical and human.

This last source of support proved indispensable to Legend's rapid success. The company's first blockbuster product was an add-on card that could be inserted into a computer to make it capable of Chinese-character word processing. The product had been developed initially at the ICT, and the technology, with its key developer, was then transferred directly to Legend. Several other high-tech products were developed either by people who transferred to Legend from the ICT, often with product prototypes, or were developed directly in the laboratories of the Institute under contract arrangements with Legend.[3]

Critics often argue that these advantages are unfair. But even if true, the argument doesn't make such benefits a less potent fact of life in the coming round of global competition. Nor are these benefits likely to disappear in the near future because they are largely a product of China's transition to a modern economy. During the early phases of development, an important first step for a transitional economy such as China's is to improve the allocation of resources—many of which were poorly utilized under the former, centrally controlled system. The problem is that transitional economies almost by definition lack the institutions and commercial infrastructure that allows these resources and assets to be smoothly and transparently transferred into the hands of those who can use them most productively. China's stock markets, for example, simply weren't capable of handling enough initial public offerings (IPOs) to cope with the magnitude and diversity of assets that had to be restructured. So much of the job was done by entrepreneurs who consolidated a mix of state, collective, and private resources to create strong companies with a bright future.

This mechanism may not have been transparent and it usually didn't follow what American lawyers like to call "fair process." But by helping to put the right resources where they could be used more productively to create commercial value, it has underpinned much of China's economic growth and rising prosperity as well as created personal wealth. It also gave emerging Chinese companies a good head start on the path to global success by furnishing them with a solid asset base at modest cost.

In fact, most of the companies who are successfully launching themselves into the global market are "hybrid" companies with a mix of public and private ownership. Even today, for example, although Lenovo's primary operating subsidiary has a majority of private ownership (through a listing on the Hong Kong Stock Exchange) it is linked back to a parent company largely owned by the Chinese Academy of Sciences.

An important implication for Western managers is the need to carefully analyze the ownership of the dragons when sizing them up as potential competitors. Avoid the temptation to cate-

gorize Chinese companies as "public" or "private." The ownership structures of Chinese companies and their relationship with
local, provincial, and national governments may be almost completely unrecognizable to executives from the rest of the world. It
is all the more important, then, to ask whether the structure of
your Chinese competitor will afford it access to assets or intellectual capital at prices that allow cost innovation—such as the provision of high technology at low cost.

In this arena, China stands apart from many other developing economies; it does have a significant stock of indigenous
technology, knowledge, and capability inherited from the central
planning age. Hitherto it had been locked up in government research institutes and the military-industrial establishment and
hence underutilized. But now that it is being transferred into the
commercial sector, the emerging Chinese dragons are using this
indigenous cache of technology to fuel cost innovation.

Of course this source of cost advantage will fade away over
time as China's financial and asset markets develop and become
more efficient and transparent. In the future, therefore, it will be
the ability to build on this initial "leg-up" of cheap assets from
the government that will distinguish those Chinese companies
that are able to sustain their initial success from those who will
falter. Today China sucks in five units of capital for every additional unit of output. This compares with three units of capital
per unit of output in Japan during its growth phase and just 2.5
in Korea.[4] So the process of moving from reliance on cheap assets and IP to becoming efficient at adding value still has a long
way to go. The leading dragons described in this book, such as
Lenovo, have made just that transition.

Exceptional Management Autonomy

Another peculiarity of China's corporate structures is that they
often lead to a greater separation between ownership and control,

and more management autonomy in practice, than in many U.S. and European companies. This means that management has the elbow room to make decisions quickly, largely independent from constraints imposed by shareholders. The case of the global port-equipment champion, Shanghai Zhenhua Port Machinery Co. Ltd. (ZPMC), illustrates how this can come about and the implications for Chinese companies to pursue cost innovation.

ZPMC's ultimate parent company is China Harbour Engineering Company (Group) Ltd., a large state-owned enterprise (SOE) that is directly supervised by the Chinese government through its State-owned Assets Supervision and Administration Commission. In practice, however, the management of ZPMC has a great deal of autonomy because of a shareholding structure that, outside China, might be regarded as unusual.

Instead of owning all the shares in ZPMC directly, China Harbour established ZPMC as a foreign-affiliated joint venture. One of the partners was China Harbour's unit in Shanghai. The "foreign" partner in the joint venture was a Hong Kong company, at least in name. But in fact the Hong Kong partner was itself a subsidiary of China Harbour.

This unusual arrangement (which amounted to China Harbour forming a foreign joint venture with its own Hong Kong unit) was chosen precisely in order to bypass the traditional constraints imposed on SOEs. Because ZPMC was officially a foreign-affiliated enterprise, it was able to enjoy policy treatment and the freedom to choose a management structure and compensation system normally accorded only to subsidiaries of foreign multinationals. Despite ultimate ownership by the state, therefore, ZPMC's management was effectively autonomous.

This separation between ownership and control was further widened in 1997 when ZPMC added a diverse set of foreign shareholders into the mix by issuing a tranche of B shares (the class of shares restricted to foreign investors) through flotation on the Shanghai Stock Exchange. The resulting shareholding structure is shown in figure 1-1.

After the flotation the state-owned China Harbour Engineering Company Group retained at least indirect control of more than 50 percent of the total shares outstanding. But because of the many layers between ZPMC and its ultimate Chinese parent and the need to be seen to protect the foreign minority shareholders, ZPMC's management was effectively in control. Its freedom to run the company with minimal shareholder involvement was further increased by its role as a government experiment in how the problems of traditional SOE structures might be overcome and the fact that its general manager was a trusted official with a long career in the Ministry of Communications.

Despite common perceptions in the West that most Chinese companies are state-run bureaucracies and therefore handicapped from competing in the global market, quite the opposite is more often true: the fact that China is in the process of transitioning

FIGURE 1-1

Separation of ownership and control at ZPMC

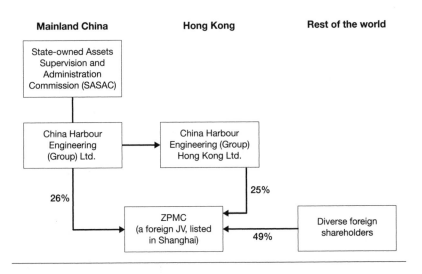

from central planning to a "market system with Chinese characteristics" means that the managers of the emerging dragons are well placed to act as entrepreneurs.

Like ZPMC, many of the other dragons we have mentioned above, such as Pearl River Piano, CIMC, and Lenovo, are all hybrid companies with a mix of state and private (often foreign) ownership. All of their CEOs have been with their companies for decades, since early economic reform. This combination of stability and autonomy at the top management level has enabled these ambitious Chinese firms to pursue aggressive, long-term goals that are often impossible for Western managements under the constant short-term pressure of the stock markets.

Cost innovation harnesses this entrepreneurial autonomy. For example, autonomy from shareholder demands is enabling the emerging dragons to bet on risky, emerging technologies that would obsolete much of the installed base and accumulated experience of their established global rivals. High levels of management autonomy are also helping Chinese companies set new standards for customer responsiveness and service. ZPMC, for example, won an early deal by accepting the customer's demand for a delivery lead time so tight that most established players in the industry would have regarded it as impossible. Through extraordinary efforts ZPMC was on track to meet the deadline, but disaster loomed when it failed to get a slot in the shipping schedule of the only carrier with the capacity to transport the finished cranes to its customer. Facing heavy penalties and the prospect of being lumbered with a reputation for unreliability, ZPMC took a bold move to ensure on-time delivery: it bought a 60,000-tonne cargo ship for $2 million, converted it into a crane carrier, and sailed its four-crane order direct to the customer! What was originally a force majeure subsequently became a channel for reinforcing ZPMC's customer-service orientation, allowing the company to break into new markets against entrenched competitors. "Whatever needs the customer has," says the CEO Guan Tongxian in an interview with the authors, "we will satisfy them." The company now has a fleet of eight specialized vessels that greatly improves its levels of efficiency and customer service, which in turn provides a significant competitive advantage against its rivals.

This means that rather than expecting the Chinese threat simply to come from imitating established products and technologies more cheaply, Western managers need to prepare for disruptive competition from the emerging dragons. An effective response will require a serious rethink about how new technologies and approaches could be used to dramatically cut costs, not just to improve the functionality of products and services, and how low Chinese costs can be used to deliver higher levels of service and customization.

Strong Incentives to Succeed

A high level of personal incentive completes the unique confluence of advantages enjoyed by the emerging dragons. Take the example of Yuandong Group, a family of companies that together have sales of $250 million and directly employ thirty-five hundred people across a range of businesses spanning electric wire and cable, pharmaceuticals, and advanced materials. Yuandong was established in 1990 by Jiang Xipei with a total investment of just $225,000, 80 percent of which came from Jiang and the rest from his brother and other family and friends. The ownership of Yuandong has switched back and forth between state and private shareholders several times throughout the history of the business, almost in synchrony with the progress of economic reform in China. This flexibility helped it acquire underutilized assets and garnered preferential financing and market access that were often beyond reach of pure private business.

During its rise, it may not have been clear whether Yuandong was a public or a private enterprise. But as Jiang likes to remind visitors, it has already created over 100 renminbi millionaires (individuals who earned the equivalent of $125,000) and ten individuals whose wealth from Yuandong exceeded 10 million RMB (around $1.25 million).

Yuandong is hardly unique in providing opportunities for employees, and particularly senior management, to accumulate substantial wealth if their company succeeds in growing revenue, profits, and value. Many Chinese companies, whether they are state-owned, collective, private, or some complex and alternating mixture of all three, are structured in such a way that the management is handsomely rewarded for financial performance. The mechanisms used may be different from the large pools of stock options often used to reward senior management in the West, but the effect is to strongly encourage managers of the emerging dragons to become entrepreneurs and innovators—especially since the downside risks are often cushioned by affiliated state institutions.

To see the power of these incentives when combined with the high levels of managerial autonomy we have already discussed, consider the next stage of Legend's evolution. As noted above, the Institute of Computing Technology (ICT) had provided Legend full access to its science and technological resources, paving the way for Legend's initial success. In 1993, Legend renegotiated its relationship with the ICT and its ultimate parent, the Chinese Academy of Sciences (CAS). This wasn't easy, because the relative contributions of different parties to Legend's success were far from clear. After a negotiation that lasted more than a year, CAS agreed that the annual dividends would be split as follows: 20 percent direct to CAS, 45 percent to ICT (which was later transferred to CAS), and 35 percent to Legend's managers. Despite this profit-sharing plan, all of the equity remained in the hands of CAS.

In 1994 Legend floated its operating company as the Legend Group Ltd via an IPO on the Hong Kong Stock Exchange. The listing made clear that the newly listed Legend Group was controlled by Legend Holdings as the majority shareholder. However, the equity split between the interested parties in the holding company was not disclosed. It was not until 1998 that it was officially acknowledged that the holding company was 65 percent owned by CAS and 35 percent owned by Legend's management and employees.

The Beijing arm of the government didn't endorse this equity arrangement until 2001, when the Ministry of Finance issued a ruling that required the Ministry of Science and Technology to lead a reform of Legend's structure. The Ministry of Science and Technology finally ruled that Legend employees could buy their 35 percent stake at a 70 percent discount to the audited share price. The rationale was that 35 percent of the earnings retained in the company since 1993 were deemed to belong to the management (as it was the product of their efforts), and therefore, this amount of money could be deducted from the cost of their shares. So it took almost ten years to resolve Legend's ownership. But the managers ultimately shared the benefits of Legend's fast growth: a new group of dollar millionaires was born from the company's success.

The fact that the senior management of China's emerging dragons can become personally rich if they succeed in building a valuable global company, while their state affiliations often cushion much of the downside risk, encourages aggressive expansion and risk taking. Most of these managers know that they are unlikely to win big if they simply try to emulate their established global rivals. Their best chance is to innovate and the obvious place to focus is on cost innovation because it plays to Chinese strengths.

Globalization Opens New Gateways for Chinese Competition

Of course, despite these significant advantages, Chinese companies abroad face a number of important handicaps; among the most common are limited knowledge of potential customers and markets overseas, weak distribution and brands, a paucity of proprietary technology, limited breadth of capabilities, and lack of management depth—especially when it comes to people experienced in managing abroad. In the past these disadvantages might have put an end to the global ambitions of Chinese companies. But globalization of the world economy has changed the rules of the game in ways that allow the emerging dragons to quickly become a potent force in global competition despite these handicaps. Most of today's multinational giants followed the same basic path to becoming global: begin by building competitive advantage in your home market using local know-how and resources, start selling your product or service in markets with similar characteristics to your home base, and then gradually adapt your offering or sourcing strategy to suit the peculiarities of different locations around the globe. That strategy made sense in a world comprised of discrete national markets, often protected by trade barriers, where products and information flowed gradually toward isolated corners of the earth; these conditions made it possible to ride product life cycles like the gentle flow of a river from one country to the next.

The environment in which today's dragons are emerging from China could not be more different. Products and information flow almost instantly across the world, and the competition they face is already global. In many ways it's a less forgiving competitive jungle; the luxury of nurturing an organization's capabilities in a sheltered local market is largely gone, along with yesterday's leisurely product life cycles. The pressure to become world-class quickly, or to perish in the global foray, is now intense.

But globalization has also brought a new opportunity for latecomers: the fact that knowledge, technologies, and components are now more mobile and readily accessed from anywhere in the world means that a budding multinational is no longer captive to its home base. Geography is no longer destiny. To take advantage of this opportunity requires that the traditional strategy of internationalization be turned on its head: succeeding globally means developing an expertise at accessing knowledge from around the world. Only excellence at "learning from the world" will allow a latecomer to compensate for the gaps in its capability base and the limitations of a developing country home market.

This is exactly what the emerging Chinese dragons are doing. They are rapid learners and they are not afraid to hire the world's best designers, advertising agencies, consultants, and technical experts to help fill the gaps in their capabilities. And when the assets they need to succeed globally, whether these are brands or technologies, look too difficult or slow to build organically, the dragons are showing that they will try to shortcut the process by using mergers and acquisitions. The gateways opened by globalization, combined with a new internationalization strategy based on learning from the world, means that the Chinese dragons will become a bigger force in global competition faster than anything we saw when Japan and Korea entered the global market.

It is important for incumbent global companies to analyze how the entry path of Chinese competitors is being unblocked by globalization because, ironically, their own strategies are in many cases smoothing the path for the Chinese (and hence inadvertently scoring against themselves); for example, one of the most important factors opening the gates to disruptive competition from China is the growing popularity of outsourcing among Western multinationals. Other gateways that are being influenced by incumbents' strategies include:

- The increasing modularization of products and services from automobiles to software and financial services

- The so-called "Global Knowledge Economy" and the drive to codify more and more of the world's knowledge so that it can be handled by IT and communications systems

- Concentration and globalization of retailing

- A more fluid international market for talent and professional services

- A more open market for corporate control, allowing the Chinese to acquire foreign companies

Outsourcing Opens the Gates

As global competition heats up, the cost pressures on U.S., European, and Japanese firms have led to a boom in their use of outsourcing.[5] Established multinationals are concentrating on the activities whose returns are most attractive and where they see the potential to build competitive advantage, leaving other pieces of the chain—both basic manufacturing and routine services—to be supplied by others. This drive toward more focused businesses in the West has also led to the global value chain being cut into ever-finer slices.

Carving up the global value chain and outsourcing less attractive activities makes a lot of sense as a way of boosting profitability. But it is also having an important side effect: outsourcing is opening up a new gateway through which Chinese dragons can penetrate into the heart of the world economy.

In the past, when established multinationals were much more vertically integrated than they are today, a new entrant was faced with replicating an entire complex system of activities in order to compete effectively. In today's de-integrated, global value chains, where many of the participants concentrate on just one or two activities and the integrators at the top of the chain use a plethora of subcontractors and outsourced services, Chinese companies can get a foothold in the industry by capturing just one slice. Globalization and de-integration of supply chains have had the side effect of reducing the barriers to entry for newcomers like the Chinese dragons. Once they have established a beachhead, they can then use the weight of their cost advantage and capabilities for rapid learning to

DISRUPTING GLOBAL COMPETITION • 43

relentlessly expand into other activities along the chain. Starting out as junior partners, they can eventually become major players.

In yesterday's environment of fragmented national markets, each isolated by trade barriers, such a strategy would have been impossible. But as markets across the globe have become much more integrated, China has attracted a massive global share of the activities in which it excels. This means it now has close to a monopoly as the "factory of the world" for many types of goods. The explosion of outsourcing, added to the large size of their Chinese home market, gives the best Chinese companies the potential to produce enormous volumes and so reap economies of scale that make them competitive despite a narrow skill base.

Having passed through this new gateway into the global market, the emerging dragons accumulate experience that helps broaden their stock of knowledge and capabilities.

The auto business is a good example. A recent study of a typical "American car" by the World Trade Organization (WTO) found that of a vehicle notionally made in the United States, 30 percent of the value was accounted for by Korean subassembly suppliers, 17.5 percent by Japan for specialized components and advanced technology, 7.5 percent by Germany for design, 4 percent by Taiwan and Singapore for minor parts, 2.5 percent by the United Kingdom for advertising and marketing services, and 1.5 percent by Ireland and Barbados for data processing. In total, the U.S. auto manufacturer accounted for just 37 percent of the value-creating activities.[6]

To see how these high levels of outsourcing in the auto industry have opened gates through which the Chinese have been able to enter; even while their capability bases are still narrow, consider the case of Wanxiang (see "Wanxiang's Rise from Outsource Supplier of a Humdrum Component to Tier 1 Global Competitor"). The company's name, which translates to "universal joint," is a reminder of the way it was able to enter the world market by focusing all of its limited resources on just one product—universal joints—courtesy of the global automakers that chose to outsource this humdrum component.

Wanxiang's Rise from Outsource Supplier of a Humdrum Component to Tier 1 Global Competitor

Wanxiang was able to concentrate just on manufacturing universal joints and still be competitive because falling barriers and more efficient transportation meant it could operate just one large-scale operation to serve global market demand in the rural town of Ningwei, where it enjoyed the world's lowest costs. Focusing all of its human and financial resources on building a company specializing in universal joints allowed Wanxiang to pull in front of its rivals. Among fifty-six Chinese makers of universal joints at the time, Wanxiang became one of only three that survived by the 1990s, and it went on to capture over 70 percent of the Chinese market. With relentless attention to improving quality and reducing cost in this narrow product range, Wanxiang was able to win the business outsourced by first-tier auto suppliers such as Delphi, Bosch, and Visteon in forty countries to become the largest supplier of universal joints in the world, producing over 25 million units per annum. One part at a time, Wanxiang has gradually expanded its product offers from universal joints to other parts of the driveline, and then to parts of a brake system, and subsequently to the whole chassis.

"Visteon doesn't treat Wanxiang as a competitor," observed Robert Marshall, Visteon's director of Asia-Pacific purchasing in Shanghai at the time. "We are clearly treating them as a supplier of components for auto parts."[a] But as it accumulated more and more resources and capabilities in the global market, Wanxiang turned its attention to disrupt the businesses of its North American competitors.

What happened to Illinois-based Schiller is instructive. Established in 1923, Schiller was one of the main aftermarket components suppliers for the auto industry in the United States and had many patents for universal joints. In 1984, Wanxiang got its first international order—thirty thousand units—from Schiller. Seeing the need to take advantage of lower labor costs in Asia, Schiller made an offer for Wanxiang to become its sole OEM producer. When the negotiation broke down, Schiller subsequently stopped ordering from Wanxiang, and switched to suppliers in Southeast

Asia. But Wanxiang, which wanted to build its own brand name over time, persisted through the early difficult days, growing ever stronger to become Schiller's toughest competitor in the United States market. By 1998, Schiller's losses were mounting. Eventually, Schiller offered itself for sale to Wanxiang for $19 million.

Wanxiang found a local partner, LSB Industries, Inc., to take the plant and workers off its hands; it retained Schiller's brand, patents, equipment, and market channels—and supplied the products from its large-scale facilities in China. This meant Wanxiang was able to capture the key knowledge assets of Schiller for a net cost of just $420,000, while adding substantial new sales volume to feed its Chinese plants.

In August 2001, Wanxiang bought a controlling 21 percent interest in Universal Automotive Industries (UAI), a Nasdaq-listed supplier of braking systems, for $2.8 million. Again, much of UAI's production was shifted to China. Two years later, Wanxiang purchased 33.5 percent of Rockford Powertrain, an American company with more than one hundred years' experience in making drive shafts. It then bought up a number of auto components distributors, such as Powers and Sons LLC in the United States, Power-Drive Europe Ltd. and Automative Components Supply Ltd. in the United Kingdom to complete its control of the chain from raw materials to distribution. Fast growth in the United States helped Wanxiang to quickly graduate from a third-tier supplier of a minor component to become a tier-one supplier of subassemblies to Ford and GM.

Since 2003, Wanxiang has also run the American Manufacturing Fund, an investment vehicle that is devoted to acquisitions and consolidation of auto components makers in the United States. By 2005, Wanxiang had acquired, merged with, or established thirty companies in eight countries, including the United States, the United Kingdom, Germany, Canada, and Australia, eighteen of which it controls outright. It has continued to grow at a blistering pace while competitors like Delphi stumble from crisis to crisis.

---

a. Paul Gao, "Supplying Auto Parts to the World," in "China Today," special edition, *McKinsey Quarterly,* 2004, 14–19.

Outsourcing by multinationals opened the first gateway for Wanxiang to enter the global market. Falling trade barriers and more efficient transportation allowed it to build massive scale and reduce costs by concentrating global production in China. As it gained strength, today's more open market for corporate control allowed it to acquire companies around the world that gave it access to technology, customer relationships, and established brands that it could use to leverage its underlying Chinese cost advantage. These new global realities made it possible for Wanxiang to move from a repair shop for bicycles and farm tractors with just $500 in capital, to a global company with $3.2 billion in sales and forty thousand employees. Its next goal? To build a complete car under its own brand name. In fact, Wanxiang has been working on an electric car since 1999, and began testing its electric bus in early 2006 with Hangzhou Tourist Bus Company. This determination to succeed has been put vividly by its founder and chairman, Lu Guanqiu, "It's been my dream to build a Wanxiang auto brand. I've announced that if I can't realize that dream, my son will; if my son can't, my grandson will. Through the effort of many generations, someday we'll fulfill this dream. We must do it. We're training and preparing our people. When the opportunity is ripe, we'll get into the business. It's the next logical step on our journey toward fulfilling our goal of becoming a large, world-class company."[7]

Modular Products and Services

The rise of outsourcing in the global economy has clearly been an important factor in allowing Chinese companies to unlock the door to the global market at an early stage in their development. Another keyhole is modularization.

In some industries, the slicing and dicing of the global value chain is so far advanced that the chain has come to resemble a series of "plug-and-play" modules. This kind of modularity is a familiar principle in the computer business, for example. Different companies can independently design and produce components, such as disk drives or operating system software, and those modules will fit together into a complex and smoothly functioning product because the module makers obey an accepted set of design rules. When a dominant design emerges in a particular industry, modularity increases efficiency and speed of innovation. But modularization, like outsourcing, also helps frame a well-defined gateway through which emerging Chinese firms can enter the global market even while they have a limited set of capabilities.

Creating a mobile phone handset, for example, used to be a black art known only to a few global players, so entry of the Chinese dragons was forestalled. For years the big three producers—Motorola, Nokia, and Ericsson—together controlled around 80 percent of the Chinese market, while other foreign manufacturers, including Philips, Alcatel, Siemens, and Sony, shared the rest. Chinese companies only started to enter the market in 1998 and in the first few years struggled to gain a foothold in their home market, let alone break into the business abroad.

Since 2000, however, as the technology has matured the value chain has been broken down into different modules, from radio frequency circuits to RISC (reduced instruction set computing) chips and applications software. The interactions between each of these modules are now regulated by a codified set of standards available to all. Specialist companies such as Wavecom of France, which makes radio-frequency modules, and Bellwave of Korea, which specializes in mobile phone design, offer the core building blocks of mobile phones. This means new entrants can launch a phone by "picking and mixing" these modules to create a distinctive product.

The Chinese competitors grabbed the opportunity opened up by modularization with both hands. Companies such as Ningbo Bird, Amoi, TCL, and Konka launched attractive phones by combining third-party modules with the help of Korean design houses. Amoi's A8 model, a product designed by Bellwave, became one of the best-selling models in China in 2001 and 2002, and helped push Amoi to become China's number-three mobile phone producer.

What happened next is an important indicator of the threat even Chinese newcomers can pose to established Western incumbents in today's world of modularization. Wavecom's experience, for instance, is a prime example.

In 2001 the champagne corks were popping at Wavecom as its sales grew by 392 percent to reach $350 million. Celebrations continued as its turnover grew by a further 91 percent in 2002. Wavecom's stunning growth was powered by huge orders from Chinese handset makers. TCL alone accounted for 32 percent of Wavecom's sales. Selling modules to the Chinese who assembled them into a final product was a bonanza.

Modularity, however, turned out to be a two-edged sword, because it meant that when the Chinese began to go beyond simple assembly to replace Western suppliers like Wavecom with internal production, they could do so step by step, one module after another. Modularity provided gateways for the dragons to enter into the core of the industry without having to figure out how to do everything at once.

The radio-frequency modules supplied by Wavecom were one of the first building blocks the Chinese competitors targeted to take in-house. Focusing their resources on this one module, the Chinese companies learned fast. The result was devastating for Wavecom; in 2003 its sales plummeted 50 percent as its Chinese customers mastered the modular technology. Wavecom's share price, which had peaked at $195, collapsed to $4 by 2005. The company was forced to exit the mobile phone market and try to relaunch the business focusing on mobile computing and industrial applications.

The repercussions were felt throughout the industry. Modularization had allowed the dam that had held back the Chinese for a decade to be broken; Chinese handset producers captured 55 percent of the Chinese market in 2003, up from a mere 8 percent in 2000. By 2006 Ningbo Bird announced that it had signed contracts to sell customized handsets to ten global operators, including Vodaphone and AT&T. Meanwhile, it was rapidly penetrating emerging markets for handsets, such as in Mexico, where it was selling phones at the rate of 300,000 per annum.[8] As we will see in chapter 5, global leaders such as Nokia and Motorola are fighting back aggressively against the expansion of Chinese handset competition—obviously, the game is far from over. But the message is clear: modularization provided the key that opened the global market to Chinese competition.

The Codification of Knowledge

The corollary of global supply chains becoming modular is that knowledge becomes more codified. And once knowledge that used to be tacit becomes codified, it can be digitized. It is then only a short step into the global knowledge base and onto the information superhighway. Increased codification of knowledge and rapid advances in communications, not least the emergence of the Internet, mean that it is much easier for Chinese firms to fill information gaps and to keep up with leading-edge developments anywhere in the world. The CEOs of Chinese high-tech firms we interviewed, such as Dawning and TechFaith, all explained that they were now just a few months behind the global industry leaders in knowing what was happening on the cutting edge. For knowledge that is still not accessible by digital means, it is now much easier for Chinese companies to establish subsidiaries to act as their "eyes and ears" in hotbeds of new technology, customer applications, or competitor intelligence around the world. As we will see in subsequent chapters, many of the emerging dragons have a network of overseas offices for just this purpose. For example, the $5.6 billion telecommunications equipment maker Huawei Technologies maintains a research and development center just down the street from Ericsson's headquarters in Stockholm.

Concentration and Internationalization of Retailing

Increasing concentration of the retail sector has also reduced the barriers Chinese companies face in penetrating global markets. In the past—when reaching the final customer meant navigating fragmented, multilayered wholesaling and retailing in every individual country—building distribution channels took years. Today, Wal-Mart alone buys more than $18 billion worth of goods in China each year. Once a Chinese company cracks the Wal-Mart account, it is automatically on the shelves of thousands of stores in the string of countries in which the retailer operates. And because the world's retailers are under relentless pressure from customers and competitors to provide greater value for money, they are prepared to assist budding Chinese multinationals with the world's lowest costs by teaching them how to upgrade and customize their products to enhance value to the consumer. Working directly with Chinese manufacturers in this way, the retailers can cut out the middlemen and shorten the chain to remove dead-weight cost.

The story of how Haier broke into the mass market in the United States market is a good example. Haier's CEO Zhang Riu Ming recalled: "I set my U.S. general manager the target of half of the top ten retail chains in the United States. He said it was impossible—it took famous brands like General Electric, Whirlpool, and Maytag decades to do that. Eventually we came up with a way forward: we erected a huge billboard displaying the Haier brand and some of our products on the road outside Wal-Mart's headquarters in Arkansas. Seeing the advertisement from his office window, Wal-Mart's head of purchasing began to enquire into Haier and its capabilities."[9] This led to Haier working closely with Wal-Mart to fine-tune its product designs and marketing. As well as getting product onto U.S. shelves, the relationship with Wal-Mart helped the Chinese company overcome its lack of in-depth understanding of the United States and learn to better tailor its products to fit U.S. consumer needs. In exchange, Wal-Mart reaped benefits from adding a new supplier capable of offering products with outstanding value for money. Today a large proportion of Haier's U.S. sales come from the top ten retailers—Wal-Mart, Lowe's, Best Buy, Home Depot, Office Depot, Target, Sam's Club, Costco, Circuit City, and Sears. The pattern is the same in Europe and Japan, where Haier's sales are concentrated in the top five retailers. From a standing start twenty-five years ago, Haier is already global number four in white goods, just behind the leaders from the United States, Europe, and Japan, each with more than a hundred years of history.

The ongoing consolidation of global retailing to create such giants as Wal-Mart, Carrefour, or Tesco, acting in their own self-interest, is opening up a new gateway for Chinese dragons to enter the global market, helping them reduce the barriers to entry that they would otherwise face.

Globalization of the Markets for Talent and Services

Another important trend that is powering Chinese firms' ability to mount an attack on world markets, despite their lack of international experience and gaping holes in their knowledge bases, is the increasing globalization of the markets for talent and business services.

A decade ago, it was very unusual to find an experienced Western expatriate working for a Chinese company. But as the global market for talent becomes more fluid, Chinese companies now employ dozens, sometimes hundreds, of foreign experts both to fill their knowledge gaps in China and to help establish their subsidiaries abroad. Take the example of Pearl

River Piano. The Pearl River Piano Group was established in 1956 in the southern city of Guangzhou (at that time, known in the West as Canton). For decades it was just another state-owned enterprise. But in the early 1990s, as China's modernization gathered pace, Pearl River became aware that it was only earning one-third the price for its pianos in China as foreign piano makers. It also came to the painful realization that the quality of its instruments was, quite simply, dire.

With piano making hardly top of the priority list for government support, Pearl River's CEO, Tong Zhi Cheng, recognized he would have to upgrade. His first step was to search the world for expertise. His first hire was Charles Corey, former general manager of U.S. company Wurlitzer's piano plant. Corey's background had been in quality control, and he was regarded as a world expert. Pearl River's first foreign consultant, he ended up working with the company for more than ten years, helping it, as Tong puts it: "overcome dozens of technological problems."[10] In 1993 Pearl River hired two German experts to assist in improving the quality of their toning process. The quality improvements they achieved allowed Pearl River to raise prices by 10 percent. Over time, the company hired more than ten world-class consultants to assist in improving every aspect of piano making, from design to production to final finish.

Looking back, Tong observes: "Without the help and guidance of these foreign experts there are some obstacles in piano making that we probably wouldn't have solved by ourselves in a lifetime! The fees of these foreign experts were extraordinarily high compared with the salaries of local people, but the technology and know-how they brought is the accumulation of hundreds of years of experience. After absorbing these insights we can use them generation after generation. No matter how high the price, it is worth it. We had to tighten our belt, learn the technology first, and then eat."[11]

Likewise, as the market for corporate control has become more open throughout much of the world, and especially in developed economies, the dragons have increasing opportunities to use mergers and acquisitions to accelerate their international expansion and to capture assets, capabilities, and know-how that would otherwise take years to replicate. When it acquired IBM's PC business, Lenovo not only quadrupled its sales from $3 billion to $12 billion per annum, catapulting it into the number-three slot worldwide (behind Dell and Hewlett-Packard), it also gained the distribution in 116 countries that IBM had built up over decades. As part of the acquisition Lenovo also secured a broad-based strategic alliance with IBM that gave it the right to use the IBM trademark on its personal computers under license for a period of five years. Lenovo also acquired full ownership of the "Think" family of brands. Along with these benefits came the assets of IBM's personal computer division, including over ten thousand IBM employees, 40 percent already located in China, 25 percent stationed in the United States, and 35 percent elsewhere. IBM also agreed to ongoing marketing-support and demand-generation services through its existing sales force of thirty thousand professionals and through IBM.com. IBM Global Financing and IBM Global Services, the number-one IT services organization in the world with powerful existing enterprise channels, are preferred providers to Lenovo for leasing and financing services, and for warranty and maintenance services, respectively.

Of course, as U.S. congressional disquiet—over the attempted acquisition of the American oil and gas company Unocal by China National Offshore Oil Corporation (CNOOC) in 2005 and Haier's early interest when Maytag came up for sale—has demonstrated, the market for corporate control is not yet fully open to Chinese companies, even in the self-styled citadels of the free market. But the dragons will continue to knock at the doors of companies coming up for sale as they seek to use acquisitions to speed up their push into global markets. And there is mounting evidence that the door to Chinese global expansion through acquisitions is opening. According to a study by the German consulting firm Klein and Coll., Chinese firms acquired 278 German companies in 2003 alone. Most were small, with revenues of between $1 million and $10 million, but possessed know-how, patents, respected brands, and distribution relationships that their Chinese buyers hope to use to shortcut some of the slower stages of their global capability building agenda.[12]

The internationalization of professional service firms has also opened a new gateway through which Chinese companies can catch up with world best practice. McKinsey & Company, for example, has large offices in both Beijing and Shanghai. Over two-thirds of their assignments are for Chinese clients. Lenovo has a $200 million brand-building and PR contract with Ogilvy & Mather, part of the global WPP advertising and marketing services group. Since 1997, Huawei alone has spent more than $70 million in consulting fees to hire IBM, Hay Group, Towers Perrin, PricewaterhouseCoopers, and FhG to help it build up management systems, introduce best practices, and improve operation efficiency in many areas. Such investment in upgrading its processes and management capabilities has been invaluable in helping Huawei keep up its fast pace of growth. Meanwhile, many of the world's leading accounting and law firms are also working for Chinese companies.

Because China is the world's fastest-growing market for machinery and equipment (between 2000 and 2004 it accounted for nearly two-thirds of the global growth in fixed capital investment) suppliers of capital goods are falling over themselves to get a share of the Chinese market. This buying power means many Chinese companies are able to demand that their suppliers provide extraordinary levels of technical advice and support. This gives the Chinese a golden opportunity to absorb new technology and learn world best practice, accelerating the pace at which they can catch up with established multinationals.

These diverse aspects of globalization are all converging on at least one point: they are jointly breaking down the barriers that Chinese companies would otherwise face in their quest to become global players and opening up new gateways through which they can enter the global game. The fact that the Chinese are entering a world economy that is already highly globalized, therefore, means that their potentially disruptive impact is likely to be faster, more powerful, and more pervasive across industries and markets than anything we have seen in the past—Japanese and Korean giants such as Toyota and Samsung included.

A New Kind of Disruptive Competition

This novel combination of a unique, if incomplete, endowment of advantages (access to low-cost talent right across the skill spectrum; the ability to access state assets and intellectual property at low cost; a high level of management autonomy from shareholders; and strong personal incentive to innovate and take bold risks) with new gateways into world markets resulting from globalization opens the way for Chinese companies to pursue the strategy of cost innovation that delivers (1) high technology at low cost, (2) variety and customization at low cost, and (3) specialty products at low cost.

Cost innovation is bringing a new kind of disruptive competition to the global market. It is "disruptive" in the sense coined by Clayton Christensen in his seminal book *The Innovator's Dilemma*—that the result of cost innovation is often products or services that initially look inferior to existing ones in the eyes of established players, but that are typically more affordable and easier to use than those in the incumbent's product portfolio.[13] The new competition from China is also disruptive because it threatens to obsolete much of the established firms' assets, capabilities, and experience base by changing the accepted rules of the game, undermining traditional profit models, and growing parts of the market that incumbents are poorly equipped to serve.

To rise to the challenge of such disruptive competition from China, you first have to understand how Chinese firms achieve such cost innovation. Chapter 2 shows you the secrets.

2

COST INNOVATION

The Chinese Dragons' Secret Weapon

COST INNOVATION MIGHT seem like a contradictory combination. We are used to associating innovation with adding value—more functionality, more features, and entirely new products and services—for which we expect customers to pay a price premium. So the idea of innovation efforts focused primarily on reducing cost—on producing cheaper products and offering similar functionality at better value for money—seems unorthodox. Some might even regard it as business suicide: why invest in R&D and innovation to sell tomorrow's products at lower prices than prevail today?

From the Chinese perspective, however, focusing on cost innovation makes perfect sense. First, it is here that the dragons have more experience than their global competitors: in their home market of China, the key to unlocking demand is to drive prices down to the point where the mass of Chinese citizens (whose average income was still only $1,200 per annum in 2005) can afford to buy.

Second, finding ways to more fully leverage their core source of competitive advantage—lower labor costs across the full spectrum of skills—plays directly to the dragons' strengths. Their basic cost advantage can be turned into an even more powerful weapon if they can exploit low costs in novel ways that established global competitors haven't yet thought of, or would find difficult to imitate.

Third, challenging the orthodoxies of global competition gives Chinese companies a better chance of winning than adhering to rules largely set by the incumbents. So long as the global game is played on the basis of existing asset stocks and technology resources, the dragons are certain to lose. Their best chance of becoming global winners is to try and turn the tables so as to render their rivals' advantages obsolete, while harnessing the peculiar advantages of their Chinese base. From these perspectives, combining cost and innovation to create a powerful competitive weapon looks like a winning strategy.

So how do the emerging Chinese dragons, with limited resources and often little experience, pull off the cost innovation feat? This chapter explains:

- How the dragons deliver high technology at low cost by leveraging cheap R&D resources; betting on low-cost, alternative technologies; and using the rise of open architecture to blow apart competitors' high-margin, proprietary systems

- How they are able to offer customers massive variety and choice at mass-market prices through a focus on process innovation and recombination of existing technologies

- How they apply scale-intensive technology to specialty products, transforming these businesses by dramatically reducing costs and prices and hence increasing volumes

High Technology at Low Cost

The latest high technology is generally applied to the most demanding applications or sold to early adopters. What these users have in common is an ability to pay. It makes sense for established global suppliers to restrict the latest high technology to leading specialist segments, and only gradually transfer it to the mainstream markets. In this way, they capture the maximum value (or what economists call "consumer surplus") throughout the life cycle of any new technology and enhance their return on investment in R&D. This makes a lot of economic sense for established competitors. But what if a newcomer were to overturn this conventional wisdom by offering the latest high technology to mass-market customers at discount prices? This is the first face of Chinese cost innovation.

Leveraging Low-Cost R&D into the Mass Market

It is estimated that you can hire between four and five Chinese engineers of equivalent quality for every one on your payroll in the United States or Europe. This opens the possibility of Chinese companies achieving cost innovation by applying world-class R&D resource to humdrum products at everyday low prices.

One of the most striking, and probably most surprising, examples of this phenomenon is the case of Dawning, a Chinese company that makes high-performance computers (HPCs). Talk of high-performance computing generally conjures up images of supercomputers and politically charged battles to make the fastest computer on earth. As you will see later, Dawning has become one of the world leaders in that race—the Dawning 4000A ranked tenth in the global top 500 supercomputer list in 2004.[1] But growing up in the Chinese environment has also led the company in another direction: finding ways to dramatically reduce the cost of HPC technology so that it can penetrate a wide variety of applications that can change people's lives. The chief designer of Dawning's 4000A, Sun Ninghui, describes his company's aims this way:

> I feel for China, the most important goal is not technology itself. It is to dramatically reduce cost. This [the potential to

reduce cost] is the biggest advantage of the clustering technology we use. If we make HPC really cheap, every beauty salon will use it. Beauty is a personalized service, and someone will write software to customize your beauty plan . . . [Creating the information society in China] would cost 10 trillion RMB (about $1.2 trillion) if we follow the American route, which is impossible. Low-cost HPCs that can be widely adopted is the first priority. We must figure out ways to massively reduce cost of the product and the way we make it.[2]

Dawning's ideas raise an interesting prospect: that Chinese companies will start to add a new dimension to high-technology competition by challenging the speed with which their multinational rivals commercialize new technologies in low-cost mass markets.

Like many of its counterparts, Dawning faced tough challenges in its early years, despite being a spin-off from the National Intelligent Computer Research Centre of the Institute of Computing Technology (ICT). The ICT had been part of an initiative to develop large computer systems at the Chinese Academy of Sciences (where research in this area had a forty-year history). But back in 1990, even Chinese government ministries were reluctant to include Dawning in their lists of approved suppliers for HPCs. When it came to supercomputers, potential customers felt the risks of opting for an unknown Chinese company were just too high. One trading firm that had purchased from established multinationals on standard industry terms refused even to consider the Dawning product unless Dawning agreed to pay any losses incurred if the computer failed to perform. The Ministry of Railways, meanwhile, flatly refused to add Dawning to its approved list for procurement contracts. These were dark days for a company that had chosen its name in the hope of "rising like the morning sun."

Faced with these barriers to entry into a market dominated by firms like Amdahl and IBM, Dawning took the unprecedented step of donating HPC machines to a university attached to the Ministry of Railways for use in conducting research. Serendipity then intervened. The Ministry's imported HPC failed, and with the foreign supplier's engineers located on the other side of the world, it would be days before it could be fixed. As a stopgap, the Ministry turned to the Dawning computer installed at its university. To its surprise, the machine performed better than the imported one. The lock on the market had been broken: the next HPC bought by the Ministry was a Dawning.

Dawning's next challenge was how to catch up with, and ultimately even overtake, the technological lead of its global competitors. It recognized that although computing technology and performance would continue to improve rapidly, the basic technological road map had been established and embodied in international standards. So, it reasoned, investing resources in trying to come up with a revolutionary kind of computing had little chance of success. Instead, Dawning decided to take the existing international processor technology (used by companies like Intel and Motorola) as a given and ask how it could get a step change in performance by improving the capability for the processors to work together—at the time an emerging technology known as *parallel computing*. In 1993 it produced its first supercomputer, the Dawning 1, by developing its own motherboard, firmware coding, and modified UNIX operating system to network together four Motorola 88000 processors.

What Dawning realized from this experience was that of the 80 percent performance improvement computers had achieved in the previous decade, improved microprocessors (better chips) accounted for only 20 percent. Better coding of software applications to enable them to run more efficiently accounted for another 30 percent. The biggest contributor to the improved performance of computers, accounting for 50 percent in fact, was innovations in the way the chips interacted with each other. Dawning therefore focused its R&D efforts on the interactions between existing processors.

By the time it had launched the Dawning 2 in 1995, the Chinese company had made a technological advance in the hardware and software required to get standard processors to work together at superfast speeds. It dubbed this approach the "cluster system." In layman's terms, what Dawning had done was to produce a high-performance supercomputer by innovatively clustering together basic, standard hardware modules. The analogy of the human brain is apt: each brain cell is a relatively simple building block; but with the right neural network managing the interactions between these cells, the brain has amazing powers. And Dawning's model had high scalability: it could easily be improved by adding more modules and improving the capability of each of the building blocks rather than requiring a redesign of the system. Thus, while its foreign competitors were spending millions on developing new, high-performance chips and operating systems to push out the envelope of supercomputer performance, Dawning had come close to matching the performance of the world's leading supercomputers by clustering together standard modules—in this case 32 Intel i860 chips working in unison. What was even more remarkable, the chips it used to build the supercomputer weren't even state-of-the-art. The latest chips simply weren't available to Dawning because of U.S. government export restrictions on the sale of high-technology products to China. Needless to say, the cost of Dawning's supercomputers was much lower than the incumbents' proprietary systems.

In the same spirit, seeing that 64-bit computing would replace 32-bit to become industry standard, Dawning aggressively cooperated with the upstart AMD to lead the market, developing the world's first "four-route" server based on AMD's Opteron chip in 2003. Because industry leaders were hesitating to go with AMD, and Intel was rather slow in developing 64-bit chips, Dawning was able to become one of the leaders in this new technology—probably one year ahead of most competitors. It also entered into close cooperation with Sun in 2005 to integrate its new server with Sun's pioneering Solaris operating system.

Dawning continued to work on the development of supercomputers based on its clustering of standard chips. Its focus on technology was brought together with a new emphasis on customer requirements. While hardly a novel idea in most businesses, it was revolutionary in an industry that relied on the supremacy of technical prowess as its dominant design influence. Adopting a customer focus, Dawning started to direct its R&D to improving four aspects of computer performance: scalability, usability, manageability, and availability (what it later trademarked as SUMA). By 2001 it had already designed and sold two thousand supercomputers. Its Dawning 3000 model was now regarded as world-class.

Dawning's experience in working closely with its customers to deliver to their specific needs also led to its next breakthrough in a completely different segment of the market. It recognized that customers using low-end servers based on Intel's IA architecture had problems of monitoring and management similar to those encountered by their customers for supercomputers; only the scale was different. Yet the monitoring and management capabilities of most servers on the market were rudimentary, little more than a few basic checks using network software. These inadequacies caused the servers to go down when, in fact, such failures could be anticipated and avoided by using some of the maintenance functions that are routine in a supercomputer. The opportunity was obvious: why not transfer some of its supercomputer technologies to bring the benefits of HPCs to the low-end server market?

Dawning launched a low-end server, the I220, which incorporated a sophisticated but user-friendly monitoring and management system. By using its skills in designing motherboards that linked the processors of supercomputers, it was also able to cut the development cost by 30 to 40 percent compared with its rivals. The I220 integrated many high-end technologies only used in HPC before, such as intelligent hardware monitoring systems, navigation software, management software, problem alerts, and so forth. With clear blue water between Dawning and its competitors, the product was an instant hit in the market.

More important than its immediate success, however, the I220 experience led Dawning to an insight with far-reaching implications. As Dawning's chairman, Li Guojie, put it: "Low-cost product is going to be an important direction for us, as multinational firms are less motivated to do so, and China is a huge market for such products. This is going to be the driving force for our innovation, and also our biggest opportunity. Actually, low cost, just like high performance, requires innovation in high technology; low cost is not squeezed from low input costs, but by using superior technology. This will allow us to reduce our customers' cost of running their computer systems exponentially."[3] In other words, the prevailing value/cost equation will be fundamentally rewritten.

Applying this logic, Dawning's chairman sees a huge opportunity to unlock the Chinese market, which in the dash for growth with limited resources, is looking for unparalleled value for money. And he believes his multinational competitors will be loath to move in this direction, wishing to preserve high margins by restricting high technology to high-end, expensive products.

Dawning illustrates two of the major ways China's emerging dragons are challenging the conventional wisdom of global incumbents. First, the dragons are challenging the idea that latecomers who are behind on the technology curve are doomed to play a futile game of catch-up. Dawning was far behind, but by eschewing the technological road map of its established competitors and instead focusing on a neglected part of the game where new ideas were emerging—in this case how processors interacted with each other—it was able to beat incumbents in the race into the new world of HPC based on clustering.

The second conventional tenet now under challenge is the idea that the potential of high technology lies in creating more sophisticated products. Instead, the Chinese dragons are using high technology to make things cheaper, not more complex. Dawning was able to turn the market upside down by applying the technology of supercomputers to making a mass-market commodity—low-end servers—both more reliable and cheaper.

Betting on Low-Cost, Disruptive Technologies

Dawning's success also illustrates another strand of the Chinese dragons' cost innovation strategy: betting on alternative, emerging technology. By focusing on the potential of clustering standard chips to achieve superperformance, Dawning was able to change the rules of the game. It bypassed its competitors' advantage—individual chips with superior performance—and leveraged its own strengths by using low-cost R&D resources in the labor-intensive and painstaking task of developing alternative clustering technology to achieve the same high performance. As Dawning's Li pointed out in an interview: "Our spirit of innovation is to avoid following the same route as the global industry leaders. We will never catch up with large multinationals if we follow their strategies. You can't leapfrog when you are following others in the same direction. You are most likely to find the chance to jump ahead when the industry is facing a technology transition and you choose a different direction. We chose to work on a different technology and different products."[4]

The dragons are using this strategy of betting on low-cost disruptive technology (some of it written off as already obsolete by global leaders) to achieve cost innovation in another industry Western companies have long considered as their sole preserve— medical X-ray equipment. The fundamental technology embodied in an X-ray machine is more than a hundred years old and has been slow to move into the digital age. Until recently, X-ray images still had to be chemically processed onto film for viewing. However, it is possible, using an alternative technology known as direct digital radiography (DDR), to transform an X-ray scan directly into a digital signal capable of being processed by a computer, bypassing the chemical process.

There are two types of DDR systems. The first is the line scan, a technology developed by the Dutch companies Philips and Oldelft NV and the Russian Academy of Sciences. It has the advantage of high resolution that can distinguish clearly between the density of different body tissues and so works well for standard X-ray procedures such as chest scans and medical examinations. The limitation of the line-scan technology is that it takes time—about ten seconds during which the patient must not move, even breathe—to scan a particular organ, so it cannot be used for real-time applications such as imaging the function of a beating heart. The second type of DDR, known as flat-panel imaging, uses advanced semiconductor technology and can be used for real-time applications such as heart scans, but has the disadvantages of poorer resolution and higher radiation doses for the patient.

Despite being among the inventors of line scanning, leading multinationals General Electric and Philips decided to discard this technology and concentrate instead on developing more advanced, flat-panel machines for high-end users. With a price tag of between $300,000 and $400,000 for a single machine, flat-panel machines looked to have more promising profit potential.

The China Aerospace Science and Technology Corporation (CASC) acquired line-scanning technology from the Russian Academy of Sciences in 1998 when Russia was having economic difficulties. A group of CASC engineers used this technology, initially targeted for other applications, to develop a DDR X-ray machine. Despite its rather poor quality at the beginning, it was more than adequate for the high-volume, everyday radiography needs in a hospital, such as chest scans and routine medical examinations. More importantly, the machine cost around $20,000 to build, compared with between $150,000 to $200,000 for a flat-panel DDR. A disruptive cost innovation was born: a product better fit for mass-market purposes, at a fraction of the cost. And Zhongxing Medical was set up to exploit this commercial opportunity.

The machine Zhongxing launched on the Chinese market in 1999 was an immediate success. The fact that it offered high technology for high-volume, routine applications was especially attractive to the many second- and third-tier hospitals with limited budgets that make up the bulk of the Chinese market. It also allowed Zhongxing to escape being captive to foreign suppliers of the high-cost semiconductors that flat-panel machines required.

Facing a dramatic loss of market share, incumbents General Electric and Philips responded by cutting between $100,000 and $150,000 off the prices of their machines. These moves were still not sufficient to compete against Zhongxing's technology leapfrog: five years later Zhongxing had 50 percent market share in the DDR segment. Since then, Philips has withdrawn its line of scanning machines from the Chinese market altogether, and GE competes at a price little more than half of what it could charge back in 1999.

The revenues and profits that Zhongxing reaped from its majority share of the market, meanwhile, allowed it to invest heavily in R&D to upgrade the performance of its line-scanning technology so that today its much cheaper machines are almost a match for expensive flat-panel products (for example, the scanning time has been reduced from ten seconds to about two seconds and thus the procedure is much more comfortable for patients). As a result, the high-end profit pool that multinationals rely on to support their margins is now also under threat. With little room to mount a counterattack, they are left facing a classic case of disruptive innovation.

Riding the Open Architecture Wave

Open architecture has become one of the major trends in global competition in recent years: consider the rise of Linux, Java, the USB port, or Internet protocol in the IT industry; GSM in the mobile telecommunications sector; or the free publication of a universally accepted sequencing of the human genome in biotechnology. This trend challenges the strategies of many established players that have historically protected their margins by designing systems based on proprietary standards, preventing customers from reducing their costs by substituting cheaper, standard products to create a "mix-and-match" solution at lower cost. Keeping customers inside a proprietary system also helped bolster profits by ensuring healthy, ongoing profits from the provision of maintenance, support, and upgrades.

The emerging Chinese dragons view the rise of open architecture as an important force they can harness to deliver cost innovation. By blowing apart proprietary systems, they can appeal to customers who feel they are being milked by being captive to their existing suppliers. By offering these customers an open architecture alternative, the Chinese dragons can overcome their latecomer handicap because they don't need to convince customers to accept an unknown, proprietary Chinese standard. They can also sidestep the need to develop a complete system by offering compatibility with products already widely available in the market.

Teknova, another Chinese leader in the medical diagnostic equipment industry, is a good example of how the dragons are leveraging open architecture to achieve cost innovation. With the aim of using the revolution in digital technology to leapfrog established players, Teknova decided to create an all-digital machine for ultrasound scanning. The product it came up with delivered two types of cost innovation. First, Teknova brought the advantages of digital technology to routine scanning applications at a time when the global leaders in the business, such as

Siemens and General Electric, had restricted the all-digital technology only to their highest-end products—confident that they could continue to reap handsome returns from their installed base of analog machines by delaying the introduction of digital technology in everyday scanning jobs.

The second element of cost innovation in Teknova's solution was that the data produced by their digital ultrasound machines could be processed by standard IT equipment that most hospitals already had in place, obviating the need for customers to invest in an expensive, proprietary system.

Instead of leveraging the capabilities of open architecture, the incumbent multinationals fed the data captured by their ultrasound scanners into expensive computers equipped with application-specific chips (ASICs). Each of the leading multinationals had developed their proprietary ASIC in-house. The cost of developing an ASIC was so high that even established competitors had to manage their path of product and technological improvement carefully to ensure they recouped the cost of designing a new ASIC for a market in which only a few thousand units were sold in any one year. For a new entrant like Teknova that could expect to sell only a handful of units in the early years as it tried to break into the market, the cost of developing its own ASIC would be ruinous.

Faced with this discouraging scenario, Teknova decided to apply some cost innovation thinking to the problem. Its investigations turned up the fact that start-ups making equipment to power what was then the nascent Internet faced a similar problem with the high cost of programmable chips. Perhaps if it took one of the semiprogrammable chips being developed for makers of Internet equipment and added its own software, Teknova could create an ASIC without developing one from scratch?

The idea of taking a general-purpose chip borrowed from a sister industry and customizing it by means of software led Teknova to a string of other ideas in the same vein for challenging prevailing industry orthodoxies. Why not replace the other proprietary storage devices, printers, and printing papers used in medical-imaging devices with the standard devices used in a high-traffic personal computer network? Rather than ask hospitals to buy a whole slew of stand-alone equipment in the form of a proprietary ultrasound imaging system, it could sell its product as just another input device into their overall information technology platforms.

Making this dream a reality still took Teknova six years of research and development. But it is revolutionizing the medical diagnostic equipment industry. Because it uses standard hardware, the cost of Teknova's equipment is dramatically lower than competing machines. Its competitors rely on years of accumulated knowledge to produce high-accuracy images by squeezing the maximum out of each "tunnel" the scanner makes. In contrast, Teknova's system gets world-class image quality by increasing the number of tunnels, each backed by a low-cost chip, and then combining the different perspectives using advanced software. This has the added benefit of making it easy to upgrade the product: rather than designing a completely new machine, Teknova can simply upgrade the software; equally, it can leverage the R&D of others by procuring the best chips developed anywhere in the world, rather than relying only on in-house resources. It can also take advantage of the rapid reductions in the cost of standard chips that typically result as manufacturers ramp up volumes and move down the experience curve. When this happened because the Internet boom fueled rapid growth in chip demand, the cost advantage of Teknova over multinational rivals using proprietary chips widened even further. And when a hospital buys a Teknova machine, the data are ready-packaged for transmission into the hospital's existing IT infrastructure, allowing it to save cost and more easily process the images to create value-added services for its doctors and patients. Teknova's black-and-white machine is aggressively taking over market share from incumbent multinationals; its color machine is due out soon, and due to deal another heavy blow to its rivals.

Teknova's strategy has had a powerful side-effect on global competition in the medical equipment business: it has blown a hole in the wall of proprietary systems that had protected its global competitors in the past. Its Chinese sister, Neusoft, had used a similar approach in magnetic resonance imaging (MRI) equipment and digital X-ray machines to become the seventh-largest supplier of medical equipment in the world.

A Neusoft executive explained the strategy of leveraging open architecture to achieve cost innovation this way: "With an eye to competition and to retain[ing] control of the customer, competitors like General Electric and Siemens base their products on proprietary technologies. But this makes the products expensive both to buy and to maintain (specialist maintenance on a proprietary hard disk could cost $15,000 per year in early days). We use an open architecture—our hard disk is the same as in a personal computer, so it costs almost nothing to maintain and little to replace." He goes on to point out that not only is open architecture a way to provide cheaper products, he believes it can also deliver better products: "At Neusoft we focus on core software development, system design, assembly, testing, and sales and service while we outsource almost all the hardware production through global procurement. By using the best component technology available from suppliers anywhere in the world we can make the most of their skills; we are not limited to our proprietary technologies." And the bottom line: "We bring advanced technology to more hospitals."[5]

For those peering out from behind the walls of proprietary systems this formula should give pause for thought: this year Neusoft overtook Siemens in sales of computed tomography imaging (CT) in China to become number two in the market, just behind General Electric. The multinationals have had to cut prices by 30 percent—that's a discount of over $120,000 per machine—to match the Neusoft price. But Neusoft retains the edge on supplies and maintenance: its cost per patient is just $12, compared with the $48 to $60 that prevailed when multinationals were the only suppliers in China. Having transformed value for money in China, Neusoft is now exporting to the United States and Europe.

By leveraging the low-cost R&D resources available in China; betting on cheap, alternative technologies; and riding the wave of open architecture to blow apart the proprietary systems of global incumbents, the emerging Chinese dragons are bringing high technology to the global market at low cost. They are pulling the proverbial rug from under established global competitors who see high technology as the preserve of the top of the market, who rely on managing the diffusion of new technology to ensure they improve their return on investment by restricting it to customers until they are willing to pay, and who bolster their profits by locking customers into proprietary systems that inflate the size of the investment and deliver ongoing and maintenance and service revenues.

Because it threatens to cause existing business models to unravel badly, the dragons' capabilities to deliver high technology at low cost poses a major challenge to incumbents. But it is not the only way in which Chinese companies are challenging the orthodoxies of global business. They are also using cost innovation strategies to offer unparalleled product variety and customization to world markets at rock-bottom prices.

Variety at Low Cost

Another strategy being adopted by the emerging dragons is to outclass their established competitors by offering customers worldwide a wider choice of product variety from a massive lineup of different models. But this raises a question: how are Chinese companies able to offer all this variety and still maintain low costs? After all, many Western companies know only too well what happens when a product line starts to spiral out of control: time lost in setup and changeover of production lines, along with unrecouped costs and write-offs on obsolete inventory, quickly cause profits to turn to losses. The Chinese secrets to avoiding these problems are to be found in cost innovation through process flexibility and re-combination of existing technologies in novel ways.

Cost Innovation Through Process Flexibility

A good example of how the emerging dragons have been able to offer greater variety while maintaining their cost advantage is the maker of rechargeable batteries, BYD, now second only to Sanyo in global market share. In 1995 BYD's founder Wang Chuanfu, an associate professor in a ministry institute specializing in bat-tery research, was trying to figure out how to break into the inter-national market for rechargeable batteries. He saw roadblocks at every turn. The market belonged almost exclusively to compa-nies such as Sanyo and Toshiba. Together, Japanese firms held 90 percent of the global market. A Japanese law that prohibited the export of technology or equipment used to manufacture rechargeable batteries protected their technological advantage.

After much deliberation Wang felt he had found some chinks in the formidable armor of his Japanese rivals. He had read that Japanese companies were planning to phase out older-style nickel cadmium (NiCad) batteries and replace them with products using the lithium ion (Li-Ion) technology that offered improved perfor-mance at higher prices, promising better margins. But Wang be-lieved that many more basic applications where cost was more important to customers than performance, such as electrically powered toys, would continue to offer a sizable market for NiCad batteries. Moreover, as these markets matured, manufacturers would likely need to extend their product lines and offer more va-riety in an attempt to maintain growth. This trend, in turn, would lead to pressure for suppliers to deliver a wider range of battery types with the capability to flex production at short notice according to fluctuations in demand for a particular model.

For these reasons the NiCad market in simple applications like toys and cordless phones (which, unlike mobile phones, are never far from their base station and so place less demand on battery life) seemed like a good market segment to attack. But BYD needed to find a way to cut costs and increase variety and flexibility compared with the automated production lines used by Japanese competitors—which were efficient only when run continuously to make a single product at high volume.

The estimated cost of establishing a NiCad production line using industry-standard processes was in excess of $1 million. BYD had only $300,000 in start-up capital. So Wang began to address this funding gap by making some of the key equipment himself. When this proved insufficient, he analyzed where he could break the automated production processes down and replace expensive machines with manual procedures that could be completed by ordinary workers. As a result, BYD was able to develop a production line with capacity for 3,000 to 4,000 batteries per day for a cost of roughly $125,000, compared with the $1 million spent by Japanese manufacturers on an equivalent production line.

BYD subsequently developed a line with capacity of 100,000 batteries per day. It required around 2,000 employees, compared with just 200 needed to run a Japanese line with the same capacity. But the BYD line could be up and running for just 6 percent of the $100 million Japanese competitors would have to invest. One investment bank estimated that this meant financing and depreciation costs were slashed from 40 percent of total costs at Sanyo to 3 percent at BYD. Even with the extra labor required, BYD could produce a NiCad battery for a total cost of $1, compared with costs of $5 to $6 incurred by rivals in Japan.

Equally important was the increased speed and flexibility afforded by BYD's labor-intensive production process. The heavily automated Japanese production lines could produce only one product; introducing a new product often required major retooling of the production line. BYD, on the other hand, could introduce new products simply by adjusting key equipment and retraining workers. BYD was therefore in a position to switch to making a new product within weeks, compared with the three months required to retool a competitor's automated line.

In a segment where competitors were unwilling to reinvest because they saw the NiCad technology as outdated and which they were unwilling to defend as prices and margins were squeezed 20 to 40 percent by customers reeling from the 1997 Asian financial crisis, Wang was armed with dramatically lower costs and higher flexibility. He had found a way to deliver high variety at low cost.

During 1997 BYD's sales of NiCad batteries grew by 90 percent. In 1998, the company began supplying batteries to Japan's Nikko, the world's largest maker of electrically powered toys. In the same year, the company reached a deal to supply batteries to Philips and VTech, the world's largest manufacturer of cordless phones. Between 1999 and 2000 BYD won deals to supply cordless phone batteries to Panasonic, Sony, GE, AT&T, and Uniden and power tool batteries to Ryobi, Craftsman, and Techtronic Industries.

BYD did not stop there. It concentrated its R&D on coming up with other innovative ways to reduce costs. It found ways to replace expensive materials used in rechargeable batteries with cheaper substitutes without impairing performance. It learned how to make batteries at ambient temperature and humidity, avoiding the necessity to construct expensive "dry rooms" in the plant.

Meanwhile the company took the know-how it had built in NiCad batteries and started to apply it to reaching the next step on the product ladder: Li-Ion batteries for mobile phones. Wang's move into Li-Ion batteries was made against many people's advice, given the significant investment costs for what was still a small company by industry standards. Equally worrying was the fact that 90 percent of the materials for Li-Ion batteries had to be imported. The skeptics argued that BYD's competitive advantage was unclear. But Wang used the same approach that had worked in the lower-end NiCad segment—he redesigned the line, replacing much of the expensive equipment with a mixture of manual procedures and locally made machines. Again, BYD was able to reduce its capital costs while increasing its capacity to offer customers more variety and flexibility. At the same time, he set about developing local sources for the high-cost imported materials used to make Li-Ion batteries. These moves resulted in costs falling from around $40 for each battery down to $12.

In November 2000 BYD secured a landmark deal: Motorola decided to allocate 30 percent of its global battery purchases to BYD. Ericsson quickly followed, giving BYD a 15 percent share of the world market. Its ability to offer high variety and fast response due to its unique manufacturing process made BYD very attractive to customers in the mobile industry, who are constantly under pressure to introduce new product ranges into the market quickly.

As their customers defected, many of the Japanese competitors headed into the red. Meanwhile, buoyed by its proposition of variety and flexibility at low cost, BYD hopped from segment to segment up the value-added ladder, notching up global battery market shares of 75 percent in cordless phones, 38 percent in toys, 30 percent in power tools, and 28 percent in mobile phones.

BYD is not alone in successfully finding ways to deliver variety at low cost. Another example is Chint, a maker of electrical equipment such as transformers and power supply units that has recently entered into an alliance with General Electric to penetrate the global market. Chint, however, has taken cost innovation to achieve variety at low cost one step further to develop a set of sophisticated systems and processes to support this capability.

Like its cousin BYD, Chint began looking at how to reengineer its production process in an attempt to eke out its scarce investment capital. Its first plant was divided into two areas. On one side were four fully automated production lines, brimming with advanced equipment and run by just two operators. Adjacent were manual lines with thousands of work stations, swarming with people. These manual lines didn't even have a conveyor belt; when they finished a subassembly stage, the young workers simply snapped on a rubber band to hold it together, then someone else picked it up and delivered it to the next step in the production line.

Comparing the lines in the two areas, Chint found that the maintenance costs of the complex automated equipment alone were four times higher than the entire wage bill for the workers it had replaced! By substituting labor for automation, Chint was able to achieve much lower operating costs. In addition, using the manual process saved it $600,000 in capital investment for every line. Chint also found that automated lines were actually less efficient for small batch orders, especially when customized features were required. The lesson, as the CEO Nan Cunhui put it: "Don't have blind faith in automation."[6] Taking this to heart, Chint built its business on finding the right balance between automation and manual processes to create the flexibility to produce high variety at low cost. Today it runs twelve automated production lines for its standard, high-volume products. Some 70 percent of its output, meanwhile, is produced on largely manual lines. Chint's plant is the world's largest production center, with a daily output of 240,000 units.

Had Chint stopped there, it would be just another example of a company exploiting China's labor-cost advantage. But interestingly, the experience of reengineering its lines launched Chint on the road to building a new capability for cost innovation through process flexibility. In managing labor-intensive processes it learned how to deliver highly customized products with minimal extra cost; as the production management team put it: "When customization is required, we know how to add the right procedures to the workflow, which is impossible for automated lines."[7]

Chint then took the capabilities and systems it had pioneered in manual lines and started reconfiguring the automated lines originally designed by equipment makers in the United States and Europe to deliver cost innovation. Every automated procedure was broken down and systematically analyzed. Wherever engineers identified a step that could be better performed manually, they parceled it out from the automatic process. Step by step this allowed them to squeeze variety at low cost out of the automatic lines as well.

Chint began to apply this same cost innovation mind-set to other areas of its business, such as procurement and raw-material management. As the general manager of procurement explained: "Machines require a high level of standardization, but men can adapt. If a component is slightly out of shape, a manual operator can adjust it slightly to put it back in place. But an automated process cannot; instead, it will discard the parts. This actually increases the cost of procurement and the cost of waste also rises."[8] So Chint separates its incoming raw materials into different grades, optimizing their overall utilization by directing low-grade inputs to the manual lines, while using the high-grade ones in its automatic processes.

To manage the elaborate balance between manual and automated processes, Chint developed sophisticated systems for coping with poorly educated recruits and high employee turnover, including graphics-based training, knowledge management, and incentive systems to systematically improve efficiency of workers. It also learned how to deploy advanced information technology to closely monitor, analyze, and improve the performance of each worker on a line. Since it commenced introducing computer-integrated manufacturing systems in 1994, Chint has spend more than $15 million on IT infrastructure to support the flexible, low-cost manufacturing system.

Powered by its accumulated capabilities in delivering variety at low cost, backed by annual R&D spending equivalent to 5 percent of sales, Chint reached turnover of $1.5 billion in 2004 to become the world's fifth-largest manufacturer of electrical products.

What had started with the necessity for capital-starved Chinese companies to substitute cheap workers for machines subsequently spawned the development of a host of capabilities in cost innovation that spanned sophisticated process analysis, IT-based monitoring and control, graphics-based training, and the use of knowledge management and incentive systems in process improvement. Ultimately both BYD and Chint built the capability to improve on process technologies imported from abroad to squeeze out more flexibility at lower cost in ways their established foreign competitors hadn't thought of.

The threat to Western companies is clear: the emerging dragons are using cost innovation to redefine the accepted trade-off that says a customer who wants variety and flexibility must pay a hefty premium for it. By focusing on how to use Chinese cost advantage to increase flexibility without losing efficiency, and building the necessary process and systems to deliver, they are offering customers choice and customization at no more than the price of a standardized product. As a consequence the price premiums incumbents enjoy in the global market for providing a broad and flexible product range are sure to be eroded, disrupting existing business models.

Recombinative Innovation

Another tool the Chinese are using to deliver variety and customization to the global market at low cost is what Haier's CEO, Zhang Rui Min, has dubbed "recombinative innovation": creating new, improved models by recombining existing ideas and technologies in novel ways, rather than by developing additional products internally from scratch.

For established global players with deep pockets and ambitious development staff, it's easy to be sucked into the idea that successfully differentiating means funding new R&D. But for Chinese companies with limited resources in a hurry to find a low-cost way of breaking into the global market, a lavish, long-term R&D project isn't a viable option. Instead, they look for ways to innovate on the cheap and avoid reinventing the wheel. The "not invented here" mentality is a luxury the emerging dragons simply can't afford. As latecomers to the global market, meanwhile, learning from others anywhere in the world comes naturally. So it's perhaps not surprising that the Chinese have come up with the idea of cutting the cost of innovation through recombinative innovation.

A classic example is Haier's approach to the launch of a new, high-performance line of washing machines. It observed that washing machine technology and design in Asia, Europe, and North America had historically followed independent development paths. Each had different advantages and drawbacks. European machines, for example, used less water; American ones were usually faster; while Asian models generally made better use of electronic sensors.

Lacking the baggage of decades in the industry that led companies from different parts of the world to vehemently disagree on the relative merits of the different approaches, Haier decided to make a machine that combined the best of all three. This model harnessed a single engine to create two separate washing actions: one emulating the washing action of an American machine and the other mimicking the European approach to removing dirt. Adding the kind of electronic sensing and control circuitry found in a typical Japanese machine completed the product.

The result was a machine that used only half the water of conventional machines and achieved close to 50 percent improvement in cleaning power at twice the speed. As an added benefit it also reduced the wear and tear on garments by 60 percent. It's true that none of the underlying technology was really new. But this low-cost recombinative innovation was awarded the only gold medal for any new product presented by the industry at the International Invention Expo held in France in May 2004.[9]

This is just another example of how the emerging dragons are turning the orthodox approach to innovation on its head by constantly asking the question: how can we offer a wider range of new products to customers by focusing our creative juices on how to innovate at the lowest possible cost? Similar thinking is behind the final type of cost innovation: bringing the benefits of scale economies and low costs to specialty products by transferring technologies between them.

Specialty Products at Low Cost

We know that serving the specialist needs of a limited set of customers in a market normally jacks up costs. One reason is that a niche market generally lacks the volume to spread the fixed cost of specific investments in R&D and product or solution design that are necessary to innovate. The result is that suppliers either slow down the rate of innovation or demand a substantial price premium from customers when new products are introduced.

But the Chinese dragons are using cost innovation to change the rules of the game for specialty products. First, they find a segment demanding specialist products, often inside China, and apply their low R&D, design, and operating costs to cut prices. Owing to their lower breakeven they can still turn a profit early on. Then, as lower prices build volume, they reap economies of scale and learning that allow prices to be cut still further, resulting in a virtuous cycle that fuels continuous volume expansion. The dragons then reuse as much of the technology and experience already amortized in producing a previous specialty as a launching pad to cut prices in an adjacent specialized market. The idea of riding the cycle of economies of scale and learning certainly isn't new; it's a strategy global companies have used for decades to penetrate mass markets that had entered the take-off phase. But it was seldom applied to specialty products, either because the breakeven point required by high-cost, Western suppliers was too large relative to the perceived market potential, or because incumbents enjoying high margins looked over the horizon at the prospect of a cost-competitive volume market and shied away.

Now along come the Chinese dragons with costs, especially in R&D and design, that have given them a much lower breakeven. They see the opportunity to further reduce breakeven by sharing costs across multiple specialties. Low breakeven means that the risk, should they fail in their attempts to drive up volume, is reduced.

The Chinese also enjoy direct access to the massive and fast-growing Chinese market where even a specialty product can deliver a substantial initial volume of sales. The price umbrella and high margins prevailing in the market for specialties give them ample potential to undercut existing suppliers. So instead of trying to come up with a differentiated product, they focus their efforts on cost innovation that will allow them to slash prices and turn the market into a volume game where the existing specialist players don't have the cost structures or the experience to compete. The story of how Shinco used VCD technology to transform the economics of specialist video players shows how this final kind of cost innovation is done.

Transforming the Economics of Specialty Products

Back in the mid-1990s when the dominant standard for recording and replaying movies was videotape based on the global VHS format, a new, but small, market emerged in China for video compact discs (VCDs). In 1994 just twenty thousand VCD players were sold in the whole of China.

Because VCDs offered only a minimal improvement in viewing quality compared with VHS tapes, the established consumer electronics multinationals looked at VCD technology and decided it would never be more than a specialist business. So when Sony, Philips, and Samsung entered the market for VCDs they followed a classic strategy for a specialist product: limit R&D spending consistent with what a low-volume business can support and set prices high. Samsung, for example, created a VCD by taking an existing CD-player circuit and bolting on a standard MPEG decoder of the type that personal computers use to play video files—thereby minimizing its R&D investment. Sony set a high price for its machine and refused to invest in adapting the features of its products to the needs of what it saw as a fringe of Chinese consumers. Philips, meanwhile, concentrated on maximizing the profits from supplying a core component that went into making VCDs, selling it at around $75 per unit. At first this strategy seemed to be working: the multinationals captured 90 percent of the market and earned a tidy profit while they waited for the next mass-market technology, digital video discs (DVDs), to be ready for launch in a few years' time.

· Shinco took a different view. It believed that it could use cost innovation to slash the price of VCDs and deliver what was then a specialist product to the mass market. So Shinco's senior management set its development team two challenging targets. First, to produce a product that could be profitably launched at no more than 3,000 RMB (around $400)—the price point it believed would unlock China's mass market. Second, to create a system that could deliver a high-quality picture to customers who relied mostly on cheap, poor-quality, pirated VCDs—because this error-correction capability was identified by market research as the key driver of satisfaction among potential mass-market consumers.

Seeking to create a mass-market product using this technology, over the next seventeen months Shinco developed its own VCD system from scratch. Unlike Samsung, Shinco didn't cobble together a design by combining an existing CD player with a standard MPEG decoder. Instead it used its lower-cost R&D resources and commitment to driving volume to create a purpose-built system designed to enable consumers to get quality viewing even from poorly duplicated pirated disks.

To meet its tight price ceiling, Shinco had to find a way to break the monopoly of high-priced component suppliers that set prices designed to skim margin from what they saw as a niche market. It achieved this by developing a strategic alliance with a new entrant, ESS Technology, a Silicon Valley start-up founded by a Taiwanese. In addition to paring back the cost, Shinco's objective was to promote an alternative supplier that was willing to support Shinco's own mass-market ambitions and support the drive for superior error correction demanded by mainstream Chinese consumers. As part of the alliance Shinco negotiated exclusivity on the ESS chip for three months after launch in exchange for Shinco's support in the development phase.

The strategy was highly successful. While the rest of the world stuck with videotape, China enthusiastically adopted the new VCD technology, with sales of VCD players topping 11 million units per annum by 1997. Shinco rapidly pulled ahead of its competitors in volume and market share to become the leader in VCDs in China, overtaking Samsung, whose design failed to cope with poor-quality disks. Meanwhile, as Shinco reaped the benefit of economies of scale it was able to drive down the cost of the critical decoding chip from ESS to just $15 per unit, compared with the $75 the incumbent niche suppliers had originally demanded.

But Shinco did not stop there. By helping transform the economics of making VCDs, it now had sufficient volume over which to spread the fixed costs of a new round of investment in R&D. This included establishing an R&D center in the United States to act as Shinco's "eyes and ears" for the identification of new technology and to facilitate codevelopment with American partners.

The first fruits of combining this investment in U.S. R&D with extensive Chinese engineering resources came in 1998 when Shinco launched a VCD that processed the formerly separate signals for sound and images through a single chip. This new chip offered world-beating performance in terms of functionality, reliability, and speed—all at a 5 percent lower cost, allowing Shinco to grow its market share still further.

Seeing that VCDs would soon be displaced by the new DVD format, however, Shinco also established a parallel project to develop its own IPR (intellectual property rights) around the new standard. It put a team of a hundred engineers to work on the problem of designing a DVD to obsolete its own product. Again, the objective was to achieve cost innovation that would rapidly take the new technology from a niche among geeks to a mass market.

When it was launched in 1999 Shinco's DVD player offered superior error correction—and cost $120 less than its nearest global competitor. The product took the China market by storm. Shinco built a $40 million new plant to mass-produce the product and by 2002 it had captured 28 percent of the Chinese market, compared with an 11 percent of all its foreign competitors combined.[10]

Hopping from Specialty to Specialty

Shinco next decided to try and break into the global market. Again, it looked for a specialist product where it could reduce the breakeven using cost innovation. The product it alighted on was the newly emerging portable DVD player. As well as offering the attractions of a high price umbrella that Shinco could undercut with its lower costs, the portable DVD segment was appealing for another reason: it offered the opportunity for Shinco to leverage the superior error correction technology it had developed for the Chinese market. This time, however, the benefit didn't come from an ability to handle pirate DVDs, which were rare in developed markets, but because it allowed Shinco's players to compensate for errors generated as the DVD is shaken around (as a car goes over bumps, for example). It was also capable of playing a wide variety of hitherto incompatible CD and DVD disks in different formats on the one machine.

Being able to leverage lower Chinese R&D and design costs, and by using error correction technology for which much of the cost had already been amortized in the Chinese market, Shinco was able to launch a superior, portable DVD player at a price between 30 percent and 50 percent below the competition in the global market.

The next specialty products Shinco set about disrupting using its cost innovation capabilities were a high-priced compact DVD player (a "theatre in the palm of your hand") and a wide-screen, portable DVD with an 8-inch display—the largest display in the industry—which won the Technology Innovation Gold Award at the twenty-second Hong Kong International Electronics Exhibition. Again it was able to transform the cost economics of supplying these specialties. Today Shinco sells more portable DVD players than any other company in the world.

Even more importantly, this strategy has allowed Shinco to rewrite the rules for how Chinese and foreign companies interact in the global value chain. Rather than being a cheap manufacturer of others' products, Shinco is leading the market with its innovative designs, technologies, and insight into customer preferences. And it has turned the traditional buyer-supplier relationship on its head: foreign companies now design and manufacture components to fit Shinco's product architectures.

Look no further than Shinco's relationship with Sony to see the implications for how this kind of cost innovation can turn the tables on established competitors. With high price and product features ill-suited to local customer needs, Sony's own product sold poorly in China. As a result, Sony relied on Shinco's sales to benefit from the country's booming VCD market. Shinco, on the other hand, wasn't captive to Sony: when Sanyo developed a better optical lens, Shinco shifted its business. The traditional relationship between an incumbent multinational and the Chinese ended up being reversed. Rather than being a subcontractor to its global rivals, Shinco was designing the product, leading the market, and calling the tune.

The Cost Innovation Challenge

It's clear that cost innovation isn't rocket science. But it should be equally clear that it is a powerful competitive weapon with the ability to disrupt global markets. By leveraging low-cost Chinese R&D and engineering resources; betting on cheaper, alternative technologies; and riding the open architecture wave, the emerging dragons can offer the world high technology at low cost. By using China's labor cost advantage in novel ways to increase their process flexibility without undermining efficiency and via recombinative innovation, Chinese competitors are offering increased variety and customization at the same rock-bottom prices as standardized products—transforming the economics of supplying today's high-priced, specialty products.

Today's global leaders need to take these unconventional strategies seriously because they expose even products and activities requiring leading-edge technologies to competition from the Chinese—and, worse still, competition that comes completely from left field. Faced with new rules, much of the incumbents' accumulated experience can be rendered irrelevant. And if an emerging Chinese competitor is able to apply high technology to a formerly lower-technology game, to deliver massively greater variety and choice, or to transform the economics of supplying specialist products, established players on all sides are left with frightening challenges. Those who basked in the high margins of the past are faced with a competitor capable of undermining the foundations of their business model by innovative use of cost advantage to deliver more for less. Those who relied on managing product life cycles to recoup their R&D costs and maximize profitability by gradually migrating new technology from high-end segments to the lower-price, mass market will find this strategy stopped dead if an emerging dragon starts to deliver high technology directly to mass-market products almost from day one.

Having lifted the veil on how the emerging Chinese dragons are achieving cost innovation, the key question Western managers need to be asking is: "Where are we most vulnerable?" Working that out is the subject of chapter 3.

3

Loose Bricks

Rethinking Your Vulnerabilities

When the Chinese dragons start to expand abroad, their initiatives are carefully targeted. Few Chinese companies have the luxury of trying to outgun their established competitors through overwhelming resources. They may be big in China, but most cannot afford to accumulate significant losses in the course of achieving their global ambitions. So the power of their thrust into new markets doesn't come from breadth or deep pockets. And despite the perceptions of some, it's not government backing that makes the Chinese entry hard to resist. What makes the dragons dangerous is the fact that their challenge is likely to come from left field: in the form of cost innovation as a tool to precisely target "loose bricks"—those market segments where existing players are potentially most vulnerable.

The tactic of breaking into a market by concentrating their attack where established competitors will be most vulnerable to cost innovation is so well developed by the Chinese dragons that Huawei even has a name for it—the "pressure point" principle.[1] This approach originally grew out of necessity when Chinese firms had very limited resources with which to face powerful global rivals inside China. Today, the principle has become a conscious tactic.

Using this approach, the Chinese dragons are already demonstrating an uncanny ability to identify and pry open loose bricks in their established competitors' defensive walls. By finding these loose bricks the dragons can improve their chances of successfully breaking into the global market against entrenched competitors who have experience, brands, and an established customer base on their side.

Once the first few bricks are knocked away the wall starts to look shaky; a few more bricks and it can even collapse under its own weight. Haier's CEO Zhang Min describes the same idea for how a new market can be captured with a slightly different metaphor: "It is like slicing wood. In the previous years, we cut a small opening (a niche) here and there, and then we push further. What we need now is to add pressure . . . until you hear that loud 'popping sound' as the whole log splits and cracks open."[2]

In order to defend against these tactics, it is critical that established companies identify exactly where their vulnerabilities lie and reassess the risk of knock-on effects—losing share in one segment leading to the collapse of their position elsewhere. This means that it is important to avoid the trap of dismissing early Chinese incursions as insignificant. It's easy for the unwary to fall victim to complacency; in our research, we often observed that established companies rationalized early losses to the emerging dragons with statements such as: "These products are not really our company's future—they were only making a contribution to covering overhead to begin with," "While one never likes to lose a sale, they were our troublesome customers," or "Who cares about a few peripheral markets in Africa anyway?" Early losses of business to the Chinese may not even make it onto the top management radar screen because they don't seem to be "strategic," or they may be the result of a voluntary retreat to high-end business. When the importance of those early loose bricks becomes clear with the benefit of 20:20 hindsight, it may already be too late.

It's not always easy for an established company to recognize the loose bricks that are obvious to the emerging dragons. This is because the Chinese are looking at your company, and your customer base, through a different prism—a prism shaped by their unique cost structure, lower breakeven, and emerging economy environment and experience. By understanding this different perspective and the loose bricks it highlights, you have a much better chance of identifying your key vulnerabilities to emerging Chinese competitors and taking actions to address those exposures before they do—and before it's too late.

Loose Bricks in Your Defenses

The loose bricks being targeted by the Chinese dragons all share two basic characteristics. First, they are segments in which cost innovation (not just low labor costs) provides a potentially powerful source of competitive advantage. Second, and equally important, they are segments in which Western incumbents are reluctant or ill equipped to mount a strong counterattack.

These loose bricks then fall into a number of categories. Perhaps the most obvious of the ones the dragons have targeted (like their Japanese and Korean competitors before them) is a bottom-end segment where the unit value is so low that the earnings on every unit sold are microscopic. A TV or DVD player that retails at $99, or a baby carrier at under $20, for which the profit is measured in a few dollars, or even cents, is not the kind of segment multinationals are likely to fight to death to defend. Once the Chinese enter, causing margins to sink further, the incumbents who take a short-term view tend to write these segments off as a lost cause. Strategically, however, surrendering a low-margin segment may afford the Chinese a beachhead from which they go on to attack more profitable segments higher up the market.

A less obvious category of loose bricks are peripheral geographic markets, such as Africa, developing Asia, or Eastern Europe, that established multinational firms tend to see as low priority, or even ignore. It is often difficult for multinationals to make money in these markets because they are small, demand low prices, suffer from poor infrastructure, or all of these woes. However, because Chinese firms grew up in an environment that is very similar to many of these peripheral markets, they know how to thrive in these circumstances. The Chinese use these peripheral markets to gain experience and build more volume. These markets therefore act as a launching pad for the dragons' subsequent international expansion.

We term the sequence of global expansion that follows as *periphery to core*—building strength in far-flung, peripheral geographies before attacking the European and U.S. markets. As we will discuss, the Chinese have followed this road with devastating effect to gain ground in a number of industries.

Low-end products and geographically peripheral markets generally become loose bricks because of the low strategic priority accorded them by established firms, which are under constant pressure to focus their resources where profit potential is highest. But intriguingly, the Chinese dragons are also starting to discover loose bricks even in markets to which the incumbents are fully committed and assume are safe from attack from competitors based in China—a developing country across the ocean. Vulnerability here is increased by an element of surprise.

One of these unexpected loose bricks is "troublesome" customers—often businesses or retailers—who ask for a uniquely customized product. Incumbents are frequently reluctant to accede to demands for something that doesn't fit their standard business model, especially if supplying it involves retooling manufacturing lines or organizational processes as well as altering the product itself. But with low costs and flexible, labor-intensive production processes, Chinese companies often see serving these "misfit" customer demands as an attractive gateway into the market.

A final, perhaps surprising, type of loose brick is the niche segment, where established suppliers believe there is only a small market among dedicated, even idiosyncratic, customers. As we saw in earlier chapters, Chinese cost innovation has the potential to blow these niches apart, turning them into much lower priced, mass markets—recall the case of refrigerated wine-storage units. By transforming niche markets in this way, Chinese companies again build experience, capabilities, and volume that they can subsequently leverage to attack more mainstream markets.

In the rest of the chapter we describe how different Chinese dragons have attacked these loose bricks and dislodged them as a critical first step in weakening their incumbent competitors' defensive walls. Then we illustrate how the Chinese firms are launching one wave of attack after another, sometimes across multiple loose bricks, and rapidly winning more and more business from established players. This understanding is essential to help Western managers rethink where their vulnerabilities to disruptive competition from China might really lie. By understanding where Chinese competitors see loose bricks, and why, the task of shoring up their defenses can begin.

Low-End Segments

Naturally, the emerging Chinese competitors look for segments where their cost innovation weapon is potentially powerful. Low-end segments are obvious candidates. Attack from this quarter is familiar to most managers, as domestic low-cost and no-frills competitors have emerged in industries from air travel to generic drugs to stock broking. What is particularly noteworthy about the new challenge from China, however, is that even when targeting the low end, the best Chinese competitors seldom compete just by imitating the strategies of existing players. The reason is simple: low price alone isn't enough to build a profitable business against other Chinese competitors and multinationals that are already sourcing the low end of their product line direct from China. What makes the rise of the dragons a new and disruptive source of competition is their use of cost innovation to target low-end segments in novel ways. Rather than simply being low-price or no-frills, they are offering better value for money with an innovative twist.

Take the example of Haier's incursion into the American market for home appliances. The loose brick they targeted was the market segment of small refrigerators that serve as minibars in hotel rooms and can be squeezed into student dormitory rooms. This segment was regarded as a low-margin, standardized commodity by the likes of GE, Whirlpool, and Maytag. But Haier's experience with China's low-priced, but fast-changing, environment led it to believe otherwise: innovation didn't have to be the preserve of the high end of the market.

Haier sent a team of design people to study the way college students use their refrigerators in their dorms. Their aim: to find a way to differentiate the Haier product by bring innovation to a market others saw as a commodity. What they came up with was a small refrigerator with foldable top that turned into a computer desk when opened. The combination of a compact refrigerator and a computer desk was a godsend to students in cramped dormitory rooms. The product became an instant hit. More broadly, the lesson for Haier was that a low price point didn't have to mean lack of innovation. Once the nexus between innovation and cost had been broken, the way was open for Haier to produce a stream of innovative, keenly priced products. Two other small refrigerator designs created specifically for use in offices and hotel rooms quickly followed. Since that time, Haier has offered some two hundred distinctive products to distributors in the U.S. market, and captured around 50 percent of this market segment.

In addition to the direct benefit of differentiating the Chinese products, even at the low end, the strategy of breaking the nexus between innovation and cost had powerful spillover: it meant that Chinese firms started building their R&D and product development capabilities even while they were competing at the low end of the market.

Peripheral Markets

In selecting where to launch their international expansion, many companies traditionally follow the impeccable logic of infamous bank robber Willy Sutton who, when asked why he robbed banks, replied: "Because that's where the money is!" But instead of simply looking for the richest pickings, Chinese companies have often begun their internationalization by targeting poorer, developing-country markets that many of their Western competitors regard as peripheral. Only once they are established as the dominant suppliers in the developing world do these Chinese companies launch into first-world markets in the United States and Europe. The case of Lifan's international expansion shows how and why, if an established company neglects far-flung, low-priced markets that might appear strategically unimportant, it lays itself open to the dragons suddenly appearing at the front door.

From Periphery to Core

By the late 1990s Lifan had pulled ahead of its domestic competitors to become one of the leading suppliers of motorcycles in the China market. Having achieved scale and experience at home, the company then set its sights on markets abroad.

Lifan chose Vietnam for its first joint venture overseas in 1999. With an attractive line of products, knowledge of how to distribute and supply parts in a developing country, and a price point 50 percent below the incumbent Japanese suppliers, it rapidly took market share. It next went on to develop in Nigeria, the Philippines, Iran, and Indonesia. Together with Vietnam, Lifan calls these markets its "five flowers." Many of its multinational competitors probably thought they looked more like weeds. But Lifan sold more than $10 million worth of motorcycles in each and every one of these countries. Its volumes in Iran alone were sufficient to justify setting up a full assembly plant in there.

The experience and volume it gained from the five flowers gave it the platform to expand into other markets in the Middle East, South Asia, Africa, and Latin America. It built a plant in South Africa, becoming a major player in the African markets. Even then, most of its competitors did not regard Lifan as a threat. By 2004, most of its sales were still outside the more profitable markets of Japan, Europe, and the United States, where the established global players were focusing the lion's share of their efforts. But almost under the radar screens of the competition, Lifan had built a presence in high-volume markets across a large swath of the globe. It now enjoyed substantial economies of scale. Moreover, it had successively broadened and deepened its experience as each step from one country to the next brought it into contact with ever more highly developed markets.

Having dislodged the loose bricks on the periphery, Lifan was ready to launch its assault on the Japanese, European, and U.S. markets. Its scale and the cost innovation experience it had gained, first in China and then in other emerging economies, allowed Lifan to offer a wide range of products at low cost. Customers responded enthusiastically. And the prize for its gradual march from peripheral into core markets was worth the wait: Europe and the United States now account for 25 percent of Lifan's sales outside China, but 50 percent of its overseas profits.[3]

We observe the same pattern being repeated in the broader auto industry. Chery's first car exports were to Syria. In 2003 it established a joint venture with Iranian parts maker SKT in Iran's northeast province of Mashlad to assemble, weld, and paint cars imported in completely knocked down (CKD) kit form. In October 2004, Chery announced plans to build its first assembly plant on the African continent, in Egypt, and is negotiating to build plants in Pakistan, Syria, Venezuela, and several Eastern-European countries. Its periphery-to-core strategy was under way. The final stop, five new models scheduled for launch in the United States in 2008 through Chery's American importer, Visionary Vehicles. Chery's aim: to be selling 1 million vehicles annually in the United States within five years of the launch.[4]

Right or wrong, Chinese companies may take a different view of the risks of operating in markets like Iran or Syria. Given that China's regulatory and legal infrastructure is far less developed, there are much lower risks of being sued by shareholders or governments at home if a foray into a foreign market turns sour. So Chinese companies may be willing to venture into global markets where others fear to tread. As one resort developer in Africa's tourism industry, where the Chinese are fast becoming the dominant investors, put it: "The Chinese don't spend months arguing about corporate governance or political risk, they just get on and build."[5]

The emerging Chinese dragons, therefore, are particularly well positioned to succeed in far-flung, difficult, and often low-priced markets where their established competitors have suspicions about the potential profitability, or neglect for other reasons. They usually have had the experience of operating at rock-bottom prices and through tortuous distribution channels throughout rural China, not just in the main cities. Success in China's huge markets means they are often able to match the scale advantages of their established global competitors even before they go abroad. Less onerous Chinese corporate governance processes and greater separation between ownership and control arguably mean they have a higher tolerance for risk. Together these capabilities allow the dragons to target the world's peripheral markets as loose bricks because they can thrive where established companies struggle to mount a solid defense.

The dragons' ability to capture share in these markets is becoming an increasingly decisive factor in overall global competition because, while each market may be small, together they constitute a significant portion of world demand. In fact, as pointed out recently by the *Economist*, and as illustrated in figure 3-1, the combined GDP of emerging and developing economies had risen to above half of global GDP when measured at purchasing-power parity by 2005.[6]

It is not only the tough segments at the bottom end of the market or the geographic periphery, however, where Chinese companies are finding cracks in their competitors' walls. They are also finding vulnerabilities in the heart of their global rivals' markets—troublesome customers and niche segments.

FIGURE 3-1

Developing country GDP passed 50 percent of world total (at PPP*)

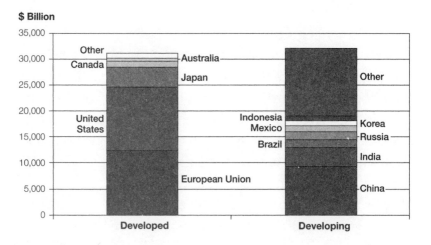

*Purchasing power parity

Source: International Monetary Fund.

Troublesome Customers

Most volume producers are reluctant to customize their products unless they have to. Customization means incurring additional fixed costs in design, setup and changeover of manufacturing lines, and risking getting stuck with nonstandard inventory if the customer curtails its orders prematurely. From a short-term profit perspective, saying no to such troublesome customers often makes a lot of sense. But what if the emerging dragons use them as loose bricks they can dislodge to undermine your defenses?

Haier is one company that has used incumbents' reluctance to serve troublesome customers to weaken its competitors' hold on the market. It reasoned that, in refusing to accede to the requests of customers for a unique product variant that would upset their well-honed supply chains designed to push through volume, the incumbents might be leaving demand unsatisfied. As Haier's vice president of sales put it: "Whirlpool and Maytag often say no to the hassle of customer tailoring."[7]

So when Office Depot sent out a request for refrigerators that could be locked for better security in offices and shared dormitories, Haier saw another loose-brick opportunity. It was precisely Haier's willingness to create this customized product, a lockable refrigerator, for Office Depot that allowed it to get initial shelf space. Out-customizing its competitors offered a win-win for Haier and the retailer. The strategy allowed Haier to leverage its lower costs of product design, plant setup, and changeover afforded by Chinese labor. For Office Depot, the vice president of procurement observes: "We usually can give our products more unique characteristics if we cooperate with Haier."[8] That uniqueness also helped Haier to achieve prices close to those of its established competitors, despite a weaker brand.

Haier's approach of looking for loose bricks in retailers' requests for customization that established competitors were reluctant to undertake has also led the company to a strategy of systematically working with the customer to develop new products. Haier routinely "tests the water" before it makes big moves. In the TV business, for example—a mature market where differentiation is difficult—Haier tests its product designs initially in the second-tier and regional retailers, and uses the lessons from this experience to improve the early designs and roll out the improved products to larger chains. Through this strategy it is able to de-risk each move forward as it chips away at competitors' market share.

Since then, Haier has started to work in even closer cooperation with retailers. In July 2004, Haier and Target staged a joint promotional event in which they set up a temporary Target store filled with Haier products within sight of Macy's in New York, offering free delivery and other promotional incentives. This innovation in guerrilla warfare marketing sold a record volume of seven thousand air conditioners in just seven hours.

Today the bulk of Haier's sales in the United States are through the ten largest retailers. The pattern is reapeated in Europe and Japan, where Haier's sales are concentrated in the top five retailers, taking it to its aim of "world-class volume" in "world-class channels."[9]

Galanz is another company that has exploited troublesome customers as a loose brick. Back in 1996 when it was producing only forty thousand microwaves per year, Galanz followed a similar strategy of out-customizing the competition to break into the international market. By contacting the Hong Kong Trade Development Bureau, Galanz found that a French importer, Wesder SA, was buying substantial volumes of standard microwaves, 23 liters and above, from another Chinese producer, Xianhua Microwave Products Co. Ltd. (later acquired by Whirlpool). Seeing a market opportunity in the cramped apartments of major European cities, however, Wesder also wanted a very small microwave with only a 17-liter capacity. Given the need for substantial redesign of the product and retooling of the production line, making such a small oven was a tough demand.

When Galanz ran the numbers, it concluded that such an awkward order would yield little or no profit and would pose considerable risk. But the company also saw it as a way to break into the European market. Despite the difficulties of customization, Galanz decided to pursue the deal. It won an order for 100,000 microwaves, setting it off on the path that was to make it by far the largest producer of microwave ovens in the world.

Some Chinese companies have gone even further: they have identified opportunities where their competitors both lack focus on a peripheral market and are reluctant to serve what they see as troublesome customers there. Looking for this kind of combination of vulnerabilities has the obvious advantage of doubling the chances of finding a weak point. But because market segments that are both peripheral and troublesome are so far out in left field, it is even less likely that the global players will recognize the threat until it's too late.

Consider what happened to the competitors of Hisense, now one of the top Chinese exporters of TV sets and home appliances. Proudly displayed in the exhibition room at company headquarters is a TV that the company customized especially for an African distributor when Hisense received its first international order in the early 1990s. It doesn't seem much out of the ordinary until you turn it on: this TV has a special capability to automatically adjust its brightness according to the light intensity in the room.

In Africa, TVs are used in a wide variety of situations—in bright sunshine and black storms, sometimes outdoors. Such a capability therefore made perfect sense. But most of the companies the African customer originally contacted had refused even to entertain the idea because, far from being straightforward, such a function required R&D, redesign of the circuitry, and installation of new production equipment.

Even though the market was dominated by Japanese and Korean competitors, Hisense saw a doubly vulnerable loose brick—a low-profit, peripheral market where customers were demanding expensive alterations to the product—so it accepted the customization brief. It organized a special task force to tackle the issue. A few months later, the new product was ready. It turned out to be the breakthrough Hisense was lookingn for. On the back of the light-adjusting TV's success, their air conditioners and refrigerators started to enter the market. Sales jumped from a few thousand to twenty-five thousand appliances per month. The company was to become the second-largest player in the African market.

Many of the other Chinese emerging dragons have similar stories. We have already seen, for example, how the now globally dominant maker of port machinery, ZPMC, adopted customization as its watchword for entering new markets. ZPMC requires its sales operation to respond to any customer request with an initial technical proposal within twenty hours after receiving the enquiry, even if it arrives over the Chinese New Year holidays. This customer-centricity has paid off. As CEO Guan Tong Xian recalls: "We won a major deal simply because we replied immediately, while our competitor took several days [to respond]."[10]

In an environment of new, disruptive competition from China, therefore, Western management needs to take another look at customers that seem to be troublesome in a new light: they might actually turn out to be loose bricks through which the emerging dragons can gain entry into the market.

Niche Segments

We often hear managers in the United States and Europe argue that the way to respond to growing competition from China is to forget the low end of the market and focus squarely on defending all those upper-end niches where customers are willing to pay a premium for differentiated offerings and appreciate the value of strong, established brands. In some cases this strategy is sound. But beware: the Chinese dragons are also finding loose bricks hidden among these segments where they can apply their cost innovation tools—in this case their ability to transform the economics of supplying specialist products—to break through and then subsequently expand into the broader market. This means that upper-end niche segments can also be a source of exposure for established players.

This vulnerability to Chinese attack through a high-end niche segment is a blind spot for many Western companies that still expect the dragons to enter only through the bottom end of a market. This makes it all the more important for them to review their exposures in this area. In making this assessment it's critical to consider how the Chinese might use cost innovation to transform a niche segment into a new playing field, rather than whether they could win in the market as it is today. What would happen, for example, if a Chinese competitor offered similar technology to a niche product, but produced it in a large facility where economies of scale allowed it to cut prices by 50 percent or more?

Exploding the Niche

As we mentioned in the introduction to this book, that's exactly the scenario that unfolded in the niche market for refrigerators specifically designed to store wine. Incumbent makers of wine refrigerators, such as La Sommelière, pitched their products to wine connoisseurs at prices starting at $1,600 for a unit capable of holding one hundred bottles. To execute this strategy they had to spend heavily on design and marketing, and also had to offer distributors a healthy margin to cover the costs of their ritzy retail outlets. Despite these high costs, business was good ($1,600 is a trivial cost if you need to protect an unbroken run of Chateau Petrus vintages!), if small scale.

Haier saw this upmarket niche as a loose brick. Their huge scale in refrigerators and the much lower costs of designers and engineers in China would enable them to come up with a specialist wine refrigerator at a fraction of the investment required to launch a similar product in Europe or the United States. Investment in branding and high distributor margins could largely be avoided if it were to distribute these special refrigerators through a well-known mass retailer (it chose Sam's Club). By dramatically reducing these investments, Haier could cut the fixed costs of the project to a fraction of the volume required by competitors. These low fixed costs could be reduced even further if Haier shared the costs with its existing volume refrigerator business wherever possible.

By applying its cost advantage to the launch of a specialty product, Haier slashed its breakeven, allowing it to make money at 50 percent of the prevailing market price level, even if sales volumes remained low. Therefore it now had a way to break into this niche market with little risk of racking up losses. The upside of Haier's application of cost innovation strategy to a niche segment, of course, was the opportunity to explode it into a volume market if average homeowners turned out to have a demand for wine refrigerators when they were offered at affordable prices.

This particular niche brick turned out to be very loose indeed: Haier captured 60 percent of the U.S. market within two years of launch and went on to repeat the strategy in other markets, including Korea and Australia. The incumbents then faced a dilemma. One option was to further increase their spending on design and R&D and to speed up the rate of new product introduction in an attempt to put clear blue water between their product offering and that of Haier. But there is an obvious problem with this approach: the extra costs would have to be absorbed by that small niche of customers willing to pay a price premium in excess of 100 percent for something only superficially different. Even if they did, Haier could afford to invest heavily in upgrading its designs and technologies, because with ten times the volume of its rivals in the market it could spread the costs more effectively.

The alternative option open to the incumbents was to restructure the business to slash costs, perhaps involving the relocation of significant activities to China itself, so as to broaden the niche market into higher volume business before its Chinese competitors could do so. We will examine the implications of these types of strategies in detail in chapter 5.

Spawning New Niches

What happens, however, if the niche the Chinese competitor chooses to target doesn't yet exist? How do you guard against the possibility that the Chinese use cost innovation to create new niches? This niche-creation scenario might sound far-fetched. But look at it from the perspective of a Chinese latecomer: rather than trying to wrestle market share away from a well-established competitor in an existing market, wouldn't it be more attractive to create a new niche, so that the competitor's advantage of incumbency was simply sidestepped?

Haier has been doing just that. The market segment: TVs for kids' rooms. The incumbent suppliers in the United States simply saw TVs that might end up in a child's room as part of the mainstream market. Most probably didn't even think to ask whether a TV was for an adult's bedroom or that of a child. By contrast, Haier saw the potential to serve the latter segment with a differentiated product. Rather than blowing open an established niche segment, it decided to use its lower breakeven for designing and producing a product to create a new one.

The functionality Haier added was extraordinary. The design, dubbed "Frog Prince," featured a frog shape whose large "eyes" doubled as night-lights. Frog Prince also included novel electronic controls, such as a system where parents could limit viewing time to between one and four hours, ensuring that children spent time on a balanced set of activities. Haier then added a simple integrated circuit that allowed kids to play educational games using their TV set. The success of the Frog Prince led Haier to develop a whole line of TVs for kids based on different cartoon characters. Another pile of loose bricks had been dislodged from its competitors' defenses.

The potential for disruptive competition as China's dragons go global obviously has many layers. In trying to "peel back the onion," we have described their strategy of cost innovation along three dimensions: delivering high technology at low cost; variety and customization at low cost; and specialty products at low cost. In this chapter we have seen how the dragons are targeting their cost innovation capabilities at loose bricks in the global market where they believe established competitors are most vulnerable: low-end market segments; geographically peripheral markets; troublesome customers; and niche segments. In practice, however, the Chinese dragons often apply multiple cost innovations to a combination of loose bricks simultaneously. In rethinking overall vulnerability, it is therefore worth taking the time to understand how these various elements interact and reinforce each other to propel the dragons forward to becoming major global players. One company that is further along this path than most is the maker of high-technology telecommunications equipment, Huawei.

Cost Innovation Meets the Loose Bricks

Up until 1995 Huawei still made most of its then-modest $200 million total sales to telecoms operators in rural China. However, even at that time its Chairman, Ren Zhengfei, already had an ambitious goal for Huawei to "become a world-class, leading global telecoms equipment manufacturer."[11] This strategy was achieved by using cost innovation targeted at a series of peripheral markets and troublesome customers as the loose bricks.

Gaining a Foothold in Peripheral Markets

Huawei's first target was a small provider of mobile telephony services in Hong Kong, the fledgling Hutchison Telecom. When the Hong Kong government swept away Hong Kong Telecom's monopoly on fixed-line services in 1995, Hutchison decided to try and enter this market. But Hong Kong was also the first region in the world to demand that consumers be offered number portability—the ability of users to change to a new telecoms provider while still keeping their existing number.[12] Reengineering the telecommunications equipment and software to accommodate this, then-novel, requirement posed challenges for all existing Hong Kong operators. But for Hutchison Telecom, the ruling threatened to delay the launch of its service, giving its rivals an unimpeded head start in recruiting new customers in the critical months after deregulation; it needed to be able to offer number portability within just three months.

Hutchison found itself boxed into a corner because the best offer Hutchison's European equipment suppliers had come up with was a six-month implementation time. Even then the established suppliers quoted high prices for what they probably saw as a troublesome customer: a nonroutine request from a start-up in a small market, demanded in a hurry. Huawei saw its chance: it committed to complete the work in three months and at a lower cost than its competitors.

By dedicating a large team of engineers and looking for a cost-innovative solution to Hutchison's problem, Huawei kept its promise. With its first satisfied customer outside mainland China, albeit an operator in tiny Hong Kong, Huawei was launched on the road to globalization. As it happened, securing that customer relationship proved to be even more fortuitous than was evident at the time because Hutchison subsequently became one of the world's largest telecoms operators through its "Orange" business (eventually sold to France Telecom) and later its "3" brand, which operates third-generation (3G) mobile services in seventeen countries.

Huawei's next win was against competition from Motorola in another market many regarded as peripheral in global terms: Vietnam. Its capability to get the Vietnamese network up and running in record time was decisive in fending off its much larger, globally recognized rival. Then in 1997 Huawei set up a joint venture with the Russian telecoms equipment maker Beto Khuavey to try to build business in the Russian market. Shortly afterward Russia was hit by a financial crisis and the telecoms equipment market came to a dead halt. Huawei sold nothing for the first two years.

Seeing the Russian market as both difficult and low priority, many multinationals in the telecoms equipment business withdrew altogether. But Ren Zhengfei remembers telling his wavering Russian representative: "If one day the Russian market recovers, but Huawei is shut out, you will jump out of the window of this building!"[13] Rather than withdraw, Huawei used the time to build its sales capabilities in Russia. It began to recruit locals and send them to its China headquarters for training; on return they were dispatched to keep visiting customers across Russia's far-flung regions with the aim of building understanding of the potential customer needs and trust.

When the Russian economy started to rebound in 2000, Huawei won its first Russian order: it was for a single switch, worth just $12! The skeptics felt they were vindicated in their view: forget the periphery and target developed economies where the certain money is. But by 2001 Huawei's Russian sales were running at $100 million per year, by 2003 it was selling $300 million in the former Soviet republics, and today Huawei enjoys a 50 percent share of the Russian market in broadband equipment.

Huawei's success in the Russian market reflects more than just perseverance. It also stems from the fact that Chinese companies' experience in China is most transferable to emerging economies such as the former Soviet bloc. It has taught them how to get their products' marketing messages and service to prospective customers despite a weak or nonexistent distribution system. They know how to deal with large rural populations spread over wide areas. Dealing with nontransparent government regulations and a backward financial system is second nature, because it's just like home. By choosing emerging- and developing-economy markets as their entry point into the global battle, the dragons can play to their experience.

Huawei then targeted the African markets. Its first opening was afforded when some of its people joined a high-level trade mission under the leadership of China's Vice Premier Wu Bangguo that visited many African countries. What struck the Huawei representatives was the potential to leverage two of the key advantages the company had honed in the course of serving the Chinese market: the ability to design telecoms networks that could efficiently service large, dispersed rural populations, and its knowledge of how to get capital costs down to meet the needs of telecom operators facing massive demand with limited investment budgets. These advantages, combined with the ability to put large numbers of Chinese installation and service support personnel on the ground in Africa at minimal cost, gave Huawei the ability to make the African markets profitable despite demanding geography, limited technical knowledge among the customers, and intense pressure for value for money. By 2004 Huawei had set up some thirty representative offices across Africa and sold its equipment in forty countries on the continent. With African sales of $442 million, it had become by far the leading competitor in the market.

Starting out by building their experience and volume in low-income markets where consumers count pennies and the investment capital available to business and government falls far short of their needs makes obvious sense for the emerging dragons such as Huawei because it is here that the cost advantage enjoyed by Chinese companies is most decisive in winning the business. With the world's lowest costs, Huawei can turn a margin on telecommunications equipment in Africa or Galanz can make money selling microwave ovens in Vietnam when higher-cost multinationals see only losses. Moreover, being able to offer rock-bottom prices means that Chinese companies can build volume faster than their competitors by unlocking latent demand.

Serving Troublesome Customers

In addition to focusing on what many of its rivals saw as peripheral, developing markets, Huawei also continued to target new entrants among the telecom operators. Its competitors might have regarded these entrants as troublesome customers who placed a premium on speed of installation and value for money, and were prepared to try innovative approaches and technologies in order to stretch their limited funding and in the hope of gaining a competitive advantage over their established rivals by breaking the rules. A good example was AIS in Thailand, a maverick company that had been set up by entrepreneur Taksin Shinawatra—a retired police chief who was later to become Thailand's billionaire Prime Minister.

In 1999 Huawei installed and tested equipment to support AIS's prepaid service in just sixty days. This allowed its upstart customer to beat DTAC, then Thailand's largest established operator, into the market by months. Following this success, Huawei then went on to supply AIS with the equipment and support to increase its network capacity eightfold to become the largest mobile telecommunications company in Thailand. In the course of these expansions, Huawei developed more than eighty unique features, tailored to meet AIS's particular needs. And it continued to deliver each, up and running, in record time, allowing AIS to be consistently first to market with new, value-added services for users, helping it go on winning market share.

Huawei then looked for an opportunity to parlay its experience with peripheral markets and new players into sales in the mainstream, developed world. An important stepping-stone was a deal with Etisalat, the operator in the wealthy United Arab Emirates (UAE). The country has a population of just 2.4 million, but it provided an opportunity to prove Huawei's capability in an advanced, 3G mobile application. Pitted against the global majors like Motorola and Ericsson in a parallel equipment trial (or "test-off"), Huawei put an incredible two hundred engineers on-site on the UAE, with many more supporting staff back in China, to continually evaluate and improve its technology. After one year, Huawei's equipment came out on top of the performance league and Huawei won the contract for full-scale implementation. This was Huawei's first overseas WCDMA (Wideband Code Division Multiple Access) contract. Just as importantly, it was the world's first project commercializing R4 technology, an emerging switching technology that effectively substituted flexible software for less flexible and more expensive hardware, and that Huawei was betting on heavily to catapult it to technology leadership. Winning such a hotly contested deal laid a solid foundation for Huawei's rapid expansion in WCDMA technology.

With the UAE as reference site in the bag, Huawei went on winning contracts to build entire 3G mobile networks at SUNDAY in Hong Kong, Emtel in Mauritius, and TM in Malaysia. So, by initially concentrating on proven technology in developing-country markets in Asia and Africa and then in emerging markets of Russia and former Soviet republics, Huawei had learned how to apply its technology to a variety of customer needs, honed its capabilities in installation, service, and support, and further reduced its costs by gaining volume. Huawei had then gone on to prove it could deliver state-of-the-art technology for 3G networks by focusing on winning the business in small markets that required advanced equipment like the UAE and Hong Kong. In both cases it exploited self-inflicted weaknesses in the way the incumbent rivals approached the business. In the first case, it relied on the perception among leading global competitors that developing-country markets were less attractive because they offered lower margins, high sales costs due to the need for heavy investment in education and relationship-building, and higher risks of problems in implementation in difficult environments. In the second case, Huawei was relying on its competitors calculating that the fixed costs of putting high technology into a small and unfamiliar market were unlikely to be worth the trouble. Like Willy Sutton, Huawei hoped its rivals would emphasize markets where the big money was to be found in a familiar environment (in this case the United States and Europe), leaving the periphery more open for Huawei to build a launching pad for its next assault.

Markets in the developing world that have only recently opened up or new, troublesome customers can act as loose bricks because it is here that the incumbent global giants are least well entrenched. The limited purchasing power and low prices that characterize these customer segments are unattractive, and Western multinationals are often unwilling to invest in marketing and distribution to properly service customers in developing markets they classify as "noncore." Nor are they usually willing to devote expensive development resources to tailor their offerings to meet the local needs of these markets and to reverse engineer their products to meet the low price points that prevail. So it is in these markets that the Chinese dragons can most easily out-deliver on customer care and service. Ask yourself whether your company would lavish on Africa or even the UAE the level of customer care and investment in local service and support Huawei delivered into these markets.

Moving from Periphery Toward Core Markets

Once its launching pad of track record, experience, and volume was firmly in place, Huawei then began to move in on more mainstream developed markets, starting with Europe. Despite its now greater depth of capabilities, experience, and reference sites across a string of countries, Huawei still faced barriers to moving further into the core of large, developed markets. But it had certainly improved its chances dramatically compared with the shape it was in when it started down the path of globalization in 1996. One main problem—brand perception—remained, because, as one manager put it: "Made in China raises an image of cheap shoes, not high tech-telecom products, so it was hard to get potential customers even to agree to let us visit." Huawei's solution was to invest $12 million each year promoting its products at established international telecoms trade shows. It was not unusual to find more Huawei representatives at a major trade show than from any other company.

Once they saw the reality, customers' perceptions started to change. After Huawei's participation in the 2002 3G World Congress, held in Cannes, France, one manager recalled the following item headlined on the French evening news: "There is 3G technology in China as well!" Huawei followed up by hosting interested customers on visits to its installed base of networks and its own facilities along what it called "the new silk road" running from Hong Kong, through the border city of Shenzhen (where Huawei is headquartered), and on to Shanghai and Beijing. Many visitors are not only impressed by Huawei's achievements, but also by the rapid development in China that made Huawei's emergence possible. In short, these visitors' perception of "Made in China" is being changed as well.

Huawei also recognized that bringing its cost innovation strategy to the areas of customization and support services would be key to winning over European customers. Its experience of developing customized solutions at low cost to meet the developing business of customers like AIS—leveraging its cost advantage to offer a more tailored solution than its competitors—proved decisive in breaking into the market. Huawei was also able to use its low-cost Chinese resources to innovate in the area of implementation support. By deploying large numbers of people on the ground next to the customer it was able to offer higher flexibility and improved responsiveness compared with Western competitors that relied more heavily on standardized processes and remote servicing.

Its first European contract to build a 3G Universal Mobile Telecommunications System (UMTS) to provide mobile broadband access to the Internet and services such as video telephony was with Telfort B.V. of the Netherlands, previously an Ericsson customer and reported by the media to be worth between $265 and $530 million.[14] During the signing ceremony, Ton aan de Stegge, CEO of Telfort, observed: "Telfort's strategy is to challenge the established norms of the mobile industry and this contract, which is the first of its kind in Europe, is exactly in line with that. We are confident that Huawei will help us to develop innovative and cost effective data solutions for our customers and look forward to a prosperous relationship with them." In a subsequent interview, Theo van der Wiel, Telfort's director of networks and systems, reemphasised the point: "We were very impressed by the innovative activities of Huawei," going on to say that Telfort chose Huawei for its technological expertise as well as its products' lower costs.[15] In short, cost innovation had won the day for Huawei in a highly competitive, developed market.

Telfort was also undoubtedly influenced by Huawei's offer to build its own support and R&D center, staffed by more than a hundred engineers, just down the road from the Telfort headquarters. Using cost innovation to provide a more customized solution was to become formalized in Huawei's service slogan: "Around the world close to you." Today, the company has four R&D centers in Europe with eleven hundred staff, 75 percent of whom are locals. In 2005 its sales in Europe exceeded $600 million.

Despite the success of the periphery-to-core strategy backed by cost innovation, Huawei's next target, the U.S. market, still proved a tough nut to crack. A central problem was lack of brand awareness. Consider what happened when Huawei opened a sales office in Plano, Texas, in March 2001. Even as they signed the lease on their property, its people noticed that Americans not only hadn't heard of Huawei, they had difficulty in pronouncing the name: the landlord kept calling it "hoo-way." Potential customers came up with variations ranging from "high-way" to "how-way."[16] Eventually, the company decided to rebrand its U.S. subsidiary "FutureWei."

FutureWei continued to struggle with lack of brand awareness and distribution connections to sell network equipment in the United States and so began to focus on simpler, smaller-unit-value routers in an attempt to pry open the market. This strategy, however, was brought to a dead halt in January 2003 when Cisco filed a suit in the U.S. District Court in Marshall, Texas, alleging that Huawei had copied Cisco's router code. Huawei was forced to suspend sales of its routers in the United States, and it was rumored that other deals in the pipeline, such as a "significant" deal with WorldCom that Huawei had hoped to announce in weeks, fell through.[17] The reputation it had tried to nurture was in tatters.

Eventually Cisco dropped the suit in July 2004 when the two companies negotiated a confidential settlement in which Huawei agreed to stop using the disputed software on the handful of products in which it had been deployed. Within weeks, Huawei announced its first major network deal in the United States: to build a 3G new generation network for NTCH Inc., operator of the ClearTalk brand, involving 358,000 points of presence (POPs) in California and Arizona.[18] In 2005 followed deals with New-York based CTC Communications, for a state-of-the-art network modernization, and a Next Generation Network (NGN) solution for Intelecom Solutions Inc., also based in New York. In the latter case the deal was described as "a significant early adoption of a solution in the United States, one that has been deployed successfully in other networks worldwide."[19]

Despite a difficult start in the United States, therefore, Huawei seems now to be making inroads into the last "ring" of its move from peripheral markets to large, developed ones. By following a systematic, periphery-to-core strategy, starting with markets that many of its competitors might consider small, difficult, or noncore, Huawei has successively penetrated the complete spectrum of global markets—from small, developing ones to the large, advanced markets in Europe and the United States. Of the nineteen licenses for new 3G mobile networks issued globally in 2004, Huawei won business from fourteen of them—that's close to 75 percent penetration of the world's most advanced contracts that were up for grabs.[20] In short, Huawei has become a potent global competitor that was able to beat both Motorola and Britain's Marconi to win a share of British Telecom (BT) Group plc's $19 billion 21st Century Network. Watching the periphery-to-core strategy at work, however, it might be more accurate to say that it took almost ten years for Huawei to become an overnight success in developed markets by targeting its established competitors' loose bricks and patiently and systematically building its capabilities through experience as it moved from the periphery to the core.

The "Experience Curve" Reinvented

Huawei's path—from chipping away at its competitors' loose bricks to becoming a major global player in its industry—illustrates the way the dragons are using a virtuous cost-scale-learning cycle to move from being minor irritants to becoming market disruptors. As they grow their sales volume and progress faster down the experience curve, the dragons are able to improve their cost innovation capabilities still further; and from a successively stronger base, they launch the next wave of attack. Having made a breakthrough in one part of the market, the dragons typically chase volume aggressively. Their objective is to bolster their cost advantage by gaining greater scale economies than any competitor in the world in the limited segments and activities they target. Ever-increasing volume also helps these emerging dragons drive down the classic experience curve to further reduce costs.

Western managers are very familiar with this classic experience curve path to lowest cost, first quantified in 1925 at Wright-Patterson Air Force Base in the United States (where it was determined that every time aircraft production doubled, the required labor time decreased by 10 to 15 percent). It was popularized in the 1970s when consultants such as Bruce Henderson, founder of The Boston Consulting Group, preached the benefits of accumulating experience through scale.[21] But here's the difference: instead of using this model as a way of achieving the lowest production costs in the business, the Chinese have revolutionized its application. The dragons are using it to drive down the costs of everything they do, from R&D to customization. And instead of using their low costs simply to further cut prices, they are deploying their cost advantages and falling breakeven in ways that enable them to deliver innovative propositions to the market: high technology at low cost, variety and customization at low cost, and specialized products at the same low costs as mass-market ones.

The pursuit of these kinds of cost innovations has led the Chinese dragons to build cost advantage across a wide swath of value-creating activities that extend far beyond volume manufacturing. Not only were they able to cut the costs of R&D, product design, and engineering, eventually their cost-reduction skills also began to be applied in the areas like customer service (as we saw with Huawei) and product customization (recall Haier and Hisense). By finding innovative ways of improving cost efficiency in these activities they were able to fashion a powerful cost innovation wedge to pry open global markets. As illustrated in figure 3-2, this wedge mostly has its base in efficient manufacturing. But ultimately the Chinese dragons extend the wedge into successively higher-value activities and closer to the customer.

Rethinking Your Vulnerabilities

Think about the kind of analyses most multinationals undertake to help decide how to allocate their resources around the globe. One typical, well-run U.S. business we know computes a "Global Prioritization Index" based on a weighting of country attractiveness measures such as disposable income per capita and political risk, market attractiveness measures such as price points and

FIGURE 3-2

The cost innovation wedge

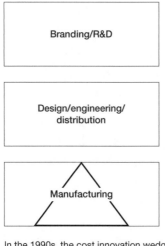

In the 1990s, the cost innovation wedge penetrated only manufacturing

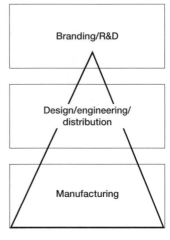

By 2005, the cost innovation wedge penetrated design, engineering, and even branding and R&D

volume growth, market saturation such as the number of competing brands already in retailers, and the rate at which new technology is adopted by customers. It's not hard to guess that on such an index, markets in Africa, Iran, or Pakistan, and most Latin American countries come out near the bottom of the pile. Their low scores tag them as low-priority, peripheral markets on the global playing field, not worthy of much investment or management attention. In the past, such a ranking probably made a lot of sense—it pays to put your cash and effort into large markets with attractive prices and a well-developed infrastructure before tackling difficult, fringe countries with low purchasing power, especially if they require products and business models to be adapted to their peculiarities.

But these calculations need to be adjusted now that the Chinese dragons use these low-priority markets as the loose bricks they can dislodge to break into the global market, building their experience and volume base there in order to launch an all-out assault on the ultimate prize—your high-margin customers in the developed world. Failure to take notice of developments in those peripheral markets could prove to be your Achilles' heel.

Likewise, the low-end segments that Chinese companies are targeting as your loose bricks are also ripe for a reevaluation. Maybe it's time to take another look at the strategy that C. K. Prahalad later described as unlocking "the fortune at the bottom of the pyramid" in a book by that name published in 2004.[22] In a nutshell, the idea was that companies could make money for their shareholders while simultaneously helping lift people out of the poverty trap by devising ways to deliver more value at much lower cost. He went on to explain that if incumbent multinationals were to take advantage of this opportunity, they would have to reexamine six widely shared orthodoxies of Western management:

- The poor are not target customers

- The poor cannot afford and have no use for the products and services sold in developed markets

- Only developed markets appreciate and will pay for new technology

- The bottom of the pyramid is not important for the long term viability of their business

- Managers are not excited by business challenges that have a humanitarian dimension

- Intellectual excitement is in the developed markets[23]

While Prahalad's ideas were perhaps novel in the West, it is not surprising that Chinese companies got there first. Not only had they thought of unlocking the fortune at the bottom of the pyramid, but they had started doing just that far ahead of most of their global competitors. Even today, their home market of China has a rural population of over 800 million people with an average per capita income of only $395 per annum. Look again at the six orthodoxies Prahalad argued multinationals headquartered in developed markets had to overturn before they could unlock the potential demand at the bottom of the pyramid. Not one of these orthodoxies is prevalent in most Chinese companies because had they believed that the poor were not target customers or had no use for the products and services sold in developed markets, they would have been writing off the mainstream consumer base in their home market.

Western thinkers came to this idea by looking at possibilities of "inclusive capitalism."[24] But wherever the idea came from the message for established companies is clear: it is not only for reasons of social responsibility that you should be taking the ideas of inclusive capitalism and unlocking the fortune at the bottom of the pyramid seriously; adopting such goals might lead you to master the principles of cost innovation in ways which would better position you to meet the disruptive impact of Chinese competition.

Given the risk that troublesome customers might turn out to be a loose brick, you might also need to reconsider the strategic implications of turning away their business. You may conclude that retaining or pursuing customers that appear difficult because they don't fit your current strategy will become critical in the future.

Finally, it could be important to jettison the notion that high-end niches aren't vulnerable to Chinese attack. The dragons' ability to transform the economics of specialty products makes niches potentially vulnerable as well.

Understanding where your loose bricks might lie, whether they are low-end segments, peripheral geographic markets, troublesome customers, or existing or new niches segments, or some combination of these, will be an essential first step toward meeting the challenge of disruptive competition from China. What makes these exposures much more dangerous is the fact they are unconventional risks. Being outside the normal run of competitive threats they may go unnoticed. It is therefore time to reassess your vulnerability in the light of the kind of cost innovation challenge that Chinese companies are increasingly mounting in the global market.

Even when you put these new vulnerabilities clearly on your radar screen, the appropriate response is far from obvious. But a response *is* necessary, because once emerging Chinese dragons have developed a solid beachhead in foreign markets they start relentlessly chipping away at adjacent segments until they suddenly seem to appear as significant players in the global market. When and if that happens, the consequences for incumbents can be dire. The question we must ask, therefore, is: having identified and exploited the established players' vulnerabilities, where will Chinese competition stop? That is the topic of chapter 4.

4

THE WEAK LINK

Limitations of the Chinese Dragons

WHERE WILL THE DISRUPTIVE Chinese competition stop? Certainly there are already signs that the dragons are far from invincible, despite all the power of their cost innovation strategy and the unique confluence of advantages that is fueling the rise of China-based companies today.

Look no further than the troubles afflicting consumer electronics maker TCL. Described by one commentator as "a quiet assassin," TCL became a huge force in the television-manufacturing industry.[1] In 2003 it became the dominant partner in TCL-Thomson Electronics (TTE), a joint venture with France's Thomson Electronics. This arrangement gave TCL the right to use the RCA and Thomson brands, as well as a network of production facilities, sales and marketing offices, and regional headquarters spread across the United States and Europe.

Today TCL remains the world's largest maker of television sets. But on October 31, 2006, it announced that it would sell its factory in Poland and close five of its seven European offices, including regional headquarters in France and six sales and marketing subsidiaries. The restructuring was estimated to cost

$57.5 million (in addition to $264 million of losses accumulated since TTE was formed) and involve making a "substantial number" of its 1,345 European employees redundant.[2] In an interview that same day, TCL's Chairman, Li Dongsheng, said that its U.S. business "remained fragile."[3]

While TCL expects the restructuring to bring these overseas operations back into profitability by 2008, its travails clearly demonstrate that the dragons do have weaknesses. And these are not limited to TCL. Chinese automakers, such as Chery, Great Wall, and Geely, have proved they can use cost innovation to develop vehicles of their own that offer attractive features at very low prices. Geely's latest Shanghai Maple model, for example, offers leather seats, antilock brakes, air conditioning, and a two-year warranty, all for a price tag of $6,500.[4] But the big push into the developed markets planned by Chery and Geely for 2007 has been delayed until 2008 or later, and plans to launch hybrid gas-electric cars have also been deferred. The evidence of these setbacks prompts two fundamental questions: Where are the weaknesses of the dragons? and, How long will they act as an important handicap to Chinese competitors' progress into the global market?

In this chapter we will put the spotlight on the dragons' weak points. These include: a limited capability to run complex, systemic businesses; their lack of strong brands; the limitations of cost innovation where industries are in the early stages of the product life cycle; and difficulty in penetrating businesses where the market is immature or nonexistent in China or the developing world.

However, we will also show that the dragons are finding novel ways to overcome these limitations or using the massive purchasing power of the Chinese state to force open opportunities they would otherwise be denied. So understanding where the dragons are weak isn't an argument for inaction. Rather it should help managers facing the challenge of disruptive competition from China in two ways: first to work out how much time they have to respond, and then how to exploit the dragons' weaknesses while they can.

Blunting the Cost Innovation Wedge

Two sets of impediments operate to blunt the Chinese cost innovation wedge and slow down the advance of disruptive competition from China. Demand-side impediments include the limited size of the Chinese market (or other developing-country markets) relative to the rest of the world and the immaturity of the industry. These factors make it difficult for Chinese competitors to use an initial focus on geographically peripheral markets to smooth their global expansion, and they undermine the potential to deliver high technology or increased variety at low cost.

The second set of impediments stems from the supply side. These include the systemic nature of an industry and the importance of intangible assets and capabilities, such as brands and brand building, which are slow and costly to imitate.

Limited Size of the Chinese and Developing Markets

Where the Chinese market is small, the dragons don't have much opportunity to build volume and experience at home before venturing into the global market. Worse still, if developing-country markets for a product or service are small or nonexistent, Chinese competitors can't use the "outside-in" strategy to build volume in peripheral, emerging markets where skills honed in China are most applicable and competition from established multinationals is arguably less intense. Limited size of the Chinese and developing markets compared with the global market, therefore, acts as an impediment to the ability of the dragons to challenge global incumbents.

The investment banking sector, especially merger and acquisition (M&A) services, is a good example. Just five years ago regulatory restrictions meant the M&A market in China was virtually nonexistent. Even by 2005, China accounted for less than 2 percent of global M&A activity by value; while total M&A in the developing world was only 5 percent.[5] As a result, Chinese banks and financial services companies had little or no opportunity to develop their skills, experience, and volume in this sector. With the U.S. market accounting for nearly half of global activity and the EU countries a further 40 percent, the periphery-to-core strategy simply wouldn't work for M&A services. Not surprisingly, the Chinese cost innovation wedge hasn't even scratched the surface in the market for investment banking services.

The small size of the Chinese and developing country markets compared with global demand has historically blunted the Chinese cost innovation wedge in other product markets, such as automobiles. For example, China's leading automaker, Chery, historically produced little more than 100,000 vehicles per year. Volume at Tianjin First Autoworks was only modestly higher, while Geely's output was even lower. These volumes paled into insignificance compared with global volumes of over 8 million cars per annum each for Toyota, General Motors, and Ford. Even Hyundai, the global number seven, churns out over 3 million vehicles per year. While the Chinese market remained small relative to the global market, disruptive competition from China was forestalled.

The message is clear: anywhere the Chinese market for a particular product or service remains small and underdeveloped, it's much harder for the dragons to make progress in bringing disruptive cost innovation to the global competitive arena.

Immature Industries

The Chinese cost innovation strategy is also generally less effective where a dominant technology has not yet emerged. Without a dominant technology it is difficult to climb aboard an experience curve that leads to reduced costs through economies of scale and learning. As a result, even when the Chinese come up with cost innovation ideas, they have trouble leveraging them up. Moreover, when a new business is emerging and early adopters are the target customers, it is novel functionality that drives the demand, rather than value for money. Technological uncertainty and an immature market comprising early adopters, therefore, expose limitations to where the dragons' cost innovation strategy can be applied.

These impediments are aptly demonstrated by the lack of Chinese penetration in the mobile phone handset business early in its product life cycle. While proprietary base technologies were competing for preeminence, the Chinese competitors were at a disadvantage to their established global rivals. They lacked sufficient knowledge and strength in the base technology and the global experience to drive proprietary approaches into the market. While the pace of technological change remained rapid—a characteristic of the early product life cycle—Chinese firms struggled to get reliable products out in a timely manner. The Chinese cost innovation wedge was blunted by an inability to keep up with a fast-moving product life cycle and the cost penalties associated with the need to buy key bits of proprietary technology from their Western competitors. Not surprisingly, the dragons' fire was sapped and, despite losing money, they made little headway in gaining market share.

The key implication for Western managers is that, while a business and its technology remain immature, it's difficult for the Chinese to disrupt them. With small volumes and the preference for technological sophistication among early adopters, the Chinese find it hard to kick-start a virtuous cycle of increased scale, rapid learning, and ever-lower cost. Delivering high technology at low cost, therefore, isn't usually viable. With the lack of an established platform and limited volume, the market isn't ready for variety at low cost. And because there aren't yet sufficient customers convinced about the technology and its benefits, the Chinese competitors can't transform the niche into a volume market even if they cut prices dramatically. After all, if consumers aren't convinced they need something or that a new technology works, they won't consider buying it at any price.

If you are able to pioneer a completely new market or technology, therefore, you can distance yourself from disruptive Chinese competition (at least for a while!).

Systemic Businesses

A third characteristic that exposes the limitations of the dragons' cost innovation strategy and impedes their advance is what economists call a *systemic* value network—in other words, industries in which a successful competitor needs to manage a complex, largely indivisible system of activities in order to deliver an attractive offering to the customer. Fast-moving consumer goods (FMCG) industries such as ready-made foods, snacks, or personal care products are a good example. These industries generally don't involve particularly high technology. But getting them right involves coordinating a complex, interrelated system that brings together sophisticated market research and product development; global sourcing of nonstandard, natural raw materials; manufacturing processes that must work as a continuous flow; and complex logistics that must take account of product variations (such as the shelf-life of different foods) and sophisticated marketing campaigns. The value delivered to the final consumer is only as good as the weakest part of this systemic network. Because a successful competitor must orchestrate the entire system to get the right result, it isn't clear where the Chinese can insert their cost innovation wedge. This is a key reason that multinational firms such as Procter & Gamble, Unilever, L'Oréal, and Henkel have dominant positions in many FMCG sectors such as personal care products and cosmetics even in China.

The drug business is another example. Traditional approaches to drug development used by the pharmaceutical industry are highly systemic, involving research, development, and clinical testing teams working together to use their tacit knowledge of interrelated, often proprietary processes.

The weakness of the dragons in these systemic industries is that they can't easily "slice and dice" the value chain into separate activity modules that require only simple interfaces and minimal coordination to deliver value to the end customer. Chinese companies can't break in by applying cost innovation to just one part of the chain. Instead they would have to tackle the complete complement of activities at once with the risk of failure caused by the handicaps they face in other activities or the fact that their limited resources would be spread too thin.

Intangible Assets

The final factor that impedes the advance of Chinese competition is the importance of intangible assets, such as brands or proprietary technology and experience that are slow and costly to build. Where these assets are critical to competitive success, the Chinese as latecomers are disadvantaged.

The power of cost innovation tends to be blunted in businesses where the bulk of customers won't even try a new supplier if they don't recognize the brand. Offering high technology, variety, or specialized products at low cost isn't enough if customers never recognize these benefits or aren't prepared to take the risk that such seemingly attractive Chinese offers might turn out to be a mirage.

Retailing is a prime example of the kind of industry in which Chinese retailers face considerable intangible asset barriers. In addition to the importance of a strong retail brand—enjoyed by the likes of Wal-Mart, Carrefour, or Tesco—success in retailing involves a plethora of intangible assets including relationships, knowledge about supplier management, logistics, shelf-space control, display, merchandising, and sales-force training.

Since labor costs are mostly driven by local wage rates, it's difficult for the Chinese to transfer the cost advantage to retail operations overseas. Meanwhile the scope for cost innovation is probably limited (although in consumer electronics retailing Chinese competitors have developed an innovative "while-you-wait" system where, after discussing a customer's requirements, a technician will assemble a customized PC or home theater to suit those exact needs from basic components in-store).

One reflection of the intangible asset advantage enjoyed by the international players over their emerging Chinese competitors is the fact that all of the fifty largest global retailers have entered the Chinese market (Carrefour has sixty-eight stores, for example, and Wal-Mart is close behind with sixty-two). While local competitors are fast imitating the capabilities of the global retailers, it is unclear that Chinese retailers will be able to develop significant sources of competitive advantage beyond local knowledge and low overhead. This will impede their ability to disrupt the global market outside China.

The importance of proprietary or uncodified technology is another factor that limits the dragons' ability to succeed in cost innovation. The petrochemicals business is a good example. Much of the key technology remains proprietary; since 1985, for instance, Exxon Mobil, Shell, and BP alone have applied for 1,770 patents in China, while Dow Chemical, BASF, and Bayer have submitted 2,560 more. Moreover, most chemical production processes are continuous, require heavy capital investment, and rely extensively on know-how accumulated over years. These characteristics make it hard to separate out one activity as a loose brick and leave little room for cost innovation by Chinese firms. While the product life cycle is mature, a few, largely standard products dominate the global markets, offering little scope for the Chinese to deploy cost innovation to outcompete the incumbents on variety and product churn as well. In the petrochemicals sector, therefore, disruptive competition from China faces many impediments.

Chinese Strengths and Weaknesses: Where Things Stand Today

In sum, we have seen that the extent to which your business is prone to disruption by the new wave of competition from China depends on four things: the size of the Chinese and other developing markets relative to global demand for your products and services; how far your offerings are along the product life cycle toward maturity; the degree to which your value network is systemic; and the importance of intangible assets in building and maintaining competitive advantage.

As part of our research we made a rough assessment of the overall strengths versus weaknesses of the emerging Chinese dragons as things stand today for different industries. By looking at the size of the Chinese and other developing markets relative to global demand and the maturity of the product life cycle in different industries, we estimated whether or not it would be difficult for the dragons to leverage their cost innovation strategy. This statistic, which we dubbed "impediments to cost innovation," was then plotted on the vertical axis of figure 4-1.

We then looked at the degree to which each industry's value network could be regarded as systemic and the importance of intangible assets in building and maintaining competitive advantage in that sector. We used the resulting statistics as a measure of the width of the "global gateway" through which the dragons might enter the global market. Thus, for example, if the value network was highly systemic and intangible assets were very important as a source of competitive advantage, we classified the global gateway as narrow—because Chinese companies would have limited ability to pass through this bottleneck to global success. This statistic was used to array different industries on the horizontal access of figure 4-1.

Some of the results will come as no surprise: toys, clothing, and shoes show up as highly exposed to disruption by Chinese competitors. But perhaps more interestingly, so do the businesses of consumer electronics, home appliances, and personal computers.

Petrochemicals, medicine, and civil aircraft appear as the businesses least exposed to disruptive competition from China. The dragons also face a weak position in retailing, banking, and FMCG, not because cost innovation can't work, but because the global gateways through which the Chinese can enter are blocked by the need to master systemic value chains and to access a large stock of intangible assets in order to be successful.

FIGURE 4-1

Limitations of the dragons today

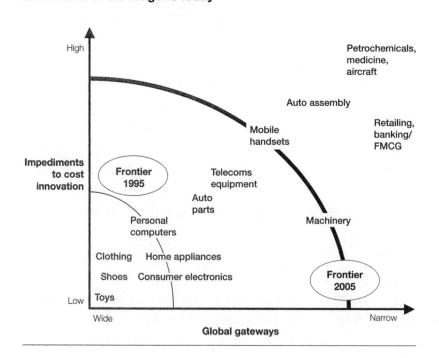

Figure 4-1 also throws up large differences between different activities within the same industry. Auto assembly, for example, is much less exposed to disruptive competition from China than is the automotive components business. There are also some salutatory warnings in the data: machinery and mobile handsets, for example, show significant exposure to disruption from the new Chinese competition in the global market.[6]

Now at first pass, these characteristics that determine where your business sits on figure 4-1 might appear to be "god-given" and hence beyond your control. But this is not the case. Each factor can be influenced by the strategy you adopt in response to the emergence of China's dragons, either directly or indirectly. There is not much you can do, for example, about how large the Chinese market becomes relative to global demand. But you can develop a strategy to neutralize some of the advantages the dragons enjoy from their large home market by stepping up your own company's capability to penetrate China's growing market—and hence match some of the advantages Chinese competitors gain from operating there.

Likewise, introducing new technology into a product line that is becoming mature may help wrong-foot Chinese competitors who thrive when a dominant technology emerges and competition shifts to variety and cost. Meanwhile, while some industry value networks are inherently more systemic than others, the speed at which a business becomes modular and key knowledge codified depends on incumbents' strategies for outsourcing and knowledge management. How fast new gateways open up to entry by the dragons, therefore, is something partly under your control.

Finally, ramping up your investments in brand building and proprietary technologies can help reinforce the importance of intangible assets, thereby increasing the barriers the new Chinese competitors face in finding ways to exploit cost innovation to win market share.

We will return to consider these strategies for exploiting the weaknesses of the dragons and responding to disruptive competition from China, as well as suggesting additional tactics, in chapter 5.

Before turning to the question of how incumbents might best respond, however, we need to recognize that the dragons' weaknesses and limitations are not set in stone. Over time, many of the weaknesses will be overcome and the limitations will be bypassed for two important reasons. First, global markets are changing in ways that will often increasingly favor Chinese cost innovation. Second, the dragons are beginning to adopt their own powerful strategies to circumvent the impediments they face in businesses that today look unpromising for cost innovation strategies: acquiring foreign companies and using China's purchasing clout to create a "demand wedge" as an alternative way to pry open global markets.

Why the Future Will Favor Cost Innovation

Let's quickly review how the market characteristics that limit the potency of cost innovation and point up the dragons' weaknesses are changing, and what we can learn from recent experience about how that might impact the likelihood of disruptive competition coming out of China.

Changing Size of the China Market

Obviously, since China is growing about four times as fast as developed economies, the relative share of China in world demand will increase. The same is probably true of other major developing countries as their growth rates exceed those in the developed world. To see how this will impact the strength of the dragons as cost innovators, consider automobile assembly, one of the businesses that our calculations suggested has only limited exposure to disruptive competition from China in today's environment.

The size of the Chinese auto market compared with global demand is now growing exponentially: it took forty years for Chinese auto production to reach 1 million units per annum; eight years to reach 2 million; two years to reach 3 million; and just one year to surpass 4 million. In 2006 China overtook Japan to become the second-largest car market in the world, after the United States. This growth is now affording Chinese firms an opportunity to develop their capabilities to build their scale and experience rapidly where they enjoy home-team advantages, collapsing the time it will take them to catch up with their global competitors.

As the impediment of China's historically small market size relative to the global market falls away in the auto industry, the potential for the dragons to apply cost innovation is kicking in. This started with the fact that the wages paid to assembly workers by budding Chinese automakers are less than half even of those paid by foreign joint-venture plants operating in China. The dragons are now finding ways to reengineer their production lines and develop process innovations that reduce their capital costs. Even today, the local firms have found ways to cut the investment required to build a plant by up to two-thirds, compared with the levels foreign joint ventures have invested on equipment for a plant of similar capacity.

As demand in the Chinese market expands and it becomes profitable to launch a wider range of models domestically, cost innovation is moving to product design (including conceiving the product concept, choosing the product platform, designing the product, and final assembly). It typically takes an established global competitor around 225,000 person-hours to design a new model. The Chinese are starting to break this total design effort down into different activities and find the ones where they can drive in their cost innovation wedge. A company such as Chery, for example, subcontracts the concept stages to Italian design houses like Bertone and Pininfarina, which are setting up operations in China. They then augment this with Chinese design and engineering staff, either in-house or from specialist design companies like TJ Innova Engineering & Technology Co. (which already has more than four hundred designers), to do the bulk of the detailed design work on salaries only one-tenth of those for designers working in the United States and Europe. Their over-all design costs are estimated at just 13 percent of the sums expended by their global competitors. In addition, since auto design is increasingly depending on 3-D design and analysis software, which is again provided by third-party software suppliers and available to all, Chinese firms are not far behind in these types of capabilities, although accumulating know-how and historical data is still critical and time-consuming.

Back in 1999 when the Chinese market for automobiles was small, there were only six new models launched in China. The Chinese cost innovation strategy of variety at low cost simply wasn't economic at these low volumes. But during the first ten months of 2005, there were already more than eighty new models introduced, of which more than twenty were launched by local firms. Today China has the fastest rate of new model introduction of any auto market in the world. As the relative size of the Chinese market grows, therefore, the industry is moving into exactly the kind of value-for-money, high-variety, rapid-churn battlefield in which Chinese competitors are likely to excel. Although its first car was launched only in 1997, Chery sold 66,400 cars in the first three quarters of 2006, putting it number three behind long-established Shanghai General Motors and Shanghai Volkswagen.

The fact that the market for automobiles is growing more rapidly in developing markets than in the United States and Europe, meanwhile, makes the Chinese periphery-to-core strategy more viable. Chery's exports reached eighteen thousand cars in 2005, making it China's number-one auto exporter. As we saw in chapter 3, most of these exports came from developing markets.

The problem is, as China's rapid growth and development is sustained, this historic limitation on disruptive global competition from the dragons is falling away across more and more businesses.

Maturing of Product Life Cycles

Businesses that find themselves moving through the product life cycle toward maturity, so that the underlying technologies become more standardized and competition shifts toward who can provide the widest variety of products or the most customized offerings, will also face an increasingly powerful threat from Chinese cost innovation. The implications of products becoming mature on the ability of the dragons to compete in disruptive ways can be dramatic, as we have seen in the Chinese market for mobile phone handsets.

By 2000, the industry reached a point in its life cycle where the rate of technological change in handsets was slowing down (certainly until prospective 3G mobile telecommunications networks had been constructed). As a result, competition in the handset market shifted from quality of reception (which was now a given using standard technology) toward appearance and features that could be engineered on top of a common technology platform. As the product life cycle ran its course, dominant technological standards emerged and the bases of competition shifted away from new technology toward volume production, a high variety of models, and rapid product churn, and the opportunities to use cost innovation multiplied.

By 2002, the terrain on the competitive battlefield had completely changed. This new terrain was well suited to the tools of disruptive competition the Chinese had perfected—high technology and high variety at low cost. Their cost wedge was now looking sharp. For so long the underdogs, the Chinese companies now had no hesitation in launching an assault: by December 2003 Chinese customers were being offered an astounding choice of 760 different models, mostly coming from the local Chinese competitors; and the reinvigorated dragons were launching so many new models so frequently that products (with the exception of a few best-sellers) were in the market for just six to nine months before they were superseded (compared with the eighteen-month product life that was accepted in the global industry at the time). Their product offerings and marketing successfully shifted consumer attention to fashion-forward design and trendy features like polyphonic ring tones, MP3 playback, voice pens, and even flashlights. The much better margins they generated as a result fed profits and cash flow that the dragons could reinvest in further cost innovation.

In short, once the mobile phone handset business started to mature, the limitations on the Chinese competitors to win market share from their established foreign rivals through cost innovation fell away rapidly

Increasing Modularization

More and more businesses are becoming modular—partly because of increasing codification of the world's knowledge combined with better communications, and partly because of the wave of outsourcing sweeping many industries in the West. As these trends continue, an increasing number of industries will be ripe for disruption by the emerging Chinese dragons.

Recall from figure 4-1 that one of the industries little exposed to the threat of cost innovation today is pharmaceuticals because of the highly systemic nature of traditional drug development. But drug development based on new biotechnology techniques is much less systemic. Biotechnology uses industry-standard protocols and lots of well-codified knowledge such as the Human Genome database, which makes available the entire gene sequence of human chromosomes. Such standardization and publicly available information makes it easier for new entrants to break into the industry by specializing in their own modular part of the activity chain and to work together with large biotech companies and established pharmaceutical giants to develop final products. Biotech may involve even higher technology than traditional pharmaceutical research, but because it is more modular and the necessary knowledge is better codified, emergent Chinese competitors are much more of a threat in this arena.

Again, therefore, as industries tend toward more modularization, we can expect the disruptive power of Chinese cost innovation strategies to increase. By riding this trend, the dragons have been able to overcome impediments to cost innovation and open up the gateways to penetrate the heart of the global market. For example, in the mobile handset industry, Chinese firms such as Ningbo Bird, TCL, and Lenovo used maturation along the product life cycle and increasing modularization to enter the low-end manufacturing part of the industry value chain. Over time, these firms upgraded their capabilities and used this deeper capability base to introduce new types of cost innovation to win market share. Other firms, such as multimedia-chip-maker Vimicro, took advantage of the same global trends that are reducing the limitations of cost innovation strategy to enter the market.

However, despite this impressive progress and all these arguments as to why the future will favor cost innovation even more than today, the emerging dragons will still have one other weakness: their lack of access to a world-class stock of intangible assets such as brands, distribution systems, business process know-how, and proprietary technologies. The problem for incumbents is that the Chinese have discovered two ways to help them overcome this weakness: acquiring and integrating foreign companies that have already built a rich stock of intangibles or using massive Chinese purchasing power as a "demand wedge" to pry open global markets they would otherwise have little chance to enter.

Dragons' Use of Foreign Acquisitions

As we noted in chapter 1, the Chinese are strategically acquiring companies that will help them overcome the impediments to winning market share in industries where cost innovation is difficult to exploit without complementary local knowledge or technology. In July 2005, for example, China's SGSB Group acquired the German-listed company Duerkopp Adler, established in 1867 and the world number-three producer of industrial sewing machines. Through this acquisition it acquired a strong brand, a wealth of customer relationships, and advanced technology. SGSB is now applying its Chinese cost innovation capabilities to deliver much better value for money than Duerkopp Adler was able to provide with its German cost base and traditional product development and manufacturing approach. By combining Duerkopp's know-how, established customer relationships, and brand with innovative ways to get costs down without threatening quality and breadth of product offering, SGSB aims to deliver high technology and variety at low cost, along with the benefits of scale to what was becoming a shrinking niche market when served out of Germany.

Piano maker Pearl River also was able to use acquisitions to overcome lack of brand awareness that were impeding its ability to grow from the mass market into higher niche segments of the global market. Rather than undergo the slow and painful process of building a high-end brand from scratch it decided to buy the rights to Ritmüller—a German brand with roots dating back to 1795. Weighed down by high production costs in Germany, this venerable firm had ceased operation in 1977. Pearl River brought the brand back to life. It subsequently acquired another respected German brand, Rüdesheimer. Having covered the traditional end of the market, Pearl River then entered into an agreement with Herman Miller, the maker of trendy modern furniture, to produce a line of pianos to complement streamlined, modern interiors. Today it also supplies pianos designed by Steinway and sold under the Boston Piano brand.

Since 2002 Chinese machine tool companies have been on an international buying spree. Shanghai Mingjing acquired a German company, Wohlenberg, and a Japanese one, Ikegai. Shenyang Machine Tool successfully took over Schiess AG in Germany. And

Dalian Machinery Company purchased Zimmerman, also in Germany, after acquiring two subsidiaries of Ingersoll in the United States. QingChuan Machine Tool acquired UAI of the United States. All the acquired companies had long histories, strong technology, recognized brands, established client bases, and wide distribution networks. However, their profitability was under threat from ever more intense global competition, where they lacked scale and the investment capital to maintain their technological and brand edge. Despite difficulties in integration, they provided a good foundation for upgrading the capability base of Chinese firms.

Huawei made a big stride in optical network technologies after buying the IP and assets of OptiMight, a U.S. company, that fell victim when the IT bubble burst in early 2001. Huawei paid just $4 million for the bankrupt operation, equivalent to only 1 percent of the total its target had invested in developing its proprietary technology. Since then it has also bought the assets of another optical network company, Cognigine, and invested in a third, LightPointe Communications Inc. Meanwhile, Beijing Orient Electronics, now a major player in flat-panel displays, entered the segment by acquiring the assets of a subscale Korean firm in 2001, followed by the purchase of the TFT-LCD (Thin-Film Transistor Liquid Crystal Display) business of cash-strapped Hynix in 2002.

In the auto sector, Shanghai Automotive Industry Corporation (SAIC) acquired 10 percent of Daewoo Motor in 2002 and 48 percent of SsangYong Motor, a maker of SUVs and RVs, for $500 million in July 2004. Nanjing Auto bought Britain's MG Rover after an extended battle against SAIC and the private equity houses in 2005. Recall also Wanxiang's multiple acquisitions in the auto-components sector. Wanxiang's CEO, Lu Guanqiu, explains his rationale this way:

> The companies we've acquired overseas aren't simply acquisitions. It's really about pooling international resources. We'll

combine whatever resources we can find to become a company that operates on a multinational basis, using the most advanced technology and playing in the key markets of the world. For instance, we acquired Schiller, Universal Automotive Industries, and Rockford Powertrain, among other companies, because they have what we lack most: markets, technology, and brands. The weakness of these companies is rising labor costs. Our strengths lie in our labor. We use a lot of labor for low-value-added products. We can bring these companies' low-value-added products to China and make them here while keeping the high-value-added goods over there. So by combining with these companies, we bring costs down and improve efficiency. This is how we were able to penetrate GM, Ford, and other major companies and markets so successfully. Everyone wins in the process.[7]

As this quotation demonstrates, the main assets Wanxiang went after in the foreign markets were technology, channels, and brands to rapidly establish its position in developed markets.

Of course, even for experienced acquirers, the acquisition game is fraught with difficulties, and buying a company has not always proven successful for the Chinese. We have already referred to the difficulties that TCL has encountered in what was effectively the acquisition of Thomson's TV business. When announcing the deal, TCL's CEO was of course optimistic, stating that: "The merger is a major initiative in our global business expansion that brings TCL to a new era. This strategic alliance fulfils our objective of being one of the top five players in multimedia electronic devices in the global marketplace, setting solid foundations in competing with international rivals."[8]

In reality, integration of the acquisition has proved difficult. Increasing productivity and cutting costs in Thomson's European operations turned out to be more difficult than TCL had expected, aggravated by restrictive labor laws and historical baggage in a number of the countries where Thomson operates. TCL's losses in the business it acquired have mounted, and revitalizing venerable, but aging, brands like RCA can prove a costly exercise. To anyone watching this experience, it is perhaps not surprising that Haier walked away from its potential acquisition of Maytag, believing its money might be better spent in building its global brand organically from a clean slate.

Nonetheless, the fact remains that the Chinese dragons are now on the foreign acquisition trail in the kinds of industries where intangible assets like brands, customer relationships, and proprietary technology or systemic value networks keep them from using cost innovation alone to grow globally. Like their Western counterparts, the Chinese will learn from experience about how to acquire, integrate, and leverage foreign companies as a way of strengthening their push into markets where their lack of intangible assets is a decisive weakness. In industries where acquisition isn't practicable (such as petrochemicals where firms with a rich stock of intangible assets, including Exxon and BP, are too big to swallow), budding dragons are likely to appeal to China's huge purchasing power to break in.

Using the Demand Wedge

The other tool the dragons are deploying to speed up their penetration into markets where they face impediments is what we call the *demand wedge*—the use of China's clout as a large and rapidly growing buyer in the global market to secure a position for Chinese companies where their learning can be maximized, and so overcome the barriers they would otherwise face. In this way the dragons use China's importance on the demand side of the global market (not only on the supply side) as a wedge to drive their global penetration into systemic businesses, those with immature technologies, or those with a heavy dependence on intangible assets that would otherwise be hard to crack.

Take the example of the massive hydropower-generation turbines used in major dams. In 1997, the Three Gorges Dam project invited bids for power-generation equipment. The specifications demanded turbines capable of generating 700 megawatts per unit—some of the largest, heaviest, and most powerful machines in the world. Just a handful of global suppliers such as General Electric, Siemens, and Mitsubishi had the know-how to design, manufacture, and install this complex equipment. Even they had installed only twenty-one machines of this size and complexity in the world.

At the time, the barriers faced by the Chinese players in entering this industry looked insurmountable. Chinese firms were only able to produce 320-megawatt machines, and were decades behind in technology. So the Chinese government announced that it would accept bids only from consortia comprised of a lead foreign company and Chinese firms. It further stipulated that, during the project, the winning foreign firms must actively transfer core technology to their Chinese partners. Faced with such an onerous condition, in effect requiring the multinationals to surrender their technology and know-how in order to win a single contract, the global players would normally have walked away. But the contract the Chinese were putting out to tender was for fourteen machines, a single order equal in size to two-thirds of the total capacity previously installed worldwide. With such massive prospective global sales up for grabs, the bidders lined up, despite having to share their proprietary technology and know-how with future potential competitors.

Once the Chinese government had used its massive buying power to pry open the market for its local companies, the dragons were quick to learn. By 2005 the Chinese firms were capable of producing the 700-megawatt machines independently and at lower costs; in consequence, they won a 67 percent share of the orders put out to tender in the second phase of the Three Gorges Dam.

The dragons' next horizon, of course, would be to take their cost advantage into the global market. This is exactly what happened in 2006. A consortium of four Chinese firms, of which three were involved in the original Three Gorges deal, won a contract to build power stations with 10 million–megawatt output over the next three years in Indonesia. This project is worth between $7 billion and $8 billion—equivalent to one-third of the total installed power station capacity in Indonesia.

In those industries where the Chinese cost innovation wedge alone isn't effective in breaking down the barriers around the global market, therefore, beware the possibility that a demand wedge might take its place. The pattern has been repeated in other sectors where the dragons face high barriers because of complex, systemic value chains and limited potential for labor cost advantage. Take the example of petrochemicals. Sinopec, the largest integrated petrochemical company in China, has sales of $75 billion per annum (ranking it 31 in the global *Fortune* 500). When such a powerful global buyer says it would like to join as a partner in a foreign oil or gas project from which it can gain invaluable knowledge and experience to build its own capabilities, few are willing to demur. Using this demand wedge, Sinopec now has active participation in oil and gas development in six countries. Meanwhile its state-owned rival, China National Petroleum Corporation, with turnover of $68 billion, has been invited to invest in more than forty projects across twenty countries. It is only a matter of time before the cycle of learning and cost innovation kicks in, and their entry into the global market as independent competitors follows.

Another industry where this strategy is at work is aircraft manufacturing, an industry in which, as we saw in figure 4-1, the dragons are currently very weak. Coordinating an aircraft's value chain is the epitome of system complexity; the global market is controlled by a handful of players, each with massive stocks of proprietary high technology, and the product life cycle begins anew almost every time a new model of aircraft, using the latest materials, is introduced. Lagging decades behind global leaders like Airbus and Boeing, surely the Chinese don't have a chance.

Even in aircraft manufacturing, however, the Chinese dragons are starting to catch up. Their strategy involves three stages. First, they find a pressure point where they can participate in the global value chain on the basis of even their narrow cost advantage. Thus, quite a few Chinese firms have become subcontractor component suppliers or subassemblers for minor pieces of Boeing and Airbus planes.

Once they have traveled some way down the experience curve and have a better understanding of how the complex system that delivers an aircraft works, the Chinese firms bid to supply higher-value components and subsystems. The fact that China is now one of the largest markets for aircraft, and that offering to increase local content is often decisive in the politicized world of aircraft procurement, helps the emerging dragons win a disproportionate share of the business. This, in turn, creates opportunities for further learning. Airbus, for example, recently awarded contracts to the Chinese company AVIC (Aviation Industries of China) equivalent to 5 percent of the total work involved in producing its new, narrow-body jet, the A350. As part of the deal, Airbus agreed to set up a joint R&D center with AVIC in China.

At the same time, Chinese firms have learned how to build a complete aircraft. For instance, using the demand wedge, they convinced McDonnell Douglas to have the Chinese deliver 70 percent of local content for two models of their long-haul MD-90 jet in the late 1980s. By the time McDonnell Douglas discontinued the relationship—shortly after it was taken over by Boeing—much of the necessary systemic know-how had already been absorbed by its Chinese partners.

Using what they learned through the Airbus and McDonnell Douglas deals, the same Chinese firms or their associates are now targeting the market for regional jets. By applying a dose of cost innovation, Xi'an Aircraft Co. has developed a sixty-seat regional jet that costs 30 percent less than competing aircraft on the market. While still meeting global standards in safety and reliability, Xi'an's plane also offers customers 10 percent lower operating costs relative to comparable aircraft.

AVIC, meanwhile, is investing $600 million to develop the ARJ21—a 110-seat regional jet. Again, its weapon is cost innovation, so instead of using leading-edge design concepts to try and produce a more sophisticated aircraft, it has taken the same advanced technology and applied it to the problem of how to build a uniquely cost-competitive plane using mostly standard components from a mature supplier base. The resulting plane will start commercial operation in 2008. AVIC's target? To sell three hundred planes in China and two hundred globally within the next twenty years. Using the demand wedge may not be subtle, but it seems to be effective in allowing the dragons to overcome their lack of intangible assets to break into complex businesses. Once in the door, they are proving adept at using cost innovation to win market share.

A Window of Opportunity

Like all strategies, it is clear that Chinese cost innovation has its limitations. Moreover, lack of intangible assets and the need to master a complete systemic value chain hampers the dragons' ability to penetrate the global market for certain types of products and services. There is still a frontier beyond which disruptive competition from China cannot reach. But that frontier has already engulfed industries like home appliances, car parts, and machinery. It is poised to move into the heart of the auto business, and a wave of disruption has buffeted the medical equipment and mobile handsets industries. And there are the first, early signs of new Chinese competition in complex, high-value businesses—such as biotechnology, aircraft manufacture, and petrochemicals—long thought beyond the reach of the emerging dragons.

One would be foolhardy, therefore, to believe that the dragons' current weaknesses and limitations provide watertight protection against their potential to unleash a new type of disruptive competition across global markets. What the dragons' weaknesses buy established competitors is that most precious commodity: time. This means there is a window of opportunity for incumbents to consider how to match or neutralize the dragons' cost innovation advantages, how to reduce their own exposure to loose bricks, and how to exploit Chinese companies' weaknesses while they last. It is this challenge, crafting an effective response to the gathering wave of disruptive competition from China, to which we must turn in chapter 5.

5

YOUR RESPONSE

Winning in the New Global Game

JUST LIKE OTHER FORMS of disruptive competition, the global advance of the dragons creates a particular problem for managers: tried and tested strategies that have proven successful in dealing with traditional rivals are unlikely to work in addressing this new challenge from China. As we have seen, cost innovation threatens to undermine some of the fundamental mind-sets and business models that established companies in the United States, Europe, and Japan hold dear. Faced with such a disruptive challenge, all too many organizations respond in the following way: first, "it's not happening"; then, "it is happening, but it doesn't matter"; and eventually, "it is happening, it does matter, but we don't need to do anything now—let's wait and see how it evolves." Soon it is too late. Like it or not, the coming disruption to global competition from China demands a timely response.

The Need to Act Now

To see both the necessity and the urgency of doing something to respond to the ways Chinese firms will disrupt global competition, look no further than that venerable American institution, Maytag. In August 1999, Maytag's stock price reached its historical high of $65.25. After that it continuously dropped, reaching a low of $9.21 per share by April 2005. In June 2005, Haier made a bid for Maytag. Then Whirlpool trumped Haier's price in what many observers interpreted as a defensive move. In August 2005, it was clear that Maytag, after trading for more than a hundred years, was going to lose its independence.

Maytag's response to growing competition had been to move upmarket, focusing on larger appliances with more features and trying to leverage the strengths of its brands (including Maytag, Jenn-Air, and Magic Chef) and its extensive service network. Another prong of its strategy was to diversify by acquiring compatible brands in related products: in 1999 it bought Hoover, one of the pioneers of vacuum cleaners; and in 2002 it purchased Amana, the respected U.S. manufacturer of kitchen appliances.

For a while these defensive strategies seemed to be working. But as Maytag moved upmarket, U.S. retailers were presenting consumers with ever more attractive value-for-money alternatives out of Asia (Haier alone offered over two hundred different models).

At first, no one took much notice of the upstarts. Then in 2001 the dot-com bubble burst and U.S. economic growth slowed. As consumers were forced to tighten their belts, they started to take a fresh look at the challenger brands. Maytag's price premium no longer seemed justified against the newcomers' products, which offered a wider range of features at lower prices, backed by the stamp of approval from retailers. It wasn't long before consumers started to switch. Maytag was dropped by three major retailers— Circuit City, Montgomery Ward, and Heilig-Meyers—and by 2003 its sales and profits were in free fall.

Some commentators chastised Maytag for ignoring this new threat until it was too late. Quite to the contrary, however, China had already been on Maytag's radar screen since the mid-1990s. In our view, the company's mistake was to regard China as just another new market. It didn't recognize the possibility that the right engagement with China could be the catalyst to revolution-izing its global, and even its U.S., strategy.

This myopia led Maytag to establish a joint venture with a Chi-nese company, Royalstar, focusing just on making washing ma-chines and refrigerators for the Chinese market. At first, things went well. But as the joint venture attempted to ramp up produc-tion and expanded its product line, its performance took a dra-matic turn for the worse.

With hindsight, Maytag's problem was to equate innovation with increased sophistication. This meant Maytag used its R&D dollars to develop new, top-end products for the Chinese market and import a high-technology production line with a capacity of 1.2 million appliances per annum, virtually identical to those in its best U.S. plants. In sharp contrast, its leading Chinese com-petitors, including Haier and Rongsheng Electric Appliances Holding Co Ltd., focused on cost innovation. Rejecting the idea that innovation is only about developing more sophisticated products, the dragons focused on using new technology to im-prove costs and increase variety, while maintaining keen prices.

The result of this contest was a debacle for Maytag's China ven-ture. Utilization fell to just 10 percent in the gold-plated manufac-turing facility. The red ink started to flow. Maytag's response was to send in a crack team of expatriates to sort out the problem, putting Americans in all of their key Chinese management positions.

Unfortunately, the extra expense of using expatriates put May-tag even further behind its cost-innovative Chinese rivals. In 2004, with its growth ambitions forestalled and losses mounting, Maytag sold out its China operations to its local partner. But its troubles were not over. Having pulled back to its U.S. base, Maytag was now under siege. Haier and its fellow dragons had disrupted the Maytag business model. The takeover bid that followed, how-ever ignominious, was hardly a surprise.

Salvation, of a sort, came in the form of a sale to Whirlpool. But that may not be the answer, because Whirlpool itself has had a rough time competing with the Chinese. Like Maytag, Whirlpool had seen China primarily as a fertile market where it could deploy its superior know-how, rather than as an opportunity to learn new tricks such as cost innovation. In an ambitious move, it set up four joint ventures, each one covering one of its major product lines—refrigerators, washing machines, air conditioners, and microwave ovens—within just eighteen months in the early 1990s.

Whirlpool followed the orthodoxy that advanced technology was applicable only to high-end products that were beyond what the mass of Chinese customers could afford. Again, when put up against Chinese cost innovation, this orthodoxy proved damaging. It led Whirlpool, for example, to delay deployment of an advanced technology designed to remove environmentally damaging chloro-fluorocarbons (CFCs) from its Chinese product line. The problem was that the Chinese dragons used the cost innovation strategy of high technology at low cost to launch CFC-free, "green" products immediately into their mass-market models—making the Whirl-pool refrigerators look inferior.

A bevy of similar problems soon led to ballooning losses; between 1996 and 1998 the washing machine joint venture lost $40 million; the refrigerator business drained another $10 million. And in microwave ovens, Galanz's combination of large scale and cost innovation virtually drove Whirlpool out of the local market, so that its plant became solely a source for its U.S. affiliates. Frustrated and facing chronic losses, Whirlpool withdrew from the China market in 1999.

In 2002, Whirlpool made another push into the China market. This time it took a lesson from the dragon's playbook and introduced more than thirty new products. But it still hadn't cracked the strategy of cost innovation. Lacking this trump card, Whirlpool has yet to make any significant inroads into the market, other than a very limited presence in the refrigerator business. Despite its scale and brand equity, it remains exposed to disruptive competition not only in China, but also in the U.S. and global markets.

Fight Fire with Fire: The Need for New Responses

The Maytag-Whirlpool experience demonstrates the folly of taking a narrow approach both to the role of China and its disruptive potential in the global market. It is no longer sufficient to approach China just as a huge prospective market or a source of low-cost manufacturing capacity. Retreating into high-end niches risks seeing them blown apart (recall Haier and CIMC). Your brand will provide shelter only until customers, with the help of increasingly powerful retailers, work out that they can get the same technology, features, choices, or customization elsewhere at better value for money.

Disruptive competition from China is flattening the "smiling curve" depicted in figure 5-1. It shows how Chinese cost innovation was first applied to simple assembly operations and then broader manufacturing—turning China into the factory of the

FIGURE 5-1

Margin pressure and the cost revolution

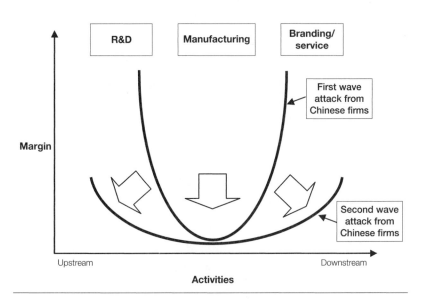

world. As we have seen, cost innovation is now being applied to successively higher-value activities, starting with engineering, then to design, and lastly R&D, putting pressure on the profits incumbent companies reap from the left-hand side of the smile. But the dragons are starting to attack the right-hand side of the curve as well, applying their experience and cost innovation strategies in new ways that also put a squeeze on the profit contribution of customization, service, distribution, and brand building.

The potential of new competition from China to cause such a fundamental shift in the structure of the global value chain and the profit potential of its different activities isn't going to be addressed by incremental improvements or tweaking of current strategies. Radical new approaches are called for. We explore three such possible responses below:

- Using cost innovation to beat the dragons at their own game

- Giving a global mandate for certain products to your China subsidiary

- Allying with the dragons to strengthen your global competitiveness

Can You Beat the Dragons at Their Own Game?

The key to beating the Chinese dragons at their own game lies in combining cost innovation with your existing strengths as an established foreign player. But can you do this at home? Or is cost innovation only possible by accessing advantages uniquely available in China? Delivering high technology at low cost, for example, might depend on being able to tap into sources of technology that are available more cheaply in China than elsewhere and leveraging the low-cost pool of Chinese engineers. Likewise, your ability to emulate the dragons' strategy of delivering specialty products at low cost might be greatly enhanced if you could benefit from the scale economies available from China's mass markets.

Other sources of cost innovation, however, do not require a company to shift more of its operations to China. The capability to deliver variety at low cost, for example, can largely be emulated by changing your strategy toward markets and segments that are currently seen as peripheral and following the Chinese strategy of determinedly "learning from the world." This strategy doesn't necessarily require the wholesale relocation of activities into China. To see how much beating the Chinese at their own game depends on reaching into the potential advantages offered by China's unique environment versus a change in your strategies and mind-sets at home, it is worth examining the extent to which each of the three main sources of cost innovation—high technology at low cost; variety at low cost; and specialty products at low cost—depend on being on the ground in China.

High Technology at Low Cost: Unlocking China's Technology Cache

We have already noted that, unlike many other developing economies, China has a significant stock of indigenous technology, knowledge, and capability inherited from the central planning age. When Dawning's president, for example, was asked why Dawning's continuous bet on emerging technologies so often turned out to be correct, he explained that this success is based on the deep understanding of computer science accumulated through fifty years of continuous research at the Chinese Academy of Science.[1]

There are now opportunities for foreign companies to access technology in China that can help them match, or better, the dragons' ability to deliver cost innovation to the market by offering high technology at low cost. Hitherto this technology had been locked up in government research institutes and the military-industrial establishment. But it is now being transferred into the commercial sector. Because of inefficiencies in the market for China's indigenous technology, it is often available more cheaply than elsewhere in the world. Moreover, because Chinese technology often has a different heritage—due to long isolation in a different institutional environment—it may have the potential to act as a catalyst for Western companies to challenge their orthodoxies and to come up with new ideas for cost innovation by combining Chinese thinking with existing corporate knowledge. And that is the key point: the potential to use Chinese technology for cost innovation lies in the fact that it's likely to be cheaper and/or different, even if, in some senses, it might be less "advanced."

So where are the sources of this Chinese technology? In the central-planning era, Chinese government institutions developed strong capabilities in basic research and development, especially in advanced technology related to military applications. As late as 2003, they still accounted for about 78 percent of total investment in basic research. Even today, much basic research is still carried out by government-owned research institutes and research universities.

Government research was structured in a tiered hierarchy.[2] The first tier was the Chinese Academy of Science (CAS), and the more than one hundred national research institutes (each containing several to dozens of research labs), and dozens of research universities for which it has oversight. Each arm of the CAS specialized in a particular scientific discipline in which it undertook both basic and applied research.

The second tier consisted of dozens of military-industrial and industrial research laboratories, each under the control of the Ministry responsible for industry to which they were related (for example, TD-SCDMA, a 3G standard developed by China, originated from such a research institute under the Ministry of Information Industry). Most of these laboratories focused on applied scientific research and development. The third tier comprised research institutes under the umbrella of the various industrial bureaus controlled by regional governments.

While highly bureaucratic, this hierarchical structure had the advantage of concentrating scarce resources into strategic sectors as well as bringing together highly talented scientists and engineers into elite corps focused on the mission set by their parent arm of government. It was particularly effective in building a comprehensive infrastructure for basic research as well as keeping China near the cutting edge of sophisticated military-related technologies despite the low level of development in the broader economy—witness China's success in developing what was dubbed *Liang Dan Yi Xing* (or two bullets, one star): the atom and hydrogen bombs—and its satellite infrastructure; as well as its more recent manned space program.

The problem with this elite, bureaucratic research structure was the lack of trickle-down of advanced technology into broader Chinese industry. There was almost a maze of brick walls separating research in the government institutes from Chinese industry. The Central Committee of the Chinese Communist Party (CCP) recognized that this structure was holding back economic development and so, in 1985, announced policies for the long-term reform of China's science and technology infrastructure.[3] The goal was clear: to forge horizontal links between research laboratories and Chinese enterprises so as to facilitate a diffusion of technologies from the state research system into industry.

The mechanism the CCP recommended to achieve this may come as a surprise to some; it believed that the best way to dramatically and rapidly improve diffusion into industry was to create a market for technologies. Several measures were introduced in order to create the market, including:

- Turning the majority of the previously 100 percent-state-funded research units into for-profit units by gradually reducing direct grants from the state

- Creating incentives for enterprises to adopt new technologies

- Reforming the personnel management system in the research hierarchy so as to improve the mobility of scientists and technicians by creating a market for talent

These reforms have been quite effective in building a bridge between state research institutions and Chinese firms and in releasing high technology that was previously imprisoned inside research establishments for commercialization. This, in turn, has begun to open up potential for foreign companies to access those technological resources, both directly and indirectly.

China now has a mixed research community spanning both state and industry. The latest complete survey available (January 2004) recorded 653 research institutes in the area of science and technology under ministries, and 2,829 under local governments. The CAS had 123 research institutes employing more than 60,000 people. Alongside this research under direct state control, there are more than 4,000 independent research institutes, 2,500 research centers within universities, and 14,000 research centers affiliated with Chinese or foreign enterprises. Today China has around 1 million people directly involved in R&D. Measured in purchasing power parity terms (PPP), China's total R&D expenditure was estimated by the Organisation for Economic Cooperation and Development to have reached $136 billion in 2006, overtaking Japan's $130 billion R&D spend and closing the gap to $330 billion spent in the United States in the same year.[4] Its ratio of R&D spending to GDP had risen from around 0.6 percent in the mid-1990s to 1.35 percent by 2006, and is targeted to reach 2 percent of GDP by 2010. This amount will still lag behind the United States, which has averaged an R&D-to-GDP ratio of 2.7 percent over the past decade, but it does underline the point that there is technology in China that can potentially deliver cost innovation.[5]

We have seen how the emerging dragons are unlocking this cache of technology. Recall, for example, that Zhongxing drew some of the critical technology for its revolutionary DDR machines from its parent, China Aerospace Science and Technology Corporation (CASC). Directly under the supervision of the State Council, with its origins in military research, CASC has world-class capabilities in launching multiple satellites from a single rocket. It is also able to develop such spacecraft as communication satellites, meteorological satellites, earth resource satellites, and scientific experimental satellites with leading technologies in satellite recovery, orbit control, and altitude control. In addition, CASC is strong in the fields of satellite applications, information technology, automatic control, and system integration. With 130 units under its direct control, comprising research centers, production sites, and companies, CASC has 110,000 employees, including 41,000 engineers, 1,300 researchers, and more than 30 members of the Chinese Academy of Engineering and Chinese Academy of Science on its staff. The fact that such an organization is now contributing to the task of building the technological resources of some of China's emerging companies is an important reason why the emerging dragons can deliver high technology at low cost.

Obviously, many Chinese sources of high technology aren't open to foreign companies operating in China. But some foreign companies have successfully begun to unlock China's low-cost technology cache and combine it with their own proprietary technologies to help them to develop this aspect of a new cost innovation capability. A good example is Intel. It was one of the first to begin tapping into China's knowledge and R&D capabilities, setting up joint labs with Beijing University and Tsinghua University in 1995. In October 2000 Intel expanded its cooperation with Tsinghua, setting up programs that, according to the

CEO Craig Barrett, would "increase the breadth of knowledge in e-business and e-commerce through hands-on research projects that couple the latest technological tools with new business practices."[6] Since then Intel has established three major research and development organizations in China: the Intel China Research center, focusing on human-computer interface research; the Intel China Software Lab, developing systems software for Intel products; and the Intel Architecture labs, an application-development organization.[7]

Foreign companies can also indirectly access competitively priced Chinese high technology by acquiring stakes in promising Chinese start-ups that have begun to combine potentially world-class technologies with a Chinese cost structure. Many of these have been started by Chinese returnees and so might be easier to integrate into a commercial global network than a Chinese research institute or purely local firm would be.

In one such arrangement, in 2002 Siemens acquired Mindit, a leading local magnetic resonance imaging (MRI) producer, and turned it into its global production and service center for MRI. Then in 2006, Siemens Communications acquired Chinese optical transmission systems specialist Photonic Bridges, with more than three hundred employees. Christian Unterberger, head of fixed network business at Siemens Communications, said, "Photonic Bridges is one of the leading companies in the SDH [synchronous digital hierarchy] market. With our commitment to Photonic Bridges, we are expanding our development capacity in forward-looking areas and securing our access to those products that offer our customers significant added value."[8]

PalmSource Inc., a maker of operating systems for mobile devices based in Sunnyvale, California, acquired China Mobile-Soft Limited (CMS), a leading Chinese mobile phone software company, in 2005. MobileSoft had developed a wide range of software for mobile phones, including more than a dozen phone applications, operating software for smart and feature phones, and a version of Linux optimized for mobile devices. The combination of Palm OS and China Mobilesoft's software products will give PalmSource one of the broadest lines of mobile software in the industry, powering mobile phones at all price points in all regions of the world.

According to Grant Thornton UK, in the twelve months to June 30, 2006, some 266 international companies from forty-one different countries made acquisitions in China. It is notable that the high-technology sector accounted for the largest number of deals within the total.[9] It seems that international competitors are beginning to see the potential of accessing Chinese technological capabilities to deliver innovation at lower cost.

Matching the Capability for Variety at Low Cost

In chapter 2 we discussed how Chinese companies have learned to deliver their customers variety at low cost by developing capabilities in process flexibility and through recombinative innovation. In theory, foreign companies outside their home countries could build these capabilities back at home base if they applied the same principles as the emerging dragons. These advantages do not necessarily depend on operating in China; much of the knowledge the emerging dragons use to deliver variety at low cost has been assembled from outside China by "learning from the world."

In fact, companies that are already global should be better placed than the emerging dragons to harness knowledge scattered around the world and use it to innovate more extensive and customized product lines. Some, such as STMicroelectronics, Nokia, and PolyGram Records, have successfully done so.[10] But when incumbents do resolve to comb the world for new types of knowledge, their search tends to focus on new technologies. By contrast, the Chinese dragons have concentrated on capturing knowledge they can use to add more variety and customization to their product lines at minimal additional cost.

To see what this involves and understand whether it is something your company should be adopting as part of your response to disruptive competition from China, consider how Chery Automobile has gone about creating attractive new offerings by learning from the world—in its case from a standing start.

Chery's CEO, Yin Tongyao, has a favorite slogan: "Learn cost control from the Japanese, craziness from the Koreans, keen pursuit of technology from the Germans, and market maneuvers from the Americans."[11] The company was set up only in 1997, but it is already a major player in China's automobile market, with plans to launch a range of models packed with options and features (all at a low price, of course) on the world market in 2008.

Chery started down the road of building the capability for cost innovation by accessing knowledge spillovers from the joint ventures between Chinese and foreign automakers such as the one between Volkswagen and First Autoworks, which produced the popular Jetta brand in China (Chery's CEO Yin, for example, had twelve years' experience as the general manager of the assembly plant that produced the Jetta). Not surprisingly, it first imitated what it had learned from foreign producers.

But then Chery started to apply a cost innovation strategy. It pared back unnecessary expenditures and looked for ways to redesign the process to cut costs. Industry sources estimate that this enabled Chery to reduce its production costs to one-third below the Chinese industry average, to build its plants at just 20 percent of the costs incurred by an equivalent foreign joint venture, and to conduct R&D more cheaply than its joint venture rivals.

Chery used this low cost to introduce just one model, the Fengyun, at two-thirds the price of the comparable Jetta. It then set out on the path of adding variety to its product line by designing a range of attention-grabbing cars that set it apart from the competition. But because it didn't have the in-house capability to deliver such variety at low cost, it launched a determined campaign to gather up the knowledge it needed from around the world. So when Volkswagen sought to leverage its global reach by centralizing its R&D in Germany, and offered early retirement to many of the engineers and technicians in its Chinese JVs, Chery promptly hired them. It then acquired a two-thirds stake in the equity of the Jia Jing Corporation, a new auto design company formed by a team of five experienced designers. Jia Jing's founders had all worked together on the development of the Elysee, a car designed at the technical center of the joint venture between Dongfeng Motor Group Co Ltd and France's Citroën, where they learned a lot through secondment to France for training and from foreign designers. As one of Jia Jing's founders, Shen Haojie, put it: "With the help of French experts we gained precious experience about modern car design day by day; I had the feeling of a fan meeting Michael Jordan."[12]

With assured funding from Chery as its majority shareholder, Jia Jing was able to hire a further twenty experienced designers from other car companies. Jia Jing's first project for Chery was a brief to develop a compact car that would appeal to young, white-collar buyers. The result was a car dubbed "QQ." Conceived as what its designers called "a natural girl" and launched six months ahead of General Motors' new offering, Spark, the QQ outsold both the GM product and Daewoo's Matiz (then the most successful compact car in the world).

Chery had proven that by accessing foreign knowledge it could deliver cost innovation: in this case the capability to build a differentiated product successfully targeted at a specific market segment while keeping costs at rock bottom by avoiding reinvention of what others already knew. Chery then scaled up this strategy. It embarked in the development of eight new models, each aimed at a different part of the market. Five of those models are ultimately targeted at export markets, so Chery needed to bolster its design capabilities with more international experience. To achieve this it hired Italian design houses Bertone and Pininfarina along with other European and Japanese design firms to work on its new models. Chery also hired international experts directly into the ranks of its staff; twelve of the engineers were headhunted from Daewoo Motor. Chery also hired an R&D director, with a PhD from a U.S. university and eight years' experience in Japan, from Ford—recruited by Chery's human resource director, who regularly makes trips to Detroit to scout for experienced talent. Chery's new head of cost management, meanwhile, was a German national who had worked for Volkswagen—a company widely credited as having been the best in the business at squeezing out excess costs—for thirty-nine years. In total, Chery has twenty foreign experts on its full-time research staff and dozens more foreign retirees on consulting contracts working on improvements at every stage of its assembly lines. The result: an unmatched capability to deliver innovative designs that extend its product variety while keeping costs low.

Chery has since applied the learning-from-the world formula to figure out how to deliver variety at low cost across core components such as engines. It began by buying the equipment from a U.K. plant closed by Ford. Then in 2002 Chery launched an engine-improvement project with the Austrian engineers AVL; together they developed eighteen different engines, ranging from 3-cylinder models to V8s and from a 0.8-liter gasoline engine to a 4-liter diesel. All these designs meet the stringent Euro IV emissions standards. With the new technology in hand, Chery then invested $350 million in a new engine factory with capacity to produce 500,000 engines per year. The new plant's staff included two hundred engineers from eight countries across Europe, the Americas, and Asia. Meanwhile, Chery formed a joint venture with a leading Taiwanese company to manufacture molds used in the pressing stages of automobile manufacture. Its end goal: to develop proprietary technology for mold making so that it could squeeze more variety and greater flexibility out of its production lines.

There is no reason at all why companies based in the United States, Europe, or elsewhere couldn't emulate this same strategy of determinedly learning from the world with the focused aim of delivering more variety to customers at lower cost. To gain this advantage, it is not necessary to be on the ground in China. In fact, global companies, with their established networks that reach into every corner of the world, should be able to beat the Chinese dragons at this game hands down. But, in our experience, it seldom happens.

If foreign firms are to successfully respond to the new wave of variety-at-low-cost competition coming out of China, two things need to change. First, Western companies need to take on board the concept of cost innovation as strategy. For many, this will mean breaking free of the straitjacket view that innovation is used almost exclusively to add more sophistication and become "leading edge"—in other words, companies must rebalance innovation in favor of finding ways to deliver a wider, more customized product line without increasing costs.

Second, even leading Western companies must recognize that they can access valuable new knowledge from China and other developing countries—especially about leveraging existing technologies and customer insights in new ways that deliver the customer more value for money.

Another approach might be to try to put clear blue water between yourself and the emerging Chinese dragons by following the principles that Chan Kim and Renée Mauborgne lay out in their book *Blue Ocean Strategy: How to Create Uncontested Market Space and Make the Competition Irrelevant*.[13] Kim and Mauborgne recommend taking strategic moves that create powerful leaps in value both for the firm and its buyers, rendering rivals obsolete and unleashing new demand. Companies such as Cirque du Soleil have successfully pulled this off. The strategy makes good sense. But beware of seeing this kind of innovation as the "silver bullet" for responding to disruptive competition from China, for two reasons. First, the Chinese are onto this game too. When the book was published, for example, the *China Daily* argued: "Chinese companies have to come up with ways to differentiate their products, retaining relatively low prices. They need to create blue oceans."[14] And as we have seen, that's exactly what the leading firms in China—the dragons—are doing. The important difference is that using their cost innovation capabilities, they have a chance of creating those blue oceans with less investment and in ways that play to their lower costs.

Second, an innovative product that creates a leap in value normally starts out with little of the knowledge codified, and with a systemic value chain, rather than a modular one—exactly the environment where the Chinese competitors' weaknesses prove to be a major handicap (as we saw in chapter 4). Most new products also start out as niche segments, serving the early adopters—a group of customers the dragons are also poorly equipped to serve. But to make substantial profits from your such a "blue-ocean" innovation, you have to defend and grow that early specialist market over time. As the market expands and matures, the technology is apt to become more widely known and more standardized, and the value chain more modular. What happens if the dragons then use the third prong of their cost innovation strategy, the capability to deliver a specialist product at low cost, to try and blow the market apart? To avoid that scenario, developing your own capability to dramatically reduce the costs and broaden the affordability of specialty products becomes an essential follow-on to blue-ocean strategy.

Delivering Specialty Products at Low Cost

Trying to beat the dragons at their own game in delivering specialty products at low cost also requires a change in mentality: breaking out of the conventional wisdom that today's niche market segments must be low-volume, high-price forever. As we saw in chapter 2, once the volume potential of a specialty product is recognized, the challenge is to dramatically reduce costs and prices and expand distribution so as to unlock latent, mass-market appeal. Again, in theory, there is no reason why a company can't execute this strategy from its home base. But perhaps being embedded in the Chinese market provides an advantage both in overcoming the orthodoxies that constrain a product to serving a niche market and in accessing the cost innovation knowledge necessary to explode the niche into a mass market. After all, when China began opening up in 1978, the market for just about every advanced product was restricted to a niche segment of wealthy early adopters. Over the past thirty years, these "specialist" products and services have today become mass-market commmodities. China, therefore, is perhaps the most fertile environment in the world to develop the mind-set and capabilities to turn a niche into a mass market.

Haier's Little Prince, for example, began as an offering targeted specifically at a niche of consumers with frequent, small-batch washing needs. It is now in its eighteenth generation, and has sold over 5 million units in more than sixty-eight countries. Immersion in the Chinese market helped Haier see the mass-market potential of the Little Prince model. Demand was opened up by the rapid social changes in China, especially the one-child policy, which led to an explosion in three-person families as well as to more people in their twenties and thirties living on their own. In addition, growing affluence and concerns about hygiene in southern China, where summers are hot and humid, led to more people wanting changes of clothes within the same day. Moreover, as lower-income consumers bought washing machines, they were apt to be more sensitive to the cost of the energy it consumed. The large potential size of the Chinese market relative to global demand and low Chinese costs that reduced the breakeven volume required to achieve profitability increased Haier's ability to deliver specialty benefits at low cost and thereby unlock latent mass-market demand.

Clearly it's possible for a foreign company to learn the tricks of delivering specialty products at low cost. To do so they must begin by adopting a single-minded focus on reducing the break-even of their specialty offerings. The key is cutting fixed costs by reengineering design, setup, and manufacturing processes in innovative ways and finding greater opportunities to share development and launch costs among different product lines.

Once breakeven has been reduced, the risks of testing the volume potential of a niche market by launching a much-lower-priced offering go down. Established suppliers of specialty products must respond to the potential of disruptive competition from China by reworking their existing cost structures so they can safely take those risks. Otherwise, they will be vulnerable to being blown away by Chinese dragons intent on exploding their niche businesses into a mass market.

Again, it is possible for Western companies to execute this response from their home base. But arguably China is the best environment in which to try and hone these skills. The facts that (1) China's vast potential as a market can only be unlocked through the ability to supply the demands of diverse customers at very low prices, (2) it is characterized by cut-throat competition between multinationals looking for increased volume and a mass of local competitors seeking to grow, (3) it is leading the world in breadth of product range in goods such as DVDs and mobile phones, and (4) it is plagued by bouts of overcapacity despite rapid growth in demand provide the ideal conditions for cost innovation to emerge and thrive. Maybe, therefore, while it is theoretically possible to master the trick of delivering specialty products at low cost back home, perhaps China's competitive "pressure-cooker" is the most conducive learning environment in which to develop this type of new skill.

Given the difficulties an inexperienced company is likely to encounter succeeding in China as a relative latecomer, another strategy might be to focus on coming up with cost innovation strategies back at headquarters and deliver them using low-cost resources from other emerging economies, such as India or Latin America. But it is clear that learning how to deliver high technology at low cost, variety at low cost, and specialist products at low cost is often easier when a company is able to access the unique benefits of the Chinese environment. This suggests that to meet the coming disruption of global competition from China, Western managers can improve their chances by giving China a new global mandate within their organization.

Giving China a Global Mandate

It is clear that many of the advantages enjoyed by the emerging dragons stem from their superior ability to harness the potential benefits of their Chinese home base, including:

- Potential labor cost advantage in everything from R&D, design, and engineering to manufacturing to customization and service

- The scale and diversity that comes from their vast and fast-growing home market, which demands cost innovation necessary to deliver unparalleled value for money

- Low-cost access to underexploited technologies now being unlocked from the Chinese research establishment

While Chinese firms continue to enjoy a lopsided ability to harness this potential in their favor, existing global players can only lose ground.

To counter the disruption the emerging dragons are bringing to the global market, established global players and national champions will have to learn the tricks of cost innovation. They will also have to become much better at harnessing the full panoply of advantages available in China and using them to augment their existing capabilities. Incumbents will have to learn how to beat the Chinese at their own game. To do so will require multinationals to fundamentally alter, and expand, the role China plays in their global network today. That means they will need to

make a lot of sometimes difficult changes—in mind-set; significant reallocation of activities between headquarters, China, and
existing subsidiaries in other countries; organizational restructuring; and a shift in relative power toward their China operations. In short, they will have to recognize China's pivotal role in
their global endeavors across a wide variety of activities, from
R&D to sales. Just how the role of China in your network will need
to change if you are to compete with the dragons depends on your
starting point. Figure 5-2 lays out the territory.

Some companies still don't have China anywhere on the chart.
But the many who do usually cast China in the role of an exciting
growth market or a low-cost source of products (or, less commonly,
low-cost services)—the bottom quadrants of figure 5-2.

Leveraging China's attractiveness as the "factory of the world"
by developing a China manufacturing operation tightly linked to
your global network can offer important advantages over rivals
who have been slower in moving into China. Companies that have
done this fall into the far right quadrant of figure 5-2—"China

FIGURE 5-2

Repositioning your China business

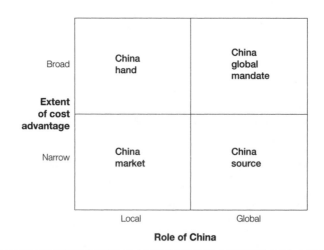

source." Logitech is a typical example. As one of the pioneers investing in China, Logitech made a big bet in 1994. It closed its plants in Ireland and the United States and moved its global production center to Suzhou. At that time, the Suzhou industrial park was still mostly surrounded by farms, there was no highway between Suzhou and Shanghai, and international phone calls had to be switched from Shanghai.

Today Suzhou has become a leading magnet for foreign direct investment in China, and a strong node in the networks of multinationals with efficient supply chain management. Some 60 percent of its components are delivered either daily or more than once every day. Logitech had 109 employees there in 1994; now there are over 5,000. Logitech already sources half of its global product needs from China and is building a new plant in Suzhou, which will increase its capacity by 30 percent. The decision to move into China sourcing in a major way earlier than its global rivals has proved to be an important fount of competitive advantage for Logitech.

But companies such as Logitech are now finding that even large investments in manufacturing operations in China are insufficient to maintain their competitive advantage against the emerging dragons who are bringing bundles of Chinese cost advantages to the global market that go way beyond manufacturing. Thus Logitech is expanding the Suzhou plant from a manufacturing center to a design center as well. There are already forty designers working in Suzhou, and the number is expected to double in the next few years.

As well as starting to broaden their base of cost advantages, China sourcers like Logitech are also having to expand their market presence in China to avoid leaving the way open for Chinese competitors to build massive scale in their home market that they can use to disrupt global competition. A few years ago, China didn't even make the top ten list of Logitech's markets globally. More recently, the company has started to invest aggressively in marketing in China, hoping to boost its China revenue and broaden the role of China to include the "China market" quadrant of figure 5-2.

Nike is making similar moves. Last year, most of its suppliers were already based in China, but its China sales accounted for little more than 2 percent of its global total. Its lack of progress in the Chinese market had left Nike's flank exposed to attack by Chinese dragons using cost innovation strategies. With the rapid rise of purchasing power among Chinese consumers, the domestic market was growing rapidly, and local competitors such as Li Ning wasted no time in filling this expanding need. To counter the emerging threat the Chinese companies posed, it was imperative for companies such as Nike and Logitech to gain a powerful base in China before their local rivals build a solid foundation for future global attack.

In the face of disruptive competition from the emerging Chinese dragons, however, it is not enough for foreign competitors to limit China's role to just another market (even an important one) or a low-cost source. The reason is simple: Chinese competitors already capture these advantages better than foreign companies can, using their home-team advantages. As we have seen, they can penetrate every corner of the Chinese market much more fully, they can gain more scale economies, and they can squeeze more out of the manufacturing and sourcing costs than a joint venture or a foreign company can. But much more important, the dragons are also able to harness Chinese costs to improve their competitiveness in a wide range of other activities—R&D, design, engineering, service, and customization. In the new value-for-money world, that ability will become decisive. In other words, if you benefit from China's peculiar cost advantages across 20 percent of your business, it's hard to beat a rival who is using Chinese costs to compete in innovative ways across 100 percent of the business.

Some companies have learned how to harness this broader range of cost advantages. Their local Chinese subsidiaries, by now largely managed and staffed by locals, have learned many of the tricks of cost innovation; they have become "China hands," moving to the top left quadrant of figure 5-2.

For some of these multinationals, China has become an important contributor within global sales, accounting for over 15 percent of their total revenue. Despite the growing importance of their China business, however, what they have learned in China has not penetrated the rest of their global organization. They have graduated to become China hands, but they haven't used these new capabilities to make themselves more competitive globally. Their own China staff understand the strategies the emerging dragons are following, they know many of the same things the Chinese competitors have learned about cost innovation, but they have no way to use this knowledge on the global battlefield. They can't fully leverage the broad potential of Chinese cost advantage beyond the China market, because the mind-sets, structures, and power bases in today's established multinationals make this impossible. Rivals such as KFC and MacDonald's; P&G, L'Oréal, Unilever, and Nestlé; SABMiller and Anheuser-Busch; Kodak and Fujifilm; and LG and Samsung are all fighting their global wars inside China. But very few have brought China fully into the battles they are fighting elsewhere in the global market.

To respond to the disruptive competition from China described in this book, that narrowness of vision has to change. Precisely because the new competition from Chinese companies is disruptive, it can't be countered purely by conventional means. Multinationals need to rethink the role of China within their global networks to make it a key weapon in their global competitive armory—China will have to be given a new global mandate, moving it into the top right-hand quadrant of figure 5-2. To have a chance of winning in the new, value-for-money game, you will need to use China as a source of new capabilities and learning. Most especially, it needs to be the means through which you bring cost innovation into your global organization.

The New Mandate for China

Crafting a new mandate for China that can achieve these goals will require:

- Changing your mind-set

- Renewing determination to win mainstream customers in China

- Shifting high-value activities to China

- Running some global business areas from China

- Changing the relationship between your Chinese subsidiaries and headquarters

Changing Your Mind-Set. The first step is a change in mind-set. Only a few companies have already adopted this broader way of thinking about China's role. One of them is Alstom, the global supplier of heavy equipment, which describes the mandate of China in one of its business units this way: "For Alstom, China means not only the center of Asia markets; this is our new global center."[15] As we will see below, a number of Western companies, including Intel, have now repositioned the role of China in their thinking, so that it now has a global mandate. Too few, however, have made this intellectual leap.

Yet even this shift in mind-set is insufficient. Rethinking the role of China in your global strategy means more than just acknowledging the importance of China as a force in your company's future. It also means embracing the concept of cost innovation. Procter & Gamble (P&G) is one company that has done so—at least in China. Gilbert Cloyd, P&G's chief technology officer, explained the shift in thinking this way: "Prior to 2000 we were always going to deliver the absolute best, then 'cost save.' We have changed that to 'cheaper and better.' That's the innovation standard, so that for the target consumer in a segment we provide them with an experience that they find better than any other competitive product in that category and price tier and at a cost structure that the competition can't match." He concedes that in the past there were some in P&G who "saw those objectives as contradictory." But he says the game is about "accepting up front that the true innovation goal is being both *better* and *lower cost*. And that has caused us to rethink a lot of things."[16] The new mind-set of cost innovation is the first step in preparing your response to disruptive competition from China.

Renewing Determination to Win Mainstream Customers in China. The second step is a new determination to win mainstream customers inside China, because what happens there will also increasingly influence who comes out on top globally. Pursuing a "skimming" strategy in China (keeping margins up by focusing only on the top-end market in leading Chinese cities and ignoring the rest) looks increasingly dangerous. Skimming may look attractive to Western incumbents in the short term, but it risks leaving a company without the scale necessary to compete in a world where China is rapidly emerging as the largest market for many goods and services (this has already happened in sectors as diverse as beer, photography, and nuclear energy). Such a strategy also reduces the likelihood that your company will learn the secrets of Chinese cost innovation. This knowledge gap could leave you dangerously exposed when disruptive competition ultimately hits your home market. Better to enter the fray knowing your enemy.

The dangers of skimming are well illustrated by the experience of VW in China. The automaker entered China in 1985, long before most of its multinational rivals. In what had long been a market heavily constrained by regulation, tariff walls, and restrictions on entry, VW was content to maintain margins rather than go for volume growth. In 2003, VW sold about 700,000 cars in China (less than its sales in Germany alone). Margins were high— 80 percent of VW's global profit came from China that year. Product introduction was leisurely: VW continued to rely very heavily on the Santana, a model developed in Europe in the 1970s and sold in China since 1985.

When the market took off through a combination of deregulation associated with China's entry into the WTO, a rush into China by all VW's multinational rivals, and the emergence of Chinese competitors in the auto industry, however, VW paid the price for its conservative emphasis on maintaining margins by serving a limited market segment. By 2005 its market share had collapsed by two-thirds from its peak of 50 percent in 2001 to just 16 percent. Its cherished China profits turned into mounting losses. VW is now struggling to reverse the skimming strategy; to regain competitiveness VW hopes to introduce ten new models to ramp up volume and reduce its cost 40 percent by 2008.

Contrast this with P&G. Back in 2000 P&G began to worry about the long-term implications of the fact that at the time it was selling its laundry detergent only to the wealthiest 8 percent of China's consumers—those sitting at the top of a three-tier pyramid it now uses to categorize the Chinese market. P&G decided that winning in the Chinese market would be key to its long-run global competitiveness. Taking a leaf from the Chinese cost innovation book, P&G created two additional versions of its existing, top-tier Tide product. Tide Triple Action was launched in 2001 and aimed at the middle-tier, mass-market consumer. Tide Clean White, launched a year later, was targeted at the lowest-income tier. A 320-gram bag of Tide Clean White sells for 23 cents, compared with 33 cents for 350 grams of Tide Triple Action. While the Clean White version did not offer all the stain-removal and fragrance benefits of its pricier cousin, it was more affordable and still outperformed every other brand at that price point.

P&G backed this product strategy by sustained initiatives to build a national distribution network covering more than eleven thousand cities and towns in China. It also invested heavily in fundamental market research. For example, it abandoned the practice of cloning a toothpaste commonly sold in the United

States for the Chinese market and went back to basics. In order to discover exactly what mass-market Chinese consumers required in the product, and what they were willing to pay for them, it billeted hundreds of researchers with Chinese families in cities and on farms to learn how they use everything from detergent to toothpaste. P&G's determination to win over China's mainstream consumers is buttressed by heavy advertising spend. In 2005, for example, it spent $48 million advertising on China's most popular TV channel, Central Television (CCTV) alone, becoming its largest single advertiser in a concerted effort to win against Chinese competitors.

Today sixteen of the seventeen brands P&G sells in China are leaders in their category, from Head & Shoulders shampoo and Cover Girl makeup to Pringles potato chips and Pampers diapers. Even in the detergent market, where it lags its Chinese rival Nice, Tide is number two.

A new determination to win mainstream customers in the China market will need to become a necessary element in many companies' strategies for responding to the disruptive competition emerging from China. As the importance of the China market grows as a percentage of global demand and the need to tap into cost innovation possibilities increases, China strategies will need to go beyond supplying top-tier customers in the affluent east-coast cities and seriously tackle the challenge of becoming one of the top players in China from the top to the bottom of the market.

Shifting High-Value Activities to China. Strategies for capturing a substantial share of the Chinese market can open the way to learning what the Chinese competitors are doing in cost innovation. It also helps ensure the dragons won't have a monopoly of the scale advantages afforded by China's massive market. But to internalize the secrets of cost innovation, multinationals need to do more than simply manufacture and sell their products and services in the Chinese mass market. They also need to have high-value activities like engineering and R&D in China. By performing these activities in China, multinationals can tap into its low-cost engineering and design resources, then build a group of employees who can bring cost innovation thinking to improve the competitiveness of products and services originally created abroad, and eventually develop cost-innovative offerings from scratch.

One of the earliest companies to recognize and act on this potential was Motorola. It set up an R&D center in China back in 1993—one of the very first multinational companies to do so. Since then, Motorola has built sixteen R&D centers with more than eighteen hundred people. In 1999, Motorola set up its China Research Institute in Beijing, which is among the largest facilities of its type in China, and also a world-class center within Motorola. Between 1985 and 2003, Motorola China has applied for 2,305 patents, making it among the biggest patent applicants in China. The research centers conduct not only fundamental research, but also global product research and local product development. In 2000, Motorola's software center attained the coveted Capability Maturity Model Integrated (CMMI) Level 5 certification of the Software Engineering Institute at Carnegie Mellon University — the first foreign organization in China to do so. It now has two other software centers with this certification. Motorola's mobile phone design center in Beijing has already become its largest overseas design center. Some of its high-end mobile phones have been successfully developed in China and sold globally, clearly establishing the role of China's R&D center in Motorola's global network.

Recognizing that it needs to leverage Chinese advantages at every stage of the value chain in order to strengthen its global competitiveness, Korea's LG group has gone even further, moving key R&D to China. In 2005 LG hired two thousand engineers and scientists into its Chinese R&D center, making it LG's largest R&D site outside Korea. LG has submitted more worldwide patent applications based on research conducted in China than any other company, with the exception of Huawei. By placing such emphasis on China-based R&D, LG is tapping into the secrets of how to deliver high technology at low cost to strengthen and differentiate its competitive position against rivals such as Sony, Matsushita, and its archrival Samsung.

Others are following suit: foreign companies now operate seven hundred R&D centers in China. Microsoft alone has five technology development centers, staffed 95 percent by locals, many with master's or PhD qualifications. And a recent survey of multinational corporations conducted by the United Nations found that 61.8 percent planned future investment in R&D capabilities in China, far higher than the 41.2 percent of multinationals planning future R&D investment in the United States and the 14.7 percent planning expansion of R&D in India.

Beyond the sheer magnitude of these figures, the important point is this: today a multinational's R&D investment in China should not be seen simply as a way to reduce R&D costs; even more significantly, it is a way to tap into cost innovation and counter disruptive competition from China by honing your own capabilities in delivering high technology, variety, and specialty offerings, all at low cost.

Undertaking these kinds of knowledge-based activities in China, however, does require steps to manage potential leakage of intellectual property (IP). Over the past twenty years, China has created IP laws that generally adhere to international standards, and the situation is gradually improving. As Jiang Zhipei, Chief Justice of the Intellectual Property Tribunal of the Supreme People's Court, optimistically puts it: "We started much later than developed nations, but we are catching up quickly; faster than anyone could ever have expected."[17] In practice, however, the ability of foreign companies to rely on the legal system to protect their IP rights is limited. Despite the intentions of the umbrella legislation, weaker implementing regulations and judicial interpretations, procedural barriers, and poor enforcement all render the protection of IP a continuing problem.

While there are no easy answers, multinationals have found ways to mitigate the risks. The key is building a strong and, as far as possible, loyal organization in China under your direct control. This is one reason why more and more foreign companies are using Wholly Owned Foreign Enterprises (known locally as WOFEs), rather than joint ventures, for their knowledge-based activities in China. Building a loyal organization begins with HR policies, including running careful background checks on key hires and putting R&D staff and design engineers in a different location from sales and marketing people. It also takes time; some companies have tried to ramp up too quickly, hiring large numbers of knowledge workers without allowing enough time to imbue them with a culture of IP protection and career attachment to the company. In addition, protecting IP in China means time and resources must be devoted to keeping a close eye on competitors, detecting violations, and taking legal action—a company's legal rights mean little in China unless the company acts determinedly to protect them. When conducting high-value activities in China, it is important for companies to make IP protection a core responsibility of the entire China management team, not merely a function of the legal department.

You will never make the ship completely watertight against IP leakage. But there is a trade-off to be made: either surrender the potential advantages of undertaking more knowledge-intensive, high-value activities in China as a way of tackling the challenges posed by the emerging dragons; or reap those advantages by giving China a more significant role and carefully managing the IP risks. As the wave of disruptive competition from China gathers strength, we believe it will pay more and more to choose the latter option: shifting high-value activities to China.

Running Global Business Areas from China. The logical extension of these moves is to transfer the global mandate for running certain businesses, products, or worldwide customer segments, including strategic decision making, to China. Few companies have yet taken the step of giving their Chinese subsidiaries global responsibility—of moving firmly up into the top-right quadrant of figure 5-2. One of the pioneers here is Intel.

Intel has been expanding aggressively in China since the early 1990s. Around the mid-1990s, when most multinational PC firms still saw China as a market where they could extend the life cycle of their obsolete models, Intel decided to promote the latest technology in the Chinese market. Since then it has built five plants in China, all using the latest technologies. To tap into China's distinctive technological developments, Intel Capital has invested in almost fifty companies in China and in 2005 it set up a $200 million Intel Capital China Technology Fund to take shares in promising technologies emerging there.

Perhaps the most significant realignment of China's role in Intel's global network, however, came in August 2005, when it announced that global responsibility for its Channel Platforms Group (CPG) would be shifted to Shanghai. This was the first time Intel had ever transferred the global leadership of one of its five major strategic business units (SBUs) outside the United States. Intel's rationale for giving the global mandate for CPG (whose charter is to expand Intel's worldwide presence by accelerating global channel growth through innovative business models and platform solutions tailored to meet local market needs), is instructive. In addition to China's huge market potential, an Intel vice president William Siu noted that it was giving its Shanghai center global responsibility because "Shanghai is becoming increasingly important as a commercial and technology centre, not only for China, but for the worldwide IT industry."[18] Intel went on to say that running the SBU from China would be particularly important in allowing it to unlock potential demand in emerging markets and in the cost-competitive segments of the developed world that required advanced technology at demanding price points. The Chinese head of the unit added: "While CPG will be based out of China, we are an international organization whose charter is to serve the needs of the channel worldwide." Put another way, Intel has given China a global mandate to help it bring cost innovation to world markets—a strategy the headquarters was less well equipped to pull off.

Philips is another company that has taken the step of giving its Chinese subsidiary the global mandate for a business unit. Its global business supplying TV sets—from R&D through design, manufacture, and global marketing—is now managed from China.

General Electric (GE) Medical Systems is a good example of the potential benefits of transferring a global mandate for a certain product line to China—especially one likely to face threats from the dragons' global market ambitions. Today GE Medical's Chinese subsidiary is responsible for the bulk of GE's global R&D in CT medical scanners. China also accounts for a slice of GE Medical's global R&D effort in magnetic resonance, and X-ray ultrasound diagnosis equipment. In 2002, GE Medical's subsidiary in Wuxi fully developed and launched the LOGIQ Book—a high-end ultrasound diagnosis machine the size of a laptop PC. Despite being portable, it was capable of high-quality color imaging with performance that matched existing bulky, desktop machines. Using the cost innovation capabilities available in China, GE Medical was able to put high technology into a portable, cost-effective offering. Perhaps not surprisingly, the product has proven a global hit. As its local general manager put it: "We have a strong belief: that is, if we can produce something at 'China cost,' but also of high quality, high functionality, and high technology, it will become a very popular mass-market product, and it will be truly welcomed by customers."[19] Seeking to replicate this success, GE Medical has now established twenty-eight specialist development laboratories, each focusing on a different product line, across five SBUs in China.

A big part of GE Medical's success in CT scanners today has evolved from its strong commitment to China since early 1990s. Back then, instead of just importing products and technology from the United States, GE decided to design products that met both local environments and price level. Incorporating U.S. technology, it designed systems with much lower costs (for example, by using as many local component suppliers as possible), but that were still technologically advanced for its target markets; its scanners quickly won local market share. At the same time, GE's China operation persuaded headquarters to designate China as the global production base for CT scanners, exporting products with high value for money to the global markets. The scale economies reaped by serving a global market helped further reduce costs, which in turn increased market share—today it sells over a thousand CT scanners annually, about one-third of the world market. Transferring the global mandate for CT scanners to China was instrumental in kick-starting this virtuous cycle that has won GE Medical global dominance in the sector.

As yet, however, such examples are rare. But we believe that, in responding to the threat of disruptive competition from China, more and more multinationals will need to consider running global business lines—especially where cost innovation could be decisive—from a Chinese base. It's clearly time to rethink the role of China subsidiaries in building global competitive advantage.

But for any of these strategies discussed above—changing mind-set, renewing determination to win in the mainstream Chinese market, shifting higher-value activities into China, and charging Chinese subsidiaries with global mandates—to have a chance of success, the relationship between the Chinese subsidiary and headquarters will also need to change.

Changing the Relationship with Headquarters. If China is to play a much more significant and potentially global role in your company's network, three changes need to be made in the traditional way most headquarters deal with China:

- If the Chinese organization is to learn capabilities of cost innovation, it must be given significant autonomy to experiment and develop new ways of doing things and new product offerings. If it simply follows the corporate blueprint religiously, its potential to come up with cost innovations will be fatally undermined.

- The Chinese operation needs to be able to make decisions quickly, rather than working through a slow and tortuous chain of command that reviews and second-guesses every initiative. Without speed and flexibility the Chinese subsidiary of a multinational will be ill-equipped to respond to disruptive competition coming from the emerging dragons.

- The subsidiary needs to be staffed by people with the qualities necessary to lead a global line of business, rather than execute with a manufacturing, sourcing, or local market sales brief.

Samsung Electronics is a good example of a company that has implemented such changes. In 2005, the China operations of Samsung Group accounted for revenues of $25.3 billion—25 percent of the company's global total. Sales of Samsung Electronics alone in the Chinese market amounted to $9.8 billion, with another $7.8 billion from export of products manufactured in China. With China becoming Samsung's largest market in 2006 and with accumulated investment of $5.1 billion, its Chinese subsidiaries are playing an increasingly important role in the company's global network. Samsung is pushing aggressively to strengthen R&D operation in China, and the head of Samsung's

China operations is now one of the three executive directors on Samsung's main board holding global business responsibilities.

A Successful Fightback

Multinationals in the mobile handset business, led by Nokia, Motorola, and Samsung, have demonstrated the effectiveness of the strategies outlined above in fighting back against new competition from Chinese rivals. In the Chinese market for handsets, for example, the market share of foreign companies fell from 95 percent in 1999 to just 45 percent by 2003.[20] Today the multinationals have won back customers to take their market share up to 65 percent.

Core to the fightback has been the foreign players' ability to learn from their Chinese competitors and to combine their own strengths with typically Chinese cost innovation strategies and capabilities. Taking a page from the Chinese "high-technology-at-low-cost" playbook, the multinationals have taken cutting-edge technologies and used them to create products such as camera phones with 1-million pixel definition, phones with MP3 music player features, and a myriad of other types of smart phones, all at demanding Chinese price points. Once outflanked by local competitors offering customers a massive choice of varieties and a rapidly evolving range of fashionable models, the multinationals have dramatically expanded their product ranges—including popular features such as recognition of handwritten Chinese characters as a means of inputting SMS messages. Foreign mobile handset companies are now introducing two or three new models every month in China, having mastered the trick of delivering variety and fashion at low cost. Far from confining themselves to the upper end of the market, multinationals have been aggressively targeting the low and low-middle segments of the market—another key element of their fight-back strategy. Motorola now offers a phone that retails at just $40 without any subsidy from the telecommunications operator. By 2006, meanwhile, Nokia had edged out local competitors to become the market leader in the low-end segment (as well as dominating higher priced segments of the market). Over the past two years, Nokia has also appointed over a hundred distributors in provincial cities across China, established three hundred franchised sales outlets, and recruited more than five thousand salespeople to promote Nokia products to every corner of the market.

Such successes signal that Motorola and Nokia, at least, have decided to meet the threat of disruptive competition from China first by mastering the capability for cost innovation, and second, by fighting the emerging dragons aggressively on their home turf.

This comeback started with a change in mind-set about the role of their China subsidiaries in these companies' global strategy. It has also necessitated substantial restructuring of their international networks. Nokia, for example, has consolidated its four joint ventures into a single China holding company that ranks with Europe and North America as one of its five "regional" units covering the world. The boss of China operations reports directly to the head of the mobile phone division at headquarters. Nokia's Chinese handset design centers account for some 40 percent of its global design activities. And the company's R&D center in China is among the largest in Nokia's global network.

Motorola and Nokia's determined efforts paid off handsomely. In 2006, Nokia sold 51 million mobile phones in China, a 39 percent increase over 2005, and took about 35 percent of the China market. Its total China sales reached $5.3 billion, with an additional $3.8 billion in exports. China became Nokia's largest market, accounting for 12 percent of global total. Motorola, meanwhile, has raised its market share to about 21 percent by the second quarter of 2006, rising from just about 11 percent in early 2005.

Clearly, therefore, one effective response to the threat of disruptive competition from China is to try to beat the emerging dragons at their own game. But there is also a potentially compelling alternative: to create a new type of alliance network that can harness the potential of the Chinese as partners to improve your own global competitiveness.

Allying with the Dragons

Suppose it were possible to find a way to combine the strengths of an established multinational—its technology, systems, brands, and the experience and reach of its existing subsidiaries—with the cost innovation advantages being built by the emerging Chinese dragons. This combination should be an unbeatable force in global competition. A pipe dream? In fact, this is exactly what a new breed of partnerships between Western and Chinese firms in the global arena is beginning to do. In their wake, the shape of global competition may well be set to change.

A New Kind of Partnership

Historically, joint ventures between foreign and Chinese companies were aimed either at breaking into the Chinese market or securing an effective, high-quality supply chain through equity involvement in the operations inside China. But consider the alliance Huawei and 3Com put together. In 2003, they formed a new joint venture company to serve the global market for communications equipment, 51 percent owned by Huawei and 49 percent by 3Com. By joining forces, the partners hoped to improve their ability to win share from the dominant global player in this sector, Cisco.

Huawei brought its cost-innovative product line, a strong market share in the developing world, and its cost-competitive service capabilities and design and engineering resources. 3Com contributed its world-renowned brand, an extensive global distribution network, detailed knowledge of customers in the United States and Europe, and a set of complementary product add-ons that completed the offering, as well as $165 million of financing.

The combination has proved powerful: Don Halsted, 3Com executive vice president and chief financial officer, noted that for the quarter ended December 1, 2006, revenue for the Huawei-3Com joint venture was $100 million, with a profit of $30 million, compared with a loss of $20 million on 3Com's other businesses. Sales of the jointly developed 5500 line of Layer 3 switches were particularly brisk, Halsted said. Huawei-3Com now has more than thirty-four hundred employees, more than half of whom are engineers, according to Bruce Claflin, 3Com president and chief executive officer, who adds, "With this growth in engineering talent, the joint venture has taken increased responsibility to develop infrastructure products for 3Com."[21] For 3Com, the global alliance provided access to cost innovation that revitalized and extended its product range, allowing it to compete effectively with Cisco for the first time in years. For Huawei, the alliance helped accelerate the global penetration of its products and technologies, especially in Europe and the United States; enhanced its reputation; and provided new sources of learning about how to build and manage an effective, multinational company.

The Coming Clash of Titan Networks

Cisco responded to the Huawei-3Com partnership in November 2005 by forming its own alliance with Huawei's Chinese archrival, ZTE Corporation, to work on 3G mobile telephony network equipment and Next-Generation Network (NGN) products. Their common goal: to bring together a product line and set of capabilities to outcompete the Huawei-3Com alliance in the global market. Again, Cisco and ZTE's products and technologies are largely complementary: Cisco dominates fixed-line routers and networking equipment, while ZTE is strong in wireless technologies. Cisco has global brand recognition and an extensive distribution network, but relative weaknesses in Asian and developing-country markets, where ZTE has strong relationships with local telecom operators.

Faced with these two large alliance competitors, some of the remaining players such as Nokia's network equipment arm (in contrast to its mobile handset business) and Siemens' telecommunications business look to be subscale and lacking in the full complement of skills, including the advantages enjoyed by the emerging Chinese dragons, necessary to compete globally. Nokia's first response, in October 2005, was to form a $110 million alliance with the Chinese company China Putian. The new entity, 51 percent owned by Putian and 49 percent by Nokia, is focusing on R&D, manufacturing, and marketing of 3G mobile telecommunications network equipment. It provided an opportunity to infuse cost innovation and low-cost design, engineering, and R&D capabilities into Nokia's telecom equipment business. Nokia's next step was to merge its network equipment business with that of Siemens to create a joint company in June 2006. Siemens itself had already formed an alliance with Huawei in February 2004 to jointly research, develop, market, and service 3G mobile telecommunications equipment.

In April 2006 telecommunications equipment makers Alcatel and Lucent finalized details of their merger to form a new $25.4 billion business. Alcatel had had a long-standing, 50:50 joint venture with China's Shanghai Bell for the development and production of telecommunications equipment. Through this company, Alcatel Shanghai Bell (ASB), the partners have been able to enhance competitiveness in what they call "a thin-margin era" by drawing on low-cost innovation, R&D, and manufacturing capabilities in China. ASB is responsible for about 20 percent of Alcatel's R&D, and over 10 percent of the companies' total world-wide patents. But the average cost of its R&D staff is about 27 percent of what it would be in Europe. ASB has also perfected the art of delivering variety at low cost: it produced more than eight hundred product types in 2005, compared with only one hundred in 2002. ASB's R&D center now has more than two thousand staff, and it is fully integrated into Alcatel's global technology databases and networks.

The merger that formed Alcatel-Lucent was finally completed in December 2006. The key role of China in its global strategy was underlined when one of the first announcements made by Patricia Russo, the CEO of the combined company, was that it would make: "China a strategic base for global research and development . . . where 40 percent of the 10,000 mainland staff are engineers."[22] In the same week, the company renewed its alliance agreement with China's Datang Telecom Technology Group to invest in further development of third generation (3G) equipment.[23]

What we are seeing in this industry, therefore, is the emergence of a small number of alliance networks that compete with each other across the globe. Each has at its heart one or more established multinational companies with proprietary technologies, brands, distribution networks, knowledge, and experience. Each has also brought in one of the emerging Chinese dragons as a significant global partner. By bringing the threat of disruptive competition from China inside the fold, potentially destructive rivalry has been redirected toward infusing Chinese cost innovation as a new strength into the global alliance—an additional strength that will improve its global competitiveness. Global competition is being transformed into a battle between titans: global alliance networks involving Chinese players as one of the parties.

Players such as Nortel Networks that are unable to match the scale and diverse set of different capabilities, including cost innovation, enjoyed by these alliances risk being progressively squeezed out of the game as the titans collide in the market. As

ASB's China president put it: "If Shanghai Bell and Alcatel were still fighting on their own, maybe neither could survive now. Only by combining the advantages of both parties into ASB, could we manage the challenge of current market conditions."[24] It was perhaps not surprising, therefore, that Nortel announced an alliance with Huawei in February 2006 to jointly develop high-speed broadband equipment for the Internet communications market.[25]

A similar pattern is emerging in global competition for mobile handsets. Here, however, the leading players such as Nokia and Motorola have built large and deep organizations in China that are fully integrated into their global networks from the highest levels down and across the complete range of activities. This has enabled them to bring cost innovation into the core of their global strategies.

Other competitors, meanwhile, have also opted to achieve these capabilities by forming alliances between Western and China players. Perhaps the best example is the strategy pursued by France's Sagem and China's Ningbo Bird. Back in February 1999, Sagem and Bird signed their first partnership agreement, under which Bird purchased GSM modules from Sagem in exchange for cash and limited transfer of technology. In 2002, a further step was taken with the establishment of a 50:50 joint venture, Ningbo Bird Sagem Electronics Corporation Ltd. (NBBSE), to produce mobile phones in a plant that today employs 2,030 staff.

In January 2006, Sagem and Bird decided to deepen their cooperation sill further. Both partners invested $3 million to form a new joint venture, Ningbo Sagem Bird Research and Development Co., Ltd. Its company mission is to develop a common product range for Sagem and Bird brands, optimizing development costs for both companies while enlarging the product range and ensuring a high quality level. This new joint venture employs over a thousand engineers and technicians working hand in hand with Sagem's existing European R&D centers. The existing production line operated by Sagem in Taiwan was moved to China, and all its products are now sourced from the new joint venture. Full integration of Chinese cost innovation capabilities has therefore been achieved by means of this close alliance.

It's still far from clear which companies will successfully survive consolidation in this fiercely competitive industry. But one fact is now beyond question: it will be necessary to fully integrate Chinese cost innovation capabilities into their global networks in order to stay in the game. 3Com underlined this point in November 2006 when it announced that it had exercised its option to buy 100 percent of Huawei-3Com for $882 million, valuing the joint venture at $1.8 billion. Commenting on the deal, Edgar Masri, president and CEO of 3Com, said: "We believe 3Com, with Huawei-3Com, can build a powerful, global technology leader."[26]

Mobile telecommunication equipment and handsets are in the vanguard of industries responding to the threat of disruptive competition from China. But the message they drive home is clear: one way or another you need to access Chinese cost innovation capabilities, whether by developing and restructuring your own operations in China to learn from your Chinese subsidiaries and provide them with a global mandate or by forming a broad-based alliance with an emerging Chinese dragon that spans functions from R&D and design to manufacturing and marketing. To respond to the coming wave of disruptive competition, China—and its cost innovation capabilities—must become a pivotal part of your competitive strategy in the global arena (not just an exciting growth market or a low-cost source).

If that is the challenge, then an obvious question remains: how is the future likely to evolve? That is the subject of our conclusion.

Conclusion

_____

CHARTING THE FUTURE

"COST INNOVATION" might sound like an oxymoron—most of us in the commercial world have gotten used to associating innovation with the business of providing more functionality and greater sophistication. But the fact that it breaks conventional wisdom is precisely why it has the potential to rewrite the existing rules of global competition. Rather than proving to be just another management fad, there are two interrelated reasons we believe it will have a significant and sustained impact on world markets.

The first reason is that 1.3 billion people (including a potentially active labor force of 800 million) can't move from economic isolation to become an integrated part of the world economy without a downward pressure on the cost of delivering products and services. And that process, which began in 1978 when China started to open up to the world, still has a long way to go: there are still at least 500 million Chinese still to move from low-productivity agriculture to be efficiently employed in manufacturing and services. That's before we even take account of another 1 billion that might make this transition in India and other developing countries over the next decades. While these shifts continue, and there is little reason to suppose they will stop, at the macro level downward pressure on costs will continue.

The second reason is that beyond their brains and brawn, these new workers have access to an ever-increasing proportion of the world's accumulated knowledge and technology because in the twenty-first century, as Thomas Friedman famously put it: "the world is flat."[1] It's because of this new opportunity to access and absorb new technology that productivity in Chinese industry has been increasing at around 17 percent per annum since 1995 (excluding public services directly provided by the State).[2] The dragons we have described in this book are in the vanguard of development, not least because many of them have demonstrated an amazing capacity to learn from the world through a multiplicity of channels—scouring the Internet; watching multinationals operating in China; hiring foreign experts, suppliers, or professional services firms to work for them in China; partnering with or acquiring foreign companies; and establishing R&D and design centers overseas.

When these two, deep-rooted trends—a sustained downward pressure on costs and a growing opportunity to access the world's knowledge—coalesced, it's perhaps not surprising that cost innovation emerged as one result. Strategies such as bringing high technology to price-sensitive mass-markets, offering buyers variety and customization at low cost, and transforming the economics of specialty products emerged and began to make headway in winning a share of global markets.

The potential to combine new ideas and technologies with low costs is set to increase as the world's knowledge is increasingly codified, moving from inside the heads of people in unique clusters such as Silicon Valley and into digital libraries or Internet sites. Some of this codified knowledge is proprietary, but as Friedman also points out, much of it will become available to anyone, anywhere in the world.[3]

At the same time, the opportunities for newcomers to break into global markets will increase with the seemingly inexorable rise in outsourcing and with it the de-integration of industry value chains into "plug-and-play" modules. This is because these developments, designed to save costs and allow increased corporate focus, also allow new entrants to play in the global league even before they have the complement of skills necessary to deliver a complete solution by concentrating on just one of these modular activities.[4]

What we see, therefore, is Friedman's "flatter world" creating gateways for Chinese companies to use their fundamental cost advantages in new ways to compete against established companies. As they do so, the differentiators separating competitors from low-cost countries from their counterparts in high-cost locations are further flattened, pushing global competition to an even higher value-for-money frontier.

That these trends will continue is no longer in doubt. The question now is: how will the dynamics play out?

Increasingly Disruptive Competition

Yesterday's competition from China might have come in the form of basic functionality at the lowest possible price. But because of the changes in the world economy discussed above, the challenge posed by China's budding global players is becoming much more disruptive. Incumbent multinationals and national champions worldwide, which used to be protected because their products were differentiated by offering high technology, a wide variety of models to choose from, or specialized features, will increasingly be confronted by competitors that use cost innovation to match many of these benefits while simultaneously offering better value for money.

High Technology at Low Prices

Pressure to deliver high technology at low prices isn't only coming out of China: look no further than the 45 percent decline between the third quarter of 2005 and the same period in 2006 in the retail value of 42-inch flat-panel televisions, where companies such as LG, Philips, and Sharp dominate.[5] But increasingly we can expect the emerging Chinese dragons to introduce high technology into mass markets in a way that truncates the ability of established players to support their return on investment in new technology by launching it only in segments willing to pay high prices and then gradually migrating it down into lower-priced volume markets. Competition that cuts short the technology-migration cycle in this way will increasingly disrupt the traditional economics on which development of new technology is based.

Recall Dawning, the company that applied the technology of supercomputers to everyday network servers. Huawei successfully penetrated the global market by offering high-technology, Next-Generation Networks to telecoms operators at a cost well below its competitors. China International Marine Containers applied path-breaking research to replace the tropical hardwood in containers with a synthetic material. Shinco deployed its experience in using advanced technology for squeezing quality images out of substandard, pirated VCDs to produce the world's best portable DVD player. Rather than shelling out $400,000 apiece for DDR machines, Zhongxing applied different high technologies to develop cost-effective direct digital radiography machines for the everyday radiography needs of a hospital. Pearl River used sophisticated, flexible manufacturing methods and high technology for drying timber to improve value-for-money in the market for pianos.

This simple idea strikes at the heart of the way many established, global companies view the role of innovation—as a way of adding value (and boosting profits) by offering the customer more sophisticated, more complex, and usually more expensive products. The emerging Chinese dragons are turning this conventional strategy on its head. They aren't using high technology to convince the early adopters on the "bleeding edge" with the hope of eventually converting the mass of consumers over time. Instead, the dragons are using high technology to slash costs and dramatically improve value for money for the kinds of products the mass market wants to buy now. That's disruptive if you are an incumbent whose business model depends on restricting high technology to high-end products. Direct digital radiography is an interesting test case for what happens when these alternative strategies go head to head. The results speak for themselves: the established global competitors such as GE and Philips had to slash the prices of their machines by 40 percent, and the emerging Chinese competitors still took over 50 percent of the market.

Falling Premiums for Variety

As cost innovation strategies allow companies to deliver huge variety in their product range or more customization, at low cost, we will see the price premiums for special features or designs come under pressure. Recall Goodbaby's offer to customers: sixteen hundred models of strollers and nursery products to choose from at prices below their competitors' standard range. CMIC offers a wider range of containers, from those suitable for dry goods to sophisticated refrigerated, tank, and foldable models, all with the low costs that have won it 55 percent of the global market. Haier provided Home Depot with a customized, lockable refrigerator that cost less than its global competitors' standard products. Hisense created a TV that was reengineered to work in bright, outdoor conditions at a price that enabled it to capture the dominant share even of a low-income market like Africa. Recall port-machinery maker ZPMC's sales pitch: "Whatever needs the customer has, we will satisfy them." The problem for ZPMC's rivals is that its words are no empty slogan. ZPMC provides its customers with an initial technical proposal customized to their needs within twenty hours of receiving an enquiry, while maintaining its cost advantage, with the result that it is now the dominant world-player in its industry.

This trend will disrupt the convention that customers need to pay a premium for variety, choice, and customization. Back in 1906

Henry Ford offered customers unrivaled value for money with his Model "T," but it came with the choice of "any color you like, as long as it's black." A century later, Chinese challengers offering the same value for money but with a choice from enormously wide product lines or customized options.

Specialty Products Coming Under New Attack

The economics of producing specialized products will also be transformed. Recall that Haier exploded the niche market for wine-storage refrigerators by finding new ways to share much of the fixed costs between these specialty products and their mass-market lines. Along with lower design and engineering costs, this cost sharing allowed Haier to reduce its breakeven to a fraction of that required by its specialist competitors. When a company reduces its breakeven it can use this windfall in one of two ways: it can choose to maintain low volume and take the benefit in higher margin; alternatively, it can cut the price in the hope of generating high volume. Haier dramatically chose the latter course and set prices 50 percent below the prevailing norm. The huge volume of demand that this stimulated meant that what had been a specialist niche exploded into a mass market. The incumbent players were snookered; their business models were built around low volume sales to a small group of consumers who were willing to pay a hefty price premium, but now they faced a market that had been flipped into much higher volume and keen pricing. Terms like "repositioning" and "change management" don't begin to capture the magnitude of the shift the incumbents were faced with. Their business models, mind-sets, and capabilities would have to be reinvented from the ground up. Given the problems of coping with this kind of dislocation, it's probably not surprising that they lost 60 percent of the U.S. market to Haier. Haier applied a similar strategy to small refrigerators for dormitory rooms and offices. The dogma in the industry was that the potential revenue from these niches was simply too low (because of low unit value combined with limited market volume) to make it worthwhile to create specific products designed to meet their peculiar need. But with lower breakeven, Haier was able to grow what were yesterday's niches into sizable markets, capturing a dominant share in the process.

CIMC did the same thing in tank containers. When they entered, the global market stood at just 12,000 TEUs per year. By acquiring the technology and applying low Chinese costs in everything from design and engineering to manufacturing and sales, CIMC was able to cut prices dramatically. The market expanded almost threefold to over 34,000 TEUs per annum as it became economical for more liquids to be shipped by sea. Yesterday's niche suppliers, who were set up to provide this specialized niche in tiny volumes, were left high and dry—they were suddenly forced to compete in a much larger market where the decisive factor was value for money. In this new competitive game, CIMC trumped them every time, leaving the incumbents from Japan, Korea, and South Africa literally bankrupt.

Challenges to Existing Market Priorities

Cost innovation will also challenge our notions about what market segments are important to focus on and protect. Conventional wisdom held that competition from emerging, third-world multinationals could be forestalled so long as incumbents could defend their positions in developed markets because a company couldn't become a significant global player unless it began by capturing a share of the large, wealthy markets in the United States, Europe, and Japan. In some industries that assumption will remain valid. But it will continue to be challenged by companies such as Huawei that have become global by first targeting countries that most of their established global competitors regard as peripheral. They achieve dominance in these geographic outposts of the world's markets—places that established global players often lump together as an afterthought dubbed "the rest of the world"—by applying a combination of their cost advantage and skills in dealing with weak distribution infrastructure and price-conscious, first-time buyers. From this solid launching pad, the Chinese dragons then prepare their assault on markets in the developed world.

Total GDP in the developing world, adjusted for purchasing power parity, now makes up more than half the world's spending power, and is growing at more than twice the rate of developing markets. As a result, the disruptive potential of today's peripheral markets—where historically it didn't pay to invest more than minimum resources and managerial attention—is set to increase.

Likewise, disruptive competition is increasingly likely to emerge from other non-mainstream segments of the market in the future as the dragons use cost innovation to successfully target them as loose bricks in their competitors' defenses. These include low-end market segments, troublesome customers, and niche markets. In a world where established companies are under ever more pressure to focus on core segments of the market that deliver highest profits in the short term, the rise of peripheral segments as a breeding ground of tomorrow's disruptive competition will pose a growing dilemma for their managers.

New Models of Management?

In this book we have focused on strategy innovation by the Chinese firms in the form of new ways of using their underlying cost advantages. However, the leading dragons have succeeded because they combine new strategies with excellent execution. In the quest to deliver their strategic goals as newcomers to the global market they are also exploring new management practices that might help them. They are seeking the right combination of the latest Western management techniques and tools with insights from traditional Chinese culture. One Chinese CEO we know, for example, reads all the major new management books published in the United States and Europe, while running his organization and alliances with the deft hand of a Chinese relationship builder. It is too early to say where such combinations will lead, but we wouldn't be surprised if these budding Chinese multinationals don't end up challenging some of our management norms, as well as innovating strategies to use cost advantage in new ways. In a decade or so, managers across the world may become fans of management ideas and processes with "Chinese characteristics" in much the same way as Japanese "Just-In-Time" systems have now been adopted almost worldwide.

Stresses on the Dragons' Source of Cost Advantage

At the same time as the wave of disruptive competition from China gathers strength, stresses are likely to appear in their source of competitive advantage. Developing and executing sophisticated cost innovation strategies in the global market will make extreme demands on the talent of a wide variety of individuals, from management to engineers and designers. At the heart of the dragons' advantage to date is the fact that large numbers of these people have been available in China more cheaply than elsewhere in the world. Their availability has enabled Chinese companies to deliver cost innovation, rather than simply standard products at low prices.

Now it's true that China will graduate another 4.13 million students from universities in 2006 (based on enrolments) and that there are 23 million people in some form of higher education, plus a further 115,000 officially registered as studying abroad.[6] China graduated over 500,000 engineers in 2005 (between two-and-a-half and eight times more than came out of U.S. engineering schools, depending on your definition).[7] And the *China Daily* reported that starting salaries for new graduates surveyed by the government had fallen from $375 per month in 2002 to under $200 per month in 2005.[8] Nonetheless, in a report published in 2006, McKinsey & Company described the market for talent in China as "white-hot." McKinsey also claimed that "Most graduates from top universities in the United States or Europe are able to be productive from day one on the job. In China, such people are few and far between."[9] There must be real questions, therefore, about whether future constraints on the available talent in China will hold back the dragons as they try to ramp up their cost innovation strategies globally.

Moreover, as ever more Chinese companies seek to expand globally, they are likely to face a growing shortage of management with the skills, let alone the experience, to manage an international organization. In the past, as we have already noted, Chinese returnees played an important role in infusing Chinese companies with this kind of capability and experience. But although the supply of returnees is growing, the pool is still quite limited. A manager with the right portfolio of skills and experience to run an international business, meanwhile, may take years to train up from scratch.

These likely future stresses on the ability of Chinese companies to deliver cost innovation to world markets cannot be lightly dismissed. Creative management solutions will be required. But the track record of leading Chinese firms in sidestepping bottlenecks and overcoming resource constraints suggest such ways will be found. Most probably, therefore, we should prepare for a future in which Chinese cost innovation presents an increasing challenge and disruptive competition from the Chinese dragons only becomes more intense.

Living in a World of Cost Innovation

The emergence of this new type of competition from China strikes at the heart of the business models that have hitherto proven successful in countering the threat of low-cost competition. You could call it "everyday low prices on steroids." As we have seen in the course of this book, moving to ever higher-end segments and activities is unlikely to provide the answer. This strategy may work as a way of maintaining profitability in the short term. But as the emerging Chinese competitors ride the virtuous cycle of scale, learning, and ever lower costs, while simultaneously investing the surpluses they generate in further cost innovation, moving upmarket risks turning out to be little more than a retreat into oblivion.

The systemic nature of industries such as FMCGs, petrochemicals, and pharmaceuticals and the difficulties Chinese dragons face in accumulating necessary intangible assets, such as brands and management systems, to compete in such industries will slow down the dragons' advance. But as we have seen, a combination of the cost innovation, Chinese acquisitions, and use of the demand wedge means that, sooner or later, few industries will be immune.

Yet we are not arguing that Chinese competitors will simply take over the world. Many will perish along the way. Others will struggle to develop organizations that can compete effectively far from their Chinese home base. Moreover, today's incumbent multinationals will learn to better protect the loose bricks in their defensive walls identified in previous chapters. They will pay more attention to the long-term implications of deemphasizing peripheral markets, shying away from troublesome customers, and assuming that niche segments cannot be transformed into a volume game. Sophisticated players are already taking notice of Chinese cost innovation and learning to incorporate this new thinking into their corporate strategies and product lines.

Recognizing these facts, our message is this: the emergence of the Chinese dragons on the world scene will fundamentally shake up the global competitive landscape. During the disruption that ensues there will be casualties among those who are either in denial or unprepared. And when the dust settles you will have to deal with a world where:

- The value-for-money equation offered to global consumers has been rewritten by the emergence of Chinese

competitors offering high technology, variety, and specialist offerings at low cost

- Cost innovation capabilities are therefore a key source of
  competitive advantage

- Today's international supply chains have been replaced
  by competition between global networks in which
  Chinese companies play an important part—either as
  foreign companies' partners or nodal members or
  leaders of a competing network (as we have already seen
  emerge in the global markets for telecommunications
  equipment and mobile handsets)

In positioning yourself for success in this new global environment, whether you are an established multinational, a national
champion, or an entrepreneurial start-up, the choices are clear: you
can take on board the notion of cost innovation and deploy some of
your distinctive capabilities and experience to beat the dragons at
their own game; you can restructure your own organization to fully
leverage the potential advantages China's unique environment offers across the spectrum from R&D and design to operations and
marketing; or you can seek to access these advantages by partnering with a Chinese firm for global (not just local) advantage.

Whichever path you choose, responding to disruptive competition from the emerging Chinese companies means tapping into
the secrets of cost innovation. So the prerequisite for all these
types of initiatives is perhaps the most difficult adjustment of all:
recognizing and accepting China as the source of deep-seated
complex learning that can help you deliver high technology, variety, and specialist offerings at low cost—and hence improve your
global competitiveness. Above all else, it will be success in achieving this shift in mind-set that determines which companies can
continue to prosper when the dragons come knocking at the door.

Notes

Introduction

1. "The Fable of CIMC," *CEO&CIO,* July 20, 2005.

2. Marcia Klein, "SA Tank Container Industry the World Leader," *Business Times* (South Africa), February 14, 1999.

3. See http://www.sassda.co.za.

4. See http://www.trencor.net and http://www.consani.co.za.

5. See http://www.ubh.co.uk.

6. See http://www.invest.uktradeinvest.gov.uk/asiapacific/site_chi /success.

7. http://www.uschina.org/info/chops/2006/foreign-trade.html.

8. http://www.csc.mti-mofcom.gov.sg.

9. In *The Writing on the Wall: China and the West in the 21st Century* (London: Little, Brown, 2007), for example, Will Hutton eloquently illustrates this case.

10. David Stipp, "China's Biotech Is Starting to Bloom," *Fortune,* September 2, 2002, 28–32.

11. Sun Tzu, *The Art of War* (Philadelphia: Running Press Book Publishers, 2003).

Chapter 1

1. Thomas L. Friedman, *The World Is Flat: A Brief History of the Twenty-First Century* (New York: Farrar, Straus and Giroux, 2005).

2. "China Report: China and the New Rules for Global Business," http://www.bcg.com/publications/files/BCG_KWspecialreport.pdf.

3. For a fascinating study of how Chinese high-tech firms get started, see Qiwen Lu, *China's Leap into the Information Age : Innovation and Organization in the Computer Industry* (Oxford: Oxford University Press, 2000).

4. See Christopher Duenwald and Jahanguir Aziz, *The Growth-Financial Nexus in China: Competing in the Global Economy* (Washington, DC: International Monetary Fund, 2004).

5. Douglas Brown and Scott Wilson, *The Black Book of Outsourcing: How to Manage the Changes, Challenges, and Opportunities* (Hoboken, NJ: John Wiley & Sons, Inc., 2005).

6. World Trade Organization, *Annual Report 1998*, 36.

7. Peter Wonacott, "China Investing in Rust-Belt Companies: Auto-Parts Maker Wanxiang Invests in U.S. Partners as Its Ambitions Expand," *Wall Street Journal*, November 26, 2004.

8. Cheng Jia, "Bird Handset Exports Go to Global Operators," *Pacific Epoch report*, January 18, 2006.

9. Interview with Zhang Riu Ming; *Dialog*, CCTV 2, December 14, 2003.

10. "Pearl River Piano Will Strike a Strong Tone of Global Brand," *Yangcheng Evening News*, June 7, 2004.

11. Ibid.

12. C. Rabe and A. Hoffbauer, "Chinesische Firmen drängen auf den deutschen Markt," *Handelsblatt*, June 9, 2005, 5; see also http://www.kleincoll.de.

13. Clayton M. Christensen, *The Innovator's Dilemma* (New York: HarperBusiness, 2000).

Chapter 2

1. See http://www.top500.org/system/ranking/7036.

2. "Interview: Sun Ninghui Chief Designer of the Dawning 4000A," *Science and Technology Daily*, June 26, 2004.

3. Li Guojie, interview with authors, Beijing, July 2005.

4. Ibid.

5. Anonymous Neusoft executive, quoted in "Bringing Advanced Technology to Hospitals," *Economic Observer*, August 2, 2003.

6. Nan Cunhui, interview with authors, Beijing, August 2005.

7. Business Media Enterprise Research Institute, "Cost Stunt: Chinese Recreation of Low Cost Belief," *China Business Review*, July 2005.

8. Ibid.

9. Hu Yong, "20 Years: The Haier Textbook," *China Entrepreneur Magazine*, May 20, 2005.

10. For a detailed discussion of Shinco and the evolution of the VCD industry in China, see Mu Ling and Lu Feng, "Local Innovation, Capability Development and Competitive Advantage: The Development

of China VCD Industry and Its Policy Implications for the Role of Government," *Management World* 12 (December 2003): 57–82.

Chapter 3

1. Huawei's 1997 "Basic Law," a document that sets out the key success factors and strategies for its future development, states that it "will insist on using the 'pressure point' principle of focusing on key success factors and selected strategic segments and allocating resources much greater than that of our main competitors. By concentrating our human, physical and financial resources in this way, we will achieve breakthrough at the key points." (Rule 23 of Huawei Basic Law, cited in Huang Weiwei and Wu Chunbo, eds., *Out of Chaos* (Beijing: China Telecom Press, 1998).

2. Hu Yong, "20 Years: The Haier Textbook," *China Entrepreneur Magazine,* May 20, 2005.

3. Interestingly, the tactic of moving from the periphery successively towards the core parallels Chairman Mao's famous rule of guerrilla warfare: "Surround the cities from the rural areas."

4. James Mackintosh, "Chinese Groups Steer Towards Low-Cost Niche," *Financial Times,* January 11, 2006.

5. Anonymous resort developer, interview with authors, London, January 2006.

6. "Emerging Economies Climbing Back," *The Economist,* January 21, 2006, 71–72.

7. Hu, "20 Years."

8. John Campi, interview with authors, Shanghai, July 2004.

9. Hu, "20 Years."

10. Guan Tong Xian, interview with authors, Shanghai, August 2005.

11. Ren Zhengfei, interview with authors, Shenzhen, April 2005.

12. See http://www.hongkongmobility.ust.hk/index_HostC.

13. "Report on Huawei's Globalization," *IT Times Weekly,* September 20, 2004.

14. http://www.unstrung.com/document.asp?doc_id=64237.

15. Quoted in Dennis Normile, "Chinese Telecom Companies Come Calling," *Electronic Business,* February 1, 2005.

16. "Haiwei in the US," *Wall Street Journal,* July 28, 2004.

17. Ibid.

18. Unstrung news feed, August 12, 2004.

19. "Technologies Implement Advanced NGN Solution," Intelecom press release, November 14, 2006; see http://www.intelecomsolutions.com/news/index.php?id=2.

20. BDA China, an independent research firm.

21. *Perspectives on Experience* (Boston: Boston Consulting Group, 1972).

22. C. K. Prahalad, *The Fortune at the Bottom of the Pyramid: Eradicating Poverty Through Profits* (Philadelphia, PA: Wharton School Publishing, 2004).

23. C. K. Prahalad and Stuart L. Hart, "The Fortune at the Bottom of the Pyramid," *Strategy and Business* 26 (Spring 2002): 1–14.

24. Ibid.

Chapter 4

1. "TCL-Thomson Electronics: A Grim Picture," *The Economist*, November 4, 2006, 89.

2. Justine Lau, "Consumer Electronics: TCL Forced to Close Units in Europe," *Financial Times*, November 1, 2006.

3. Ibid.

4. "Carmaking in China: The Fast and Furious," *The Economist*, November 25, 2006, 83–84.

5. Dealogic, 2006, http://www.dealogic.com.

6. Of course there will always be a degree of subjectivity in how each industry is scored because statistics such as "impediments to cost innovation" cannot be measured directly and precisely. There are also important variations in exposure within industries that aren't captured. Therefore figure 4-1 should not be treated as deterministic. Rather, it is intended to provide a conceptual framework that each company can use to do a thorough analysis about the potential threat from Chinese competitors.

7. Paul Gao, "Supplying Auto Parts to the World," in "China Today," special edition, *McKinsey Quarterly* 2004, 13–19.

8. News release, http://www.tcl.com, November 4, 2003.

Chapter 5

1. Li Jun, interview with authors, Beijing, September 2005.

2. For an illustration of the organization of the Chinese science and technology system, see Denis F. Simon and Merle Goldman, eds., *Science and Technology in Post-Mao China* (Cambridge, MA: Harvard University Press, 1989).

3. For details on the process of drafting the program, see Anthony J. Saich, *China's Science Policy in the 1980s* (Manchester, UK: Manchester University Press, 1989), chapter 5.

4. "China Will Become World's Second Highest Investor in R&D by End of 2006, Finds OECD," December 4, 2006, http://www.oecd.org.

5. http://www.nsf.gov/statistics.

6. http://www.english.people.com.cn/english/200010/25/eng 20001025_53583.html.

7. Ibid.

8. Siemens Press Release, "Siemens strengthens its commitment to next generation optical networks," May 16, 2006, http://www .siemens.com.

9. http://www.gti.org/pressroom/articles/pr_08212006.asp.

10. See, for example, Yves L. Doz, Jose Santos, and Peter Williamson, *From Global to Metanational: How Companies Win in the Global Knowledge Economy* (Boston: Harvard Business School Press, 2001).

11. Zhu Qiong, "Chery's Bet," CEO&CIO, July 5, 2004, 9–11.

12. Ibid.

13. W. Chan Kim and Renée Mauborgne, *Blue Ocean Strategy: How to Create Uncontested Market Space and Make the Competition Irrelevant* (Boston: Harvard Business School Press, 2005).

14. Reported in: http://www.blueoceanstrategy.com/pages/press .htm.

15. *National Business Daily,* May 17, 2005.

16. Jeremy Grant, "Check the Depth of the New Customer's Pocket," *Financial Times,* November 16, 2005.

17. http://www.chinaiprlaw.com/english/news/news5.htm.

18. "Intel Announces Plans to Open Shanghai HQ," *China Daily,* August 2, 2005.

19. Yang Guang, "GE Medical in China," *Sino Foreign Management,* May 2003, 31–34.

20. Ministry of Information Industries representative, telephone interview with authors, April 2004.

21. Transcript of 3Com's F2Q07 (quarter ending December 2, 2005), conference call, http://www.networking.seekingalpha.com/article/5319.

22. Bien Perez, "Alcatel-Lucent to Boost Mainland Investment," *South China Morning Post,* December 5, 2006.

23. Ibid.

24. Xu Yangfan, "Alcatel's Leverage Point," *CEO&CIO,* December 20, 2005, 5–8.

25. Paul Taylor, "Nortel and Huawei Sign Internet Tie-up," *Financial Times,* February 2, 2006.

26. "3Com to Buy Huawei's 49 Percent Stake in Huawei-3Com Joint Venture for $882 Million," 3Com press release, http://www.phx .corporate-ir.net/phoenix.zhtml?c=61382&p=irol-newsArticle&ID=93 6596&highlight.

Conclusion

1. Thomas L. Friedman, *The World Is Flat: A Brief History of the Twenty-First Century* (New York: Farrar, Straus and Giroux, 2005), 1.

2. Ibid.

3. Ibid., chapter 3.

4. See Dieter Ernst, "The New Mobility of Knowledge: Digital Information Systems and Global Flagship Networks," in R. Latham and S. Sassen, eds., *Digital Formations: IT and New Architectures in the Global Realm* (Princeton, NJ: Princeton University Press, 2005), 89–114.

5. Song Jung-a, "LG Philips Scales Back Screen Dream," *Financial Times*, November 30, 2006.

6. Pallavi Aiyar, "In China—Problem of Plenty?" *The Hindu*, June 22, 2006.

7. Mark Claydon, "Does the US Face an Engineering Gap?" *Christian Science Monitor*, December 20, 2005.

8. Liu Shinan, "Improved Educational Standards Required," *China Daily*, June 7, 2006.

9. http://www.mckinsey.com/locations/greaterchina/knowledge /functions/strategy/ChinaTalent.asp.

Index

aan de Stegge, Ton, 114
acquisitions. *See* mergers and acquisitions
Actions Semiconductor Co., Ltd., 21
Africa
    peripheral markets in, 96, 101–102, 109, 118
    South African firms, 9–10, 11, 199
Airbus, 146
aircraft manufacturing, 132, 145–147
AIS, 110, 113
Alcatel, 47
Alcatel-Lucent partnership, 189–190
Alcatel Shanghai Bell (ASB), 189–191
Alibaba, viii
alliance networks, 186–187, 190
alliances. *See* strategic alliances
Alstom, 174
Amana, 150
AMD, 62
Amdahl, 61
American Manufacturing Fund, 45

Amoi, 47, 48
Andersen, H. N., 4
Anheuser-Busch, 173
appliance manufacturing industry
    customization in, 99–100
    exposure to competition, 132
    recombinative innovation in, 80–81
    response to disruptive competition, 149–152
    specialty products, 103–104
application-specific chips (ASICs), 69
The Art of War (Sun Tzu), 24
ASB (Alcatel Shanghai Bell), 189–191
AsiaInfo, 18
Asian financial crisis of 1997, viii, 8, 75
ASICs (application-specific chips), 69
AT&T, 49, 75
Australia, 45, 104
automated production, 74–78, 151
automobile industry
    exposure to competition, 133
    globalization in, 43–46, 55

automobile industry (*continued*)
impediments to cost innovation,
124, 126
increasing variety in, 136
peripheral markets in, 96–97
size of China market, 134–135
strategic acquisitions in,
141–142
variety at low cost, 162–164
Automotive Components Supply
Ltd., 45
Aviation Industries of China
(AVIC), 146, 147
AVIC (Aviation Industries of
China), 146, 147
AVL, 164

Barbados, 43
Barrett, Craig, 159–160
BASF, 130
Bayer, 130
Beijing Orient Electronics, 141
Beijing University, 159
Bellwave, 47, 48
Bertone, 135, 163
Best Buy, 51
Beto Khuaveyto, 108
biotechnology industry, 20–21,
138–139
Blue Ocean Strategy (Kim and
Mauborgne), 165
Boeing, 146
Bosch, 44
The Boston Consulting Group,
117
Boston Piano, 140
BP, 130, 143
brand awareness
building, to increase entry
barriers, 133
lack of, in U.S. market, 114–115

as limitation to disruptive
competition, 124
as problem in core markets,
112–113
use in strategic partnership,
188
breakeven point
reducing, focus on, 167–168
in specialty products, 81–82,
104
British Telecom Group plc (BT),
116
BYD, 20, 73–76, 79

Canada, 45
Capability Maturity Model
Integrated (CMMI) Level 5
certification, 178
CapitalBio, 20–21
capital costs, 109
capital goods, 54–55
capital-output ratio, 33
Carnegie Mellon University
(CMU), 178
Carrefour, 51, 129, 130
CAS. *See* Chinese Academy of
Science
CASC (China Aerospace Science
and Technology
Corporation), 66, 159
CCP (Chinese Communist
Party), 157
Central Committee of the
Chinese Communist Party,
157
central planning age, technology
resources from, 33, 155–156
CEOs (chief executive officers),
36
Channel Platforms Group (CPG;
Intel), 181

Chery Automobile
impediments to cost innovation, 124, 126
learning from world, 162–164
peripheral markets, 96–97
size of China market and, 135, 136
chief executive officers (CEOs), 36
China
building loyal organizations in, 180
expanding global role of, 169–187
experience in emerging economies, 108–109
industry commitment to, 182–183
new mandate for (see new mandate for China)
overseas-Chinese diaspora, 17–18
role in global strategies, 174–175
scale advantages in production, 46
shifting high-value activities to, 177–180
as source of learning and capabilities, 173, 204
strength in domestic market, 4–5
subsidiaries run from, 49–50, 181–185
U.S. restrictions on sale of high-technology products to, 62
world share of high-technology products, 14
China Aerospace Science and Technology Corporation (CASC), 66, 159

China Daily, 165–166, 201–202
"China hands," 170, 172–173
China Harbour Engineering Company (Group) Hong Kong Ltd., 35
China Harbour Engineering Company (Group) Ltd., 34, 35
China International Marine Containers Group. See CIMC
China market
for capital goods, 54–55
competing against multinationals in, 17
as "demand wedge," 143–147
expanding presence in, 171–172
experience in, 19, 97
importance of low price in, 57
as learning environment, 168
for low-cost products, 64
scale advantages in, 177–178
size of, 19, 125–126, 134–136
specialty products in, 82
strength in, 4–5
three-tier pyramid, 176–177
winning mainstream customers in, 175–177
China Medical, 21
China Merchants Holdings, 4
China MobileSoft Limited (CMS), 160–161
China National Offshore Oil Corporation (CNOOC), 53
China National Petroleum Corporation, 145
China Putian, 189
China Research Institute, 178
Chinese Academy of Engineering, 18, 159
Chinese Academy of Science (CAS), 18, 60
infrastructure reform and, 155, 159

Chinese Academy of Science
(*continued*)
relationship with Legend,
30–31, 32, 38, 39
research hierarchy and, 156,
158
Chinese Communist Party
(CCP), 157
Chinese economy
foreign trade and, 17
growth of, viii–ix
transitional, resource allocation
and, 32
transition to new structure, ix
Chinese firms (dragons)
advantages of, 23, 172
assessing vulnerability to,
117–121
beating at cost innovation
game, 154–169
competition in high-end segments, 147–148
cost innovation strategy (*see*
cost innovation)
determining ownership structures of, 32–33
entrepreneurship by managers
of, 35–36
expanding role of, 169–187
fighting back against, 25, 133,
185
focus on process innovation,
23–24
global competition and, ix
handicaps in global market,
39–40
impediments to cost innovation by, 131–134
massive restructuring of, 16,
123–124, 204
new opportunities in global
economy, 16–17

use of foreign acquisitions,
139–143
using cost innovation to defeat,
154–169
weaknesses of, 24–25, 148,
166, 168
Chinese subsidiaries
autonomy in running, 181–183
established to access
knowledge, 49–50
relationship with headquarters,
184–185
Chint, 76–79
Christensen, Clayton, 55
CIMC (China International
Marine Containers Group),
3–10, 15, 20, 153
alliance with UBHI, 10–11
cost innovations, 196, 197,
199
establishing strength in
domestic market, 4–5
expansion abroad, 5–7
as hybrid company, 36
upmarket moves, 7–10
Circuit City, 51, 150
Cirque du Soleil, 165
Cisco Systems, 115
clash with Huawei-3Com
partnership, 188–189
partnership formed to compete
against, 187, 188
Citroën, 163
Claflin, Bruce, 188
ClearTalk, 115
Clive-Smith Cowley, 3, 13
clothing business, 132
Cloyd, Gilbert, 174–175
clustering technology, 59–60, 64
CMMI (Capability Maturity
Model Integrated) Level 5
certification, 178

CMS (China MobileSoft Limited), 160–161
CMU (Carnegie Mellon University), 178
CNOOC (China National Offshore Oil Corporation), 53
Cognigine, 141
competitive advantage
  Asian financial crisis of 1997 and, 8, 75
  during materials shortages, R&D capability and, 12–13
  strategic alliances and, 25
  sustainable, building, x
  translating strategies into, 21–22
competitive advantage, Chinese, 27–56
  access to state assets and intellectual property, 30–33
  confluence of advantages, 28–39
  cost innovation capabilities and, 204
  disruptive competition and, 55–56
  example, Wangxiang as, 39–55
  globalization and, 27, 39–55
  global market for talent and services, 51–55
  government support as, 18–19, 31
  low-cost labor and, 27–28, 169
  low-cost talent at all skill levels, 28–30
  management autonomy and, 33–37
  modularization as start of, 46–49
  outsourcing and, 28, 42–46
  personal incentives and, 37–39
  reduced barriers in retailing, 50–51

role of information in, 49–50
  "soft infrastructure" and, 18
competitive climate, change in, 2–3
competitors
  in consumer electronics industry, 15
  diversified, pressing cost advantage against, 6–7
  finding "loose bricks" in defenses of, 5–7, 24
  pressuring by squeezing costs, 6
complacency, dangers of, 90–91
computer industry
  Chinese impact on, 20
  exposure to competition, 132
  leveraging low-cost R&D, 59–65
  modularization in, 46–47
computer technology
  3-D design software, 136
  development of high-tech products, 31
  high performance computers, 59–65
Consani Engineering, 9–10, 11
consumer electronics industry
  Asian competitors in, 15
  Chinese impact on, 20
  customization in, 101–102
  exposure to competition, 132
  limitations of disruptive competition in, 123–124
  portable DVD players, 85–87
  specialty niches in, 105
  video compact discs, 82–85
  "while-you-wait" systems, 130
consumers, Chinese, ix, 119–120
container industry
  cost innovation in, example of, 3–10

container industry (*continued*)
European firms in, 3, 11, 13
Japanese firms in, 9, 199
South African firms in, 9–10,
199
core markets, 112–116
brand perception in, 112–113
"loose bricks," 116
mobile telephony market,
113–114
U.S. market, 96, 114–115, 126
Corey, Charles, 52
corporate control, market for,
53–54
cost advantage, Chinese
economies of scale and, 7, 172
extending, 6–7
global economic structure and,
28
over United States, in wage
rates, 29
in R&D, volume segments and,
12
source of, 201–202
Costco, 51
cost innovation, ix, viii, 1–25,
57–88
aspects of, 1–3
beating dragons at own game,
154–169
challenge of, 87–88
in container industry, 3–10,
196, 197, 199
in customer service, 113
disruptive competition and, 2,
55–56, 195–201
dynamics of, 3–10
global effects of, 202–204
growing competitiveness and,
20–25
high technology at low cost,
58–72

impact of, in future, 193–204
impediments to (*see* impediments to cost innovation)
less effective in immature
industries, 126–128
"loose bricks" and, 5–7,
106–117
moving upmarket with, 7–10,
153–154
need to adopt as strategy, 165
in product design, 135–136
response strategies, 154–169
risks of high-end niches,
10–14
source of cost advantage and,
201–202
specialty products at low cost,
81–87
strong position in China, 4–5
through process flexibility,
73–79, 161
unique aspects of Chinese
competition in, 15–19
value-for-money equation and,
2–3, 203–204
variety at low cost, 72–81
"while-you-wait" systems as,
130
window of opportunity for,
147–148
cost innovation wedge, 118
CPG (Channel Platforms Group;
Intel), 181
Craftsman, 75
CTC Communications, 115
customer(s)
Chinese consumers, ix,
119–120
mainstream, winning, 175–177
troublesome (*see* troublesome
customers)
customer-centricity, 102

customer requirements
in peripheral markets, 106–107
winning mainstream
customers, 176–177
working with customer in
development, 99–100
customer service
cost innovation in, 113
cost-reduction skills in, 117
new standards for, 36–37
in peripheral markets, 110–112
use in strategic partnership,
187
customization at low cost,
99–102
in consumer electronics
industry, 101–102
cost innovation strategy, 113
cost-reduction skills in, 117
to dislodge "loose bricks,"
99–100
as disruptive competition, 55
using manual production
processes, 77–78
using open architecture,
69–70

Daewoo Motor, 141, 163, 164
Dalian Machinery Company, 141
Datang Telecom Technology
Group, 190
Dawning, 1, 49, 59–65, 155, 196
DDR (direct digital radiography),
66
decision making, autonomy and,
184–185
Dell Computer, 53
Delphi, 20, 44, 45
"demand wedge"
state purchasing power as, 139,
143–147

use of, 134, 198–199
design companies, 135–136
developed markets. See core
markets
developing countries
GDP of, 98, 200
labor forces in, 193
markets in (see peripheral
markets)
direct digital radiography (DDR),
66
disruptive competition, vii
challenge to existing markets,
199–200
changes in world economy
and, 193–195
cost innovation challenge, 2,
55–56, 195–201
high technology at low cost, 55,
152, 195–197
by "kamikaze pilots," 22–23
layers of, 106
limitations of (see limitations of
disruptive competition)
narrow approach to, folly of,
153–154
new kind of, 55–56
new management models and,
200–201
response to (see response
strategies)
specialty products at low cost,
55, 198–199
systemic businesses and, 203
variety at low cost, 55, 197–198
disruptive technologies, 65–67,
197
distribution networks
building, 50
mass-market retailers, 103–104
use in strategic partnership,
188

diversified competitors, 6–7
domestic market. *See* China
  market
Dongfeng Motor Group Co., Ltd.,
  163
Dow Chemical, 130
dragons. *See* Chinese firms
  (dragons)
DTAC, 110
Duerkopp Adler, 140

early adopters, 115, 166, 167
East Asiatic Company, 4
economies of scale
  in China market, 177–178
  cost advantage and, 7, 172
  driving down component
    prices, 84
  in high-end niche segments, 103
  presence in high-volume mar-
    kets and, 96, 169
  pressing for, to reduce costs, 10
  by production in China, 46
  by serving global market, 183
  in specialty products, 81
The Economist, 98
education, 29, 201–202
efficiency, modularity and, 47
emerging economies
  Chinese experience in, 108–109
  low-cost resources of, 168–169
emerging technology, betting on,
  36
Emtel, 111
entrepreneurship, 32, 35–36
entry barriers
  breaking with marketing inno-
    vation, 60–61
  to global market, 16–17
  increasing, with brand aware-
    ness, 133

reduced because of globalization, 41, 42–43, 55
reducing in retailing, 50–51, 197
systemic value network as, 132
environmentally safe products,
  152
Ericsson, 47, 50, 76, 110, 114
ESS Technology, 84
established (Western) firms
  in China market, 5, 133
  desire to restrict technology,
    58–59, 196–197
  determining ownership struc-
    tures of dragons, 32–33
  failure to compete in periph-
    eral markets, 199–200
  inability to harness cost advan-
    tage, 173
  management orthodoxies of,
    119
  need to compete on basis of
    technology, 14
  need to learn cost innovation,
    30, 165
  need to respond to
    competition, 149–152
  options to compete in specialty
    niches, 104–105
  research and development by,
    179
  response strategies, vii, 22–23,
    25
  views of innovation, 193, 196
  vulnerabilities of (*see* "loose
    bricks")
Etisalat, 110
European firms, 42
European market, 96
experience
  in domestic markets, 19, 97
  in emerging economies,
    108–109

experience curve, x, 116–117
Exxon Mobil, 130, 143

fast-moving consumer goods
(FMCG) industries, 128–129
FhG, 54
Fillony Limited, 100
First Autoworks, 162
fixed costs, 11, 111–112
flat-panel imaging technology,
66–67
flexibility. *See* process flexibility
flexible ownership, 37–38
FMCG (fast-moving consumer
goods) industries, 128–129
Ford, Henry, 197–198
Ford Motor Company, 126, 142, 164
foreign acquisitions by dragons,
139–143
foreign direct investment
Chinese economy and, 17
joint ventures (*see* joint
ventures, Sino-foreign)
separation between ownership
and control, 34–35
foreign trade, 4, 17
Fortune magazine, 21
France, 47, 123–124, 191
France Telecom, 107
Friedman, Thomas, 27, 194, 195
Fujifilm, 173
FutureWei, 114–115

Galanz, 20, 100–101, 109, 152
Gao, Paul, 44
GDP. *See* gross domestic product
(GDP)
Geely, 124, 126
General Electric (GE), 50, 75, 94,
144

GE Medical Systems, 182–183,
197
high technology at low cost,
66, 67, 69, 71, 76
General Motors, 126, 142, 163
geographic periphery. *See* peripheral markets
German auto manufacturing, 43
Germany
acquisitions in, 140–141
container industry in, 3
mergers and acquisitions in, 45
purchase of technology from,
7–8
global alliances. *See* strategic
alliances
global competition, ix
challenging orthodoxies of, 58
"China hands," 170, 172–173
experience in domestic market
and, 19, 97
in supply chains, 204
global economy
changes in, disruptive competition and, 193–195
economic structure, 28
"Global Knowledge Economy,"
41
new opportunities for Chinese
firms and, 16–17
"global gateway," width of, 131–132
globalization
in automobile industry, 43–46,
55
Chinese competitive advantage
and, 27, 39–55
entry barriers reduced due to,
41, 42–43, 55
opportunity for latecomers,
40–41
of talent and services market,
54–55

"Global Knowledge Economy," 41
global market
  characteristics of (see market
    characteristics)
  Chinese handicaps in, 39–40
  entry barriers to, 16–17
  knowledge codification as
    entry, 49–50
  modularization as entry, 41,
    46–49
  outsourcing as entry, 41, 42–46
  serving, economies of scale
    and, 183
  shares of, Chinese, 19
  for talent and services, 51–55
  using "demand wedge" on, 134
  using strategic alliances to pen-
    etrate, 76–79
global partnerships, 190
global players, 15–16
Global Prioritization Index,
  117–118
global strategy, 25, 174–175
global value chain, See also industry value chains
  modularization of, 46–49
  shift in structure of, 153–154
  Sino-foreign interaction in,
    86–87
"go global" strategy, 22
Goodbaby, 2, 197
government regulation
  company ownership structures
    and, 34–35
  effect on acquisitions, 142–143
  of initial public offerings
    (IPOs), 5
  intellectual property laws,
    179–180
  issue of Legend's ownership, 39
  of merger and acquisition
    services, 125–126

regulatory and legal infra-
    structure, 97, 108
government support, 18–19, 31
Graaff Transportsysteme GmbH,
  3, 7–8
Grant Thornton UK, 161
Great Wall, 124
"green" products, 152
gross domestic product (GDP)
  of developing countries, 98, 200
  ratio of R&D spending to,
    158–159
Guan Tongxian, 37, 102
guerilla warfare marketing, 100
guoyou minying ("state-owned,
    non-government-run")
    principle, 31

Haier, viii, 2, 20, 53, 79, 117
  creating new niches, 105
  dislodging "loose bricks," 90,
    94, 99–100
  disruptive competition and,
    143, 150, 151, 152
  entering upmarket niches,
    103–104, 198–199
  reducing entry barriers, 50–51,
    197
  tapping mass-market potential,
    167
Halsted, Don, 188
Hangzhou Tourist Bus Company,
  46
Hay Group, 54
Heilig-Meyers, 150
Henderson, Bruce, 117
Henkel, 128
Herman Miller, 140
Hewlett-Packard, 53
high-end segments
  economies of scale in, 103

expansion into, using R&D capability, 13
new Chinese competition in, 147–148
retreating to, as poor strategy, 10–14
"skimming" strategy, 175–176
vulnerability of, 120
higher-end products at low cost, 9–10
high performance computers (HPCs), 59–65
high technology at low cost, 58–72
as disruptive competition, 55, 152, 195–197
disruptive technologies, 65–67, 197
in fighting back against dragons, 185
leveraging low-cost R&D, 59–65
open architecture, 68–72
product design and, 182–183
response strategies, 154, 155–161
upmarket moves, 7–9
using clustering technology, 59–60, 64
high-technology companies, 18, 160
high-technology products
China's world share of, 14
expansion into, 13
high margins on, threatened, 2
offered at low cost, 1, 7–9
U.S. restrictions on sale of, to China, 62
high-value activities, 177–180
high-volume applications, 67, 73–74
high-volume markets, 96, 169

Hisense, 101–102, 117, 197
Home Depot, 51, 197
Honda, 22
Hong Kong, 17, 106–107
Hong Kong International Electronics Exhibition, 86
Hong Kong Stock Exchange, 32, 38–39
Hong Kong Telecom, 106–107
Hong Kong Trade Development Bureau, 100
Hoover, 150
"horses for courses" strategy, 11
HPCs (high performance computers), 59–65
Huawei-3Com partnership
clash with Cisco-ZTE partnership, 188–189
formation of, 187–188
purchase of, by 3Com, 192
Huawei Technologies Co., Ltd., viii, 54, 117, 141, 196, 199
accessing knowledge, 49–50
alliance with Nortel, 190–191
experience in peripheral markets, 107–109
FutureWei U.S. subsidiary, 114–115??
moving from periphery to core, 112–116
partnership with Siemens Communications, 189
patent applications, 179
serving troublesome customers, 110–112
use of ?pressure point? principle, 89–90
humanitarian motives, 119, 120
Hutchison Telecom, 106–107
"hybrid" companies, 32–33
Hynix, 141
Hyundai, 8, 9, 126

IBM, viii, 20, 53, 54, 61
ICT (Institute of Computing Technology), 30, 31, 60
Ikegai, 140
immature industries, 126–128
impediments to cost innovation, 125–134
  current status of, 131–134
  immature industries and, 126–128
  importance of intangible assets, 129–131, 133, 139
  limited market size and, 125–126
  systemic value network and, 124, 128–129
incentives, personal, 37–39
incentive systems, 78
India, 193
Indonesia, 96, 145
industry value chains. *See also* global value chain
  modularization of, 46–49, 194–195
  in systemic businesses, 128–129
information technology (IT), 141
information technology (IT) industry, 181–182
infrastructure
  reform of, 155, 159
  regulatory and legal, 97, 108
  for scientific research, 156–158
  "soft infrastructure," 18
initial public offerings (IPOs), 32
  government regulation of, 5
  increasing success of, 21
  Legend Group Ltd., 38–39
innovation
  cost innovation (*see* cost innovation)
  in low-end segments, 94

  in management processes, x, 23–24
  marketing innovation, 60–61
  process innovation, x, 23–24
  recombinative, 79–81, 161
  scarce resources and, 79–80
  speed of, modularity and, 47
  views of established firms, 193, 196
innovation standard, 174–175
innovative products, 166
innovative response strategies, 153–154
The Innovator's Dilemma (Christensen), 55
INSEAD, viii
Institute of Computing Technology (ICT), 30, 31, 38, 60
"institute-run enterprise" *(suoban gongshi)* structure, 30–31
intangible assets, 129–131, 133, 139
Intel, 174
  high technology at low cost and, 61, 62, 63
  proprietary technology, 159–160
  running subsidiary from China, 181–182
Intel Architecture Labs, 160
Intel Capital, 181
Intel China Research Center, 160
Intel China Software Lab, 160
Intelecom Solutions Inc., 115
intellectual property (IP)
  access to, 30–33
  high-technology production and, 14
  potential leakage of, 179–180
intellectual property rights (IPR), 85

Intellectual Property Tribunal of the Supreme People's Court, 179
International Invention Expo (2004), 80
international networks, 186
international trade, 4, 17
Internet, 49
investment banking sector, 125–126
IP (intellectual property). *See* intellectual property (IP)
IPOs. *See* initial public offerings
IPR (intellectual property rights), 85
Iran, 96, 118
Irish firms, 43

Japan, 33, 96
Japanese firms
    in auto industry, 43, 55
    automated production, 74–75
    in container industry, 9, 199
    innovation in management processes, x
    outsourcing by, 42
    in peripheral markets, 95, 101
    protection of technological advantage, 73
    time taken to become global players, 16
Jenn-Air, 150
Jia Jing Corporation, 163
Jiang Xipei, 37–39, 179
joint ventures, Sino-foreign
    alternatives to, 180
    in automobile industry, 96–97
    CIMC, 4
    "clash of titans," 188–192
    consortia, 144, 145
        to develop proprietary technology, 164
        as entry into global market, 42
        knowledge spillovers from, 162
        in mobile telephony, 108
        new kinds of partnerships, 187–188, 204
        ZPMC, 20, 34–37, 102, 197
just-in-time manufacturing, x, 201

KFC, 173
Kim, Chan, 165
Klein and Coll., 54
knowledge
    China as source of, 173, 204
    cost-scale-learning cycle, 116
    "Global Knowledge Economy," 41
    learning from world, 162–164, 194
knowledge, accessing
    by Chinese subsidiaries, 49–50
    importance of, 165, 194
    spillovers from joint ventures, 162
    systemic knowledge, 145–147
knowledge assets, 45, 52
knowledge-based activities, 179–180
knowledge codification, 49–50, 194
knowledge gap, 175
knowledge management, 78
Kodak, 173
Konka, 47
Korea, 33, 104
Korean firms, 55
    in auto industry, 43
    competitive pressure against, 7
    in mobile telephony, 47

Korean firms (*continued*)
  in peripheral markets, 101
  research and development,
    178–179
  specialty products, 199
  time taken to become global
    players, 15–16

labor force, Chinese, ix, 193
  access to rural labor force,
    28–29
  growth of skilled labor pool, 29
  low-cost labor (*see* low-cost
    labor)
La Sommelière, 103
latecomers, 40–41
Latin America, 96, 118
learning from world, 162–164,
  194
Legend. *See* Lenovo
Legend Group Ltd., 38–39
Legend Holdings, 39
Lenovo, viii, 53, 54, 139
  development of, 30–31
  as hybrid company, 36
  as Legend, 38–39
  purchase of IBM Thinkpad, 20
leverage, in global strategy, 25
LG Group, 173, 178
  cost innovation challenge and,
    195–196
  as global player, 15–16
Liang Dan Yi Xing, 157
Li Dongsheng, 124
Lifan, 95–96
LightPointe Communications
  Inc., 141
Li Guojie, 64
limitations of disruptive competition, 123–148
  brand awareness as, 124

in consumer electronics indus-
    try, 123–124
  impediments to cost innovation,
    125–134
  intangible assets as, 129–131,
    133, 139
  market characteristics, 134–139
  role of mergers and
    acquisitions, 139–143
  using demand wedge, 143–147
  window of opportunity,
    147–148
line scanning technology, 66–67
Li Ning, 172
Logitech, 171–172
"loose bricks," 89–121
  analyzing vulnerabilities,
    90–91, 117–121
  cost innovation and, 5–7,
    106–117
  finding, in competitors'
    defenses, 5–7, 24
  low-end segments as, 91, 92,
    93–95, 119
  nature of, 91–93
  niche segments as, 102–106
  peripheral markets as, 92,
    95–98, 117–119, 203
  protecting, 203
  troublesome customers as, 24,
    92, 99–102, 203
L'Oréal, 128, 173
low-cost labor
  across spectrum of skills,
    57–58
  Chinese advantage and, 27–28,
    169
  increasing process flexibility
    with, 87
  limited scope for cost inno-
    vation, 130
  used by multinationals, 29–30

low-end segments
  disruptive competition from,
    200
  with high-end technology,
    63–64
  innovation in, 94
  as "loose bricks," 91, 92,
    93–95, 119
Lowe's, 51
LSB Industries, Inc., 45
Lucent-Alcatel partnership,
  189–190
Lu Guanqiu, 46, 141–142

McDonald's, 173
McDonnell Douglas, 146
machine tool industry, 140–141
McKinsey & Company, 54, 202
Macy's, 100
Magic Chef, 150
Mai Boliang, 4–5
management
  growing shortage of, 202
  new models of, 200–201
  separation from ownership
    structures, 33–35
management autonomy, 33–37,
  184–185
management orthodoxies
  on advanced technology, 152
  challenging, 58
  of established companies, 119
  on paying premium prices,
    197–198
management processes, x, 23–24
managers, entrepreneurship by,
  35–36
manual production processes,
  74–78
  customization at low cost,
    77–78

flexibility and speed of, 74–75
  redesigning automated
    processes, 76–77
  variety at low cost, 75–76
manufacturing. See also specific
    industries
  just-in-time, x, 201
manufacturing capabilities
  expanding on, 8–9
  linking to global network,
    170–172
manufacturing costs, 172
Marconi, 116
market(s). See also China market;
    mass market
  attractiveness measures,
    117–118
  characteristics of (see market
    characteristics)
  European, assault on, 96
  existing, disruptive competi-
    tion and, 199–200
  on geographic periphery (see
    peripheral markets)
  limited size of, cost innovation
    and, 125–126
  national, as barrier to entry, 43
  for services (see professional
    services market)
  for talent (see talent market)
  for technology, creating,
    157–158
market characteristics, 134–139
  increasing modularization,
    138–139
  maturing product life cycles,
    137–138
  size of China market, 125–126,
    134–136
marketing, 60–61, 100, 177
market research, 176–177
market share, 139–143

Marshall, Robert, 44
M&A (merger and acquisition)
    services, 125–126
Masri, Edgar, 192
mass market
    delivering high technology at
        low cost, 182–183
    delivering specialty products
        to, 83–85
    tapping potential of, 167
    turning niche segments into, 93
mass-market retailers, 103–104
materials
    pursuing cost savings in, 9
    raw materials management, 78
    shortages of, R&D capability
        and, 12–13
Matsushita, 179
Mauborgne, Renée, 165
Maytag, 20, 143
    Chinese competitive advantage
        and, 50, 53
    "loose bricks" and, 94, 99
    response to competition,
        150–151, 153
    sale to Whirlpool, 151–152
medical diagnostic equipment
    industry
    acquiring Chinese technology,
        160
    disruptive technologies in,
        65–67, 197
    exposure to competition, 132
    MRI and CT equipment, 71–72
    open architecture and, 68–71
    strong commitment to China,
        182–183
merger and acquisition (M&A)
    services, 125–126
mergers and acquisitions
    to accelerate international
        expansion, 53–54

to acquire Chinese technology,
    159–161
to build capabilities, 41, 45
as defensive strategy, 150–151
government regulation and,
    142–143
strategic, in automobile industry,
    141–142
winning market share by,
    139–143
Mexico, 49
MG Rover, 141
Microsoft Corporation, 179
Middle East, 96
military-industrial R&D, 156–157
Mindit, 160
mind-set, changing, 170,
    174–175, 198, 204
Ministry of Information Industry,
    157
Ministry of Railways, 60, 61
Mitsubishi, 144
mobile telephony
    acquiring Chinese technology,
        160–161
    "clash of titans" in, 187–189
    cost innovation in, 106–109
    early in product life cycle, 127
    maturing product life cycle,
        137–138
    modularization in, 47–49
    moving from periphery to core,
        112–116
    research and development, 178
    responses to disruptive compe-
        tition, 188–192
    serving "troublesome
        customers," 110–112
    successful response strategies,
        185–186
    variety at low cost, 75–76,
        137–138

modularization
    disruptive competition and,
        138–139
    as entry into global market, 41,
        46–49
    of industry value chains,
        46–49, 194–195
Montgomery Ward, 150
motorcycle industry, 95–96
Motorola
    Chinese organization, 191
    Chinese R&D center, 178
    cost innovation and, 61, 76
    "loose bricks" and, 107–108,
        110, 116
    modularization and, 47, 49
    successful response strategies,
        185–186
multimedia-chip industry, 20
multinational corporations
    competing in domestic market,
        17
    low-cost labor used by, 29–30
    running subsidiaries from
        China, 181–183

Nan Cunhui, 77
Nanjing Auto, 141
Nasdaq, 18, 21
national assets, 30–33
National Intelligent Computer
    Research Centre (of ICT),
    60
national markets, 43
NBBSE (Ningbo Bird Sagem
    Electronics Corporation Ltd.),
    191–192
Nestlé, 173
Netherlands, 113–114
Neusoft, 71–72
new mandate for China, 174–185

changing mind-set, 170,
    174–175, 198
high-value activities, 177–180
relationship with headquarters,
    184–185
running global businesses,
    181–183
winning customers, 175–177
New Technology Development
    Company, 30
Next-Generation Network (NGN),
    115, 188–189
NGN (Next-Generation Network),
    115, 188–189
Nice, 177
niche segments
    early adopters and, 166, 167
    exploding, 103–105
    high-end (see upmarket
        niches)
    as "loose bricks," 24, 93,
        102–106, 203
    new, creating, 105–106
    peripheral markets, 200
    specialty niches, competition
        in, 104–105
    specialty products at low cost,
        81–87
Nigeria, 96
Nike, 172
Nikko, 75
Ningbo Bird, 47, 49, 139
Ningbo Bird Sagem Electronics
    Corporation Ltd. (NBBSE),
    191–192
Ningbo Sagem Bird Research and
    Development Co., Ltd.,
    191–192
Nissan, 22
Nokia, 161
    Chinese organization, 191
    modularization and, 47, 49

Nokia (*continued*)
    partnership with China Putian,
      189
    successful response strategies,
      185, 186
Nortel Networks, 190–191
NTCH Inc., 115

Office Depot, 51, 99
Ogilvy & Mather, 54
Oldelft NV, 66
open architecture, 58, 68–72
OptiMight, 141
Organisation for Economic Coop-
    eration and Development
    (OECD), 158
outsourcing, 28, 41, 42–46
overseas-Chinese diaspora, 17–18
ownership structures
    determining, 32–33
    incentives to succeed and, 37–39
    separation of management
      from, 33–35

Pakistan, 118
PalmSource Inc., 160–161
Panasonic, 75
parallel computing, 61–62
parallel equipment trials, 110–111
patent applications, 21, 178, 179
patents, purchase of, 3, 8
Pearl River Piano Group, 20, 140,
    196
    competitive advantage and,
      51–52
    as hybrid company, 36
peripheral markets, 24. *See also*
    specific locations
    challenges to priorities,
      199–200

    cost innovation in, 106–109
    customer service in, 110–112
    limited size of, as impediment
      to cost innovation, 125–126
    as "loose bricks," 92, 95–98,
      117–119, 203
    using proven technology in,
      110–112
periphery to core expansion, 92,
    95–98
personal care products industry,
    128
personal incentives, 37–39
petrochemical industry
    exposure to competition, 132
    proprietary technology in,
      130–131
    using "demand wedge" in, 145
pharmaceutical industry, 129,
    138–139
Philippines, 96
Philips Electronics, 47, 182
    cost innovation and, 66, 67, 75,
      82–83
    high technology at low cost,
      195–196
Photonic Bridges, 160
Pininfarina, 135, 163
points of presence (POPs), 115
political influence in business, 18
PolyGram Records, 161
POPs (points of presence), 115
poverty, devising value and,
    119–120
PowerDrive Europe Ltd., 45
power-generation equipment, 144
Powers and Sons LLC, 45
PPP (purchasing power parity),
    98, 158
Prahalad, C. K., 119, 120
"pressure point" principle,
    89–90

PricewaterhouseCoopers, 54
private companies, "hybrid,"
    32–33
process flexibility
    cost innovation through,
        73–79, 161
    low-cost labor and, 87
    manual production, 74–75
process innovation, x, 23–24
Procter & Gamble (P&G), 128, 173
    innovation strategy, 174–175
    winning over mainstream cus-
        tomers, 176–177
procurement, 78
product compatibility, 68
product costs, 193, 194
product customization. See cus-
    tomization at low cost
product design
    cost innovation in, 135–136
    design centers, 171, 178
    differentiated products,
        163–164
    high technology at low cost,
        182–183
    used to cut development costs,
        63–64
    variety at low cost, 138
product development. See also
    research and development
    (R&D)
    high-tech products, 31
    working with customer in,
        99–100
product development costs, 11,
    63–64
product differentiation, 15,
    163–164
production processes
    automated, 74–78, 151
    Chinese scale advantages, 46
    cost innovation in, 75

manual (see manual production
    processes)
    modularization and, 48
    redesigning, 10, 76–77, 135,
        162
    retooling, 100
productivity, increase in, 194
product life cycles, 127
    cost innovation and, 87–88
    effect on disruptive competi-
        tion, 137–138
    globalization and, 40
product lines. See also variety at
    low cost
    expanding, 10, 44, 162–163
    wide, offered at low cost, 1–2,
        185–186
professional services market
    as entry into global market,
        42
    globalization of, 54–55
    M&A services, limited market
        for, 125–126
profit-sharing, 38
property rights, 18
proprietary technology
    combining with low-cost
        technology, 159–160
    cost of, 62
    developing with joint ventures,
        164
    importance of, 130–131, 133
    need to use, cost innovation
        and, 127
    open architecture and, 58, 68
    purchase of, 3
    rendering unnecessary, 69–71,
        72
public companies, "hybrid,"
    32–33
purchasing power parity (PPP),
    98, 158

QingChuan Machine Tool, 141

raw materials management, 78
RCA, 123, 143
recombinative innovation,
    79–81, 161
research and development
    (R&D)
  cheap resources in, leveraging,
      58, 59–65
  in cost cutting, 75–76
  by established companies, 179
  establishing capacity for, 12–13,
      95
  fixed costs of, loss of volume
      business and, 11
  as high-value activity, 177–178
  investing in, to upgrade perfor-
      mance, 67
  investment in market research,
      176–177
  by Korean firms, 178–179
  low-cost, specialty products
      and, 81, 83–84
  military-industrial R&D,
      156–157
  mixed research community,
      158–159
  of other companies, leveraging,
      70
  research hierarchy, 156, 158
  strategic alliances in, 84–85
resources
  access to, 19, 33
  allocation of, in transitional
      economy, 32
  cheap, leveraging in R&D, 58,
      59–65
  low-cost, of emerging
      economies, 168–169
  reverse migration as, 17–18

technology resources, from
    central planning age, 33,
    155–156
resources, scarce, 79–80, 89–90
response strategies, 149–192
  by established firms, vii, 22–23,
      25
  expanding China's global role,
      169–187
  fighting back successfully,
      185–187
  high technology at low cost,
      154, 155–161
  immediate action, 149–152
  innovative responses, 153–154
  specialty products at low cost,
      155, 166–169
  strategic alliances, 187–192
  using cost innovation, 154–169
  variety at low cost, 155,
      161–166
retailers
  close cooperation with, 100
  desire to cut out middlemen,
      50
  mass-market, distribution
      through, 103–104
retailing sector, 197
  concentration of, 50–51
  as entry into global market, 42
  intangible asset barriers in,
      129–130
reverse migration, 17–18
risk, 10–14, 97
risk taking, 38, 39
Ritmüller, 140
Rockford Powertrain, 45, 142
Rongsheng Electric Appliances
    Holding Co., Ltd., 151
Royalstar, 151
Rüdesheimer, 140
rural labor force, 28–29

Russia, 108
Russian Academy of Sciences, 66
Russo, Patricia, 190
Ryobi, 75

SABMiller, 173
Sagem, 191–192
SAIC (Shanghai Automotive Industry Corporation), 141
Sam's Club, 2, 51, 104
Samsung Electronics
  China's global role and, 173, 179, 185
  as global player, 15–16
  low-cost specialty products, 82–83, 84
  subsidiary-headquarters relationship, 184–185
Sanyo, 73, 74, 86
SASAC (State-owned Assets Supervision and Administration Commission), 34, 35
SBU (strategic business units), 181–182
scale advantages. See economies of scale
scale-intensive technology, 58
Schiess AG, 140
Schiller, 44–45, 142
science and technology system, 31
Sears Roebuck & Co., 51
SGSB Group, 140
Shanghai Automotive Industry Corporation (SAIC), 141
Shanghai Bell, 189–191
Shanghai General Motors, 136
Shanghai Mingjing, 140
Shanghai Stock Exchange, 35
Shanghai Volkswagen, 136

Shanghai Zhenhua Port Machinery Co. Ltd. (ZPMC), 20, 34–37, 102, 197
Sharp, 195–196
Shell, 130
Shen Haojie, 163
Shenyang Machine Tool, 140
Shenzhen Special Economic Zone, 14
Shenzhen Stock Exchange, 5
Shinawatra, Taksin, 110
Shinco, 5, 196
  adding product offerings, 85–87
  specialty products at low cost, 82, 83–85
Siemens, 47, 69, 71, 144, 160
Siemens Communications, 160, 189
Sina, 18
Singapore, 43
Sinopec, 145
skilled labor pool, 29
"skimming" strategy, 175–176
SKT, 96–97
social responsibility, 119, 120
SOEs (state-owned enterprises), 31, 34, 52
"soft infrastructure," 18
Software Engineering Institute (CMU), 178
Sohu, 18
Sony, 47, 75, 82–83, 86, 179
South African firms
  in container industry, 9–10, 199
  retreat to high-end segments, 11
South Asia, 96
Southeast Asia, 17
specialty products at low cost, 1–2, 81–87

specialty products at low cost
(*continued*)
adding specialty products,
85–87
disruptive competition and, 55,
198–199
response strategies, 155,
166–169
specialty niches, competition
in, 103–105
transforming economics of,
82–85
using scale-intensive technology,
58
speed of innovation, 47
speed of manual production
processes, 74–75
SsangYong Motor, 141
staff
to lead global line of business,
184
support personnel, 109, 110–111
start-ups, high-tech, 18, 160
state assets and intellectual
property, 30–33
"state-owned, non-government-
run" (*guoyou minying*)
principle, 31
State-owned Assets Supervision
and Administration
Commission (SASAC), 34, 35
state-owned enterprises (SOEs)
constraints on, 34
global talent market and, 52
guoyou minying principle, 31
state projects, 4
state purchasing power
as "demand wedge," 139,
143–147
using to force opportunities, 124
Steinway, 140
STMicroelectronics, 161

stock markets, Chinese
Hong Kong Stock Exchange,
32, 38–39
IPOs and, 32
Shanghai Stock Exchange, 35
Shenzhen Stock Exchange, 5
strategic alliances, 10–11,
187–192. *See also specific
alliances and partnerships*
between Chinese and foreign
firms, vii
clashes between, 188–192
to gain advantage, 25
networks of, 186–187, 190
new kinds of partnerships,
187–188
to penetrate global market,
76–79
pioneering technology and,
62–63
in R&D, 84–85
strategic business units (SBU),
181–182
strategies
cost innovation (*see* cost
innovation)
global strategy, 25, 174–175
"go global" strategy, 22
"horses for courses," 11
mergers and acquisitions as,
141–142, 150–151
"skimming" strategy, 175–176
translating into competitive
advantage, 21–22
Sui, William, 181
SUNDAY, 111
Sun Microsystems, 63
Sun Ninghui, 59
Sun Tzu, 24
suoban gongsi ("institute-run enterprise") structure, 30–31
supply chains, 42–43, 204

support personnel, 109, 110–111
sustainable competitive advantage,
  x
Sutton, Willie, 95, 111
Syria, 96
systemic businesses, 128–129,
  203
systemic knowledge, 145–147
systemic value network
  cost innovation less effective
    in, 124, 128–129
  as entry barrier, 132
  gaining systemic knowledge,
    145–147

Taiwan, 17
Taiwanese firms, 43
talent market
  creating, 158
  as entry into global market, 42
  globalization of, 51–55
  "white-hot," 202
talent pool
  at all skill levels, 28–30
  university graduates, 29,
    201–202
Target, 51, 100
TCL
  disruptive competition and,
    123–124
  modularization, 47, 48
  strategic alliances and, 139,
    142–143
TCL-Thomson Electronics (TTE),
  123–124
TechFaith Wireless, 21, 49
technological advantage, 73
technology, 8, 14. See also specific
    technologies
  acquiring through mergers,
    159–161

creating market for, 157–158
disruptive technologies, 65–67,
    197
early adopters of, 115
in expanding specialty product
    offerings, 85–86
to improve customer service,
    36–37, 197
management orthodoxies on,
    152
pioneering, strategic alliances
    and, 62–63
proven, use in peripheral
    markets, 110–112
rapid pace of change in, 127
recycling, 80–81
resources from central plan-
    ning age, 33, 155–156
restriction of, 58–59, 73,
    196–197
scale-intensive, 58
underexploited, access to, 169
using to beat dragons, 25, 133
value-for-money equation and,
    72
Technology Innovation Gold
    Award, 86
technology-transfer agreements,
    10
Techtronic Industries, 75
Teepe, Stephan, 8
Teknova, 68–71
telecommunications. See also
    mobile telephony
  cost innovation in, 106–117
Telfort B.V., 114
Tencor, 11
Tesco, 51, 129
Thailand, 110
Thomson Electronics, 123,
    142–143
3Com, 187–188, 192

Three Gorges Dam project, 144, 145
3G technology. *See* mobile telephony
3G Universal Mobile Telecommunications System (UTMS), 113–114
Tianjin First Autoworks, 126
TJ Innova Engineering & Technology Co., 135
TM, 111
Tong Zhi Cheng, 52
Toshiba, 73
Total Quality Control, x
Towers Perrin, 54
toy business, 132
Toyota, 16, 22, 126
trade barriers, 46
trade shows, 113
training, 78
Trencor, 9
troublesome customers
    cost innovation for, 110–112
    disruptive competition from, 200
    as "loose bricks," 24, 92, 99–102, 203
Tsinghua University, 159
TTE (TCL-Thomson Electronics), 123–124

UAE (United Arab Emirates), 110–111
UAI (Universal Automotive Industries), 45, 141, 142
UBHI (UBH International Limited), 10, 11
UBH International Limited (UBHI), 10, 11
Uniden, 75
Unilever, 128, 173

United Arab Emirates (UAE), 110–111
U.K. firms
    in auto industry, 43
    in container industry, 3, 11, 13
    mergers and acquisitions, 45
    in telecommunications, 116
United Nations, 179
United States
    Chinese communities in, 17
    Chinese cost advantage over, 29
    Chinese understanding of, 51
    cooperation with retailers, 100
    dot-com bubble and, 150
    mergers and acquisitions in, 45
    ratio of R&D spending to GDP, 158–159
    restrictions on sale of high-tech products, 62
Universal Automotive Industries (UAI), 45, 141, 142
Unocal, 53
Unterberger, Christian, 160
upmarket moves, 7–10, 153–154
upmarket niches
    entering, 103–104, 198–199
    high-end, risks of, 10–14
    turning into volume business, 2
U.S. firms
    Chinese subsidiaries, 114–115
    outsourcing by, 42, 43
U.S. market
    assault on, 96
    lack of brand awareness and, 114–115
    for M&A services, 126
UTStarcom, 18

value, devising, 119–120
value-for-money equation

cost innovation and, 2–3, 203–204
"flatter world" and, 195
ignoring threat of, 150–151
low-cost technology and, 72
in low-end segments, 94
van der Wiel, Theo, 114
variety at low cost, 7–9, 58, 72–81
disruptive competition and, 55, 197–198
in fighting back against dragons, 185
mobile telephony, 75–76, 137–138
process flexibility, 73–79
recombinative innovation, 79–81
response strategies, 155, 161–166
VCDs (video compact discs), 82–85
video compact discs (VCDs), 82–85
Vietnam, 95–96, 107–108
Vimicro Corporation, 18, 20, 139
virtuous cycle, 24
cost-scale-learning cycle, 116
economies of scale in, 7
in specialty products, 81
Visteon, 44
Vodaphone, 49
Volkswagen, 164
Shanghai Volkswagen, 136
"skimming" strategy, 175–176
variety at low cost and, 162, 163
volume segments
cost advantage in R&D and, 12
exploding niches into, 104
low prices and, 109
potential of specialty products, 166–167
VTech, 75

vulnerabilities. See "loose bricks"

wage rates, 29
Wal-Mart, 50–51, 129, 130
Wang Chuanfu, 73, 75, 76
Wanxiang, 20
mergers and acquisitions, 141–142
outsourcing to, 43–46
Wavecom, 47, 48
WCDMA technology, 111
weaknesses of dragons, 24–25
in innovative products, 166
overcapacity as, 168
time as, 148
wealth, personal, 37–38, 39
Welfit Oddy, 9
Wesder SA, 100
"while-you-wait" systems, 130
Whirlpool, 50
"loose bricks" and, 94, 99
response to disruptive competition, 150, 151–152, 153
Wholly Owned Foreign Enterprises (WOFEs), 180
Wideband Code Division Multiple Access (WCDMA) technology, 111
Williamson, Peter, viii
WOFEs (Wholly Owned Foreign Enterprises), 180
Wohlenberg, 140
WorldCom, 115
World Trade Organization (WTO), 17, 43, 176
WPP group, 54
Wright-Patterson Air Force Base, 116

WTO (World Trade Organization), 17, 43, 176
Wu Bangguo, 109
Wurlitzer, 52

Xi'an Aircraft Co., 147
Xianhua Microwave Products Co. Ltd., 100

Yahoo!, viii

Yin Tongyao, 162
Yuandong Group, 37–38

Zeng Ming, viii
Zhang Rui Min, 50, 79, 90
Zhongxing Medical, 67, 159, 196
Zimmerman, 141
ZPMC (Shanghai Zhenhua Port Machinery Co. Ltd.), 20, 34–37, 102, 197
ZTE Corporation, 188–189

About the Authors

Ming Zeng is Professor of Strategy at Cheung Kong Graduate School of Business, Beijing, China. Between 1998 and 2004 he was a faculty member at INSEAD.

Professor Zeng has conducted extensive research on growth strategies of Chinese companies, the competition and cooperation between Chinese and multinational firms, and how the emergence of Chinese competitors is changing global competition. He has been working closely with leading Chinese companies including Haier, Legend, TCL, and Alibaba, among others. His case on Haier's acquisition strategy won the prestigious Pedro Nueno prize of the 2000 European Foundation for Management Development (EFMD) Case Competition, and is widely used in business schools. His recent article with Peter Williamson, "The Hidden Dragons," which analyzed the globalization strategy of Chinese firms, is one of the most cited articles that have appeared in the *Harvard Business Review*. He has also conducted research on the management of strategic alliances, China strategy for multinational firms and e-commerce.

Ming Zeng has published widely in world's top management journals, including *Academy of Management Review*, *Organization Science*, *Journal of International Business Studies*, *Harvard Business Review*, *MIT Sloan Management Review*, and *California Management*

Review. His research has been highlighted in the *Wall Street Journal* and the *Economist*, and on CNBC and the BBC.

Professor Zeng received his PhD in International Business and Strategy from the University of Illinois at Urbana-Champaign (1998), and his BA in Economics from Fudan University (1991). He can be contacted at: mzeng@ckgsb.edu.cn.

Peter J. Williamson is Professor of International Management and Asian Business at INSEAD in Fontainebleau, France, and Singapore, and Visiting Professor of International Business at the Judge Business School, University of Cambridge. He was formerly Dean of MBA Programmes at London Business School and Visiting Professor of Global Strategy and Management at Harvard Business School. Peter has worked with both Asian companies and multinationals throughout the region on strategy and capability development for more than twenty years. He has been actively involved in a number of joint ventures in China since 1983 as well as numerous mergers and acquisitions. Peter is an adviser to governments on trade and investment. He also serves as a nonexecutive director of several listed companies, including the Chinese-based software company Geong International Ltd., and chairs one of the leading macro hedge fund managers, Tactical Global Management Ltd.

Peter holds a PhD in Business Economics from Harvard University. His research and publications span globalization, the internationalization of Asian companies, strategy innovation, competitive dynamics, and the use of strategic alliances to accelerate growth. His article, "Is Your Innovation Process Global?" was a prize-winner in the 2005 Sloan-PricewaterhouseCoopers Awards, which honor those articles that have contributed to the enhancement of management practice. Other publications include the books *Winning in Asia: Strategies for the New Millennium* (2004) and *From Global to Metanational: How Companies Win in the Knowledge Economy* (2001; coauthored with Yves L.

Doz and José Santos)—both published by Harvard Business School Press; *The Economics of Financial Markets* (1995; coauthored with Hendrik S. Houthakker); *Managing the Global Frontier* (1994; coauthored with Qionghua Hu); *The Strategy Handbook* (1992; coauthored with Michael Hay); and an edited volume, *Global Future: The Next Challenge for Asian Business* (2005; with Arnoud DeMeyer, Frank-Jürgen Richter, and Pamela C. M. Mar). He can be contacted at peter.williamson@attglobal.net.